Medieval Europe
Latin Christendom
1050-1150

NORWAY

SCOTLAND

IRELAND

DENMARK

North Sea

NORD-MARK

POLAND

Elbe

SAXONY

Weser

LUSATIA

Oder

MEISSEN

ENGLAND

WALES

London

FLANDERS

LOTHARINGIA

Rhine

Cologne

FRANCONIA

Mainz

Prague

BOHEMIA

MORAVIA

| ////// Holy Roman Empire |

NORMANDY

Seine

Paris

ROYAL DOMAIN

AUSTRIA

BRITTANY

BAVARIA

Augsburg

Danube

Loire

DUCHY OF BURGUNDY

KINGDOM

CARINTHIA

FRANCE

Geneva

GUIENNE

Lyons

Vienne

OF

Milan

Venice

Po

Rhône

ITALY

GASCONY

Florence

TOULOUSE

BURGUNDY

Arles

NAVARRE

ARAGON

Ebro

BARCELONA

Rome

CASTILE

APULIA

Mediterranean   Sea

CALIPHATE
OF
CORDOBA

Palermo

SICILY

Miles

0   50   100   150   200

Phoenix Frustrated

Christopher Cope

PHOENIX FRUSTRATED

THE · LOST · KINGDOM
OF · BURGUNDY

Constable · London
Dodd, Mead & Company · New York

First published in Great Britain 1986
by Constable and Company Ltd
10 Orange Street London WC2H 7EG
Copyright © 1986 by Christopher Cope

First published in the United States of America
in 1987 by Dodd, Mead & Company, Inc.
79 Madison Avenue, New York, NY 10016

Set in Linotron Ehrhardt 11pt by
Rowland Phototypesetting Ltd
Bury St Edmunds, Suffolk
Printed in Great Britain by
St Edmundsbury Press Ltd
Bury St Edmunds, Suffolk

British Library CIP data
Cope, Christopher
Phoenix frustrated: the lost kingdom
of Burgundy
1. Burgundy (France) – History
I. Title
944'.4   DC611.B775
ISBN 0 09 467290 3

Library of Congress Cataloging-in-Publication Data
Cope, Christopher
Phoenix frustrated.
Bibliography: p.
Includes index.
1. Burgundy (France) – History.
I. Title.
DC611.B775C66   1987   944'.4   86-19761
ISBN 0-396-08955-0

To my son DAVID
since our last talk prompted this book

February 1967

Phoenix

A legendary bird represented by the ancient Egyptians as living five or six centuries in the Arabian desert, being consumed by fire by its own act, and rising in youthful freshness from its own ashes and often regarded as an emblem of immortality or of the resurrection.

The paragon of excellence or beauty.

Webster's Dictionary

Contents

Illustrations   11
Maps   15
Acknowledgements   16
Preface: A Kingdom Discovered   19

I PROLOGUE – TRIER, AUTUMN 1473

Charles the Bold demands the Crown of Burgundy – the Kingdom of
Burgundy reconstituted for Charles the Bold.   27

II PHOENIX ON THE WING

Nibelungs and Merovings: The First Kingdom of Burgundy   35
'The skin of our teeth' – after the 'Disaster of the Nibelungs' the Burgundians
settle the Homeland (413–58) – the Merovingian Franks keep the Kingdom of
Burgundy separate and intact (534–726) – Queen Brunhild, prototype of the
Wagnerian heroine (550–613) – the sub-Roman Kingdom of Burgundy –
twilight over Burgundy – Burgundy is still separate until the triumph of Charles
Martel (737).

Carolings and Rudolfians: The Second Kingdom founded   57
The Moors and Charles Martel – Gerard of Roussillon – Boso and the Rudolfs
restore the Kingdom – Conrad the Peaceful (937–93) – the Fall of the Phoenix.

III THE PARAGON OF EXCELLENCE AND BEAUTY

Burgundy born again   73

Romanesque and Gothic Art   76
The mighty Order of Cluny – Cluny's and Burgundy's part in the recovery of
the West – the Cistercian Order – the magnificent architecture of Cluny –
Cluny's sculpture and painting – medieval Burgundy's most precious legacy –

Burgundian half-Gothic is spread all over Latin Christendom – Burgundian Gothic is overtaken by '*le style français*' – France and Burgundy and the coming of 'Gothic' – 'Burgundo-English' Romanesque and Gothic.

Thought and Literature   91
Reform and heresy – the Valdensians – the everyday use of 'Burgundian' – Burgundian literature.

The Power and the Glory   98

IV 'ASHES'

Under the King-Emperors   103
The permanence of Burgundy's frontiers – the governing of Burgundy – Emperor Frederick I (Barbarossa).

Richard Lionheart, William of Baux and the Kingdom   109
The Emperor promises the crown of Burgundy to Richard I – Richard as 'King of Burgundy' – Frederick II designates William of Baux as King of Burgundy.

V PHOENIX RESURGENT

The Views from the Crest (a recapitulation)   119

The Phoenix Analogy   126

Charles of Anjou: the First Near-miss   128
Master of Provence and uncrowned King of Arles – the reconstitution of the Kingdom of Burgundy (1277–82) – the Sicilian Vespers – the character of Charles of Anjou – the Angevins' prospects in the twelve-eighties – King Robert of Naples and the Angevins' last chance.

One Burgundy or Four?   140
Burgundian 'national consciousness'? – four languages, four states – Provence and the lure of Italy – the emergence of the Swiss Confederation – the Dukes of Burgundy build up a quasi-independent state – the Emperor effectively recognizes the independence of Savoy.

Amadeus VIII and the 'Lesser Kingdom' of Burgundy   149
The beginnings of Savoy – the expansion of Savoy – the Savoyards as the 'most Burgundian' of the Kingdom's dynasties – the consolidation of Savoy by Amadeus VIII – the great achievements of Amadeus VIII 'the Peacemaker' – Amadeus VIII and the Kingdom of Burgundy – Anne of Lusignan, the 'evil genius of the dynasty' of Savoy – Savoy's first absorption by France.

Charles the Bold, The King denied a Crown   159
The 'New Monarchies' – Burgundy the best placed 'new monarchy' (1425–75)
– the 'Grand Dukes' as Renaissance monarchs – Philip the Good and Charles
the Bold: a sorry contrast – the Emperor betrays Charles on his coronation day
– Charles and Edward IV plan the partition of France – Charles recovers
Lorraine but misses his chance in France – Nancy, Charles's chosen city of
destiny – the remaining match points lost at Grandson and Morat – return to
Nancy – the English alliance the match-winner.

Infelix Burgundia, Felix Austria   183
The Duchy of Burgundy is absorbed by France – the Franche Comté holds on
longer to its freedom – Northern Burgundy becomes Belgium and the
Netherlands – the Hapsburgs reap Burgundy's harvest.

The last Kingdom of Burgundy   188
Savoyards help to check the expansion of France – Duke Emmanuel Philibert
of Savoy rejects dreams of the Kingdom – Charles Emmanuel, misnamed 'the
Great' – Charles Emmanuel's first attempt on the Kingdom of Arles – Charles
Emmanuel prepares his second bid for the Kingdom of Arles – the 'Escalade' –
the death of the dream – the end of the last kingdom of Burgundy.

VI REMNANTS AND REFLECTIONS

A Language without a Country   201
The passing of a forgotten land – Savoy and Franco-Provençal, remnants
barely vanished – Savoy: the Phoenix risen? – the 'annihilation of the rags and
tatters of Feudalism and Slavery' – the survival of 'Burgundian' – the resurgence
of 'Burgundian' in north-west Italy – 100,000 speakers of 'Burgundian' today.

The Burgundian Phoenix, the fabulous 'Might-have-been'   213
Language the map-maker – 'Burgundy proper' a more likely survivor than the
Kingdom – the Valois dukes create a Middle Kingdom – Charles the Bold's
Middle Kingdom: vicissitudes 1643–1945 – Savoy as a possible survivor –
Burgundy, Italy and Germany – Burgundy and Ireland – Burgundy and
Scotland.

Conclusion   229
The reasons for Burgundy's failure – some closing reflections – Burgundy's
place in history.

CONTENTS

APPENDIX I: Burgundy and the epic of Northern Europe   236
APPENDIX II: 'Burgundian' – the language   239
APPENDIX III: Some notes on architecture   247
APPENDIX IV: Bibliography   253
APPENDIX V: Notes   260
APPENDIX VI: Dates   266
APPENDIX VII: Rulers of Burgundy   274
APPENDIX VIII: Genealogical tables   280
INDEX   287

Illustrations

between pages 64 and 65

I   A Burgundian vineyard (château de Couches). (*French Government Tourist Office, London*)
The broken bridge at Avignon. (*J. P. Bois, Avignon*)

II Geneva cathedral: the excavations. (*Canton of Geneva: Charles Bonnet, head archaeologist, Pierre George, photographer*)
A mosaic of the same period. (*Canton of Geneva: Charles Bonnet, head archaeologist, Pierre George, photographer*)
A mosaic near Vienne, probably third century. (*Office de Tourisme, Vienne*)

III Chalice of Gourdon. (*Bibliothèque Nationale, Paris*)
Tournus, Saint Philibert. (*French Government Tourist Office, London*)

IV Chapaize. (*French Government Tourist Office, London*)

V   Cluny III, arch. (*French Government Tourist Office, London*)

VI Paray-le-Monial, façade. (*Jacques Verroust, Paris*)

VII The martyrdom of Saint Vincent, Berzé-la-Ville. (*Éditions Combier, Mâcon*)

VIII Vézelay nave. (*French Government Tourist Office, London*)
Vézelay abbey, view. (*French Government Tourist Office, London*)

between pages 96 and 97

IX Anzy-le-Duc, church exterior. (*Éditions Arthaud, Paris*)

X   The Holy Lance. (*Kunsthistorisches Museum, Vienna*)
The Musician. (*Éditions Arthaud, Paris*)
The Flight into Egypt. (*Éditions Arthaud, Paris*)

XI Balaam and his ass. (*Éditions Arthaud, Paris*)
'Luxury'. (*Éditions Arthaud, Paris*)
'Eve'. (*Musée Rolin, Autun: photo A. Allemand*)

XII   Cluny, before its demolition. (*Photo. Giraudon, Paris*)

XIII   La Charité-sur-Loire, view. (*French Government Tourist Office, London*)
La Charité, the choir. (*Éditions Arthaud, Paris*)
Paray-le-Monial, the apse. (*French Government Tourist Office, London*)

XIV   Fontenay abbey, the nave. (*French Government Tourist Office, London*)

XV   Autun cathedral, the nave. (*Éditions Arthaud, Paris*)

XVI   Vézelay, the façade. (*French Government Tourist Office, London*)

between pages 128 and 129

XVII   Two 'Burgundian' abbeys in England:
Castle Acre (Cluniac), a reconstruction. (*Historic Buildings and Monuments Commission for England*)
Rievaulx (Cistercian), the present-day ruins. (*Historic Buildings and Monuments Commission for England*)

XVIII   Peter II of Savoy's palaces:
The Savoy in London. (*Author's own print*)
Château de Chillon. (*Swiss National Tourist Office, London*)

XIX   Scenes of Charles the Bold's defeats:
Château de Grandson. (*Éditions A. Dériaz, Beaulnes, Switzerland*)
Morat: the battlements, much as they were. (*Swiss National Tourist Office, London*)

XX   Dijon, the church of Notre Dame. (*Ets. Protet, Dôle*)

between pages 160 and 161

XXI   Cistercian abbeys:
Pontigny, in Burgundy. (*Éditions Combier, Macon*)
Bellapais, in Cyprus. (*Douglas Dickins, London*)

XXII   Churches of destiny:
Arles, Saint Trophîme cathedral (for Frederick Barbarossa). (*French Government Tourist Office, London*)
Palermo, Santo Spirito (for Charles of Anjou). (*Azienda di Turismo, Palermo*)

XXIII   The Grand Dukes' sculpture in Dijon:
Philip the Bold's tomb. (*French Government Tourist Office, London*)
A mourner on the tomb. (*Éditions Arthaud, Paris*)
The Well of Moses at Champmol: Isaiah. (*French Government Tourist Office, London*)

XXIV The Well of Moses at Champmol: Christ. (*Éditions Arthaud, Paris*)
Charles the Bold: a painting by John van Eyck. (*Mansell Collection, London*)

between pages 192 and 193

XXV Charles of Anjou:
The sculpture by Arnolfo di Cambio. (*Musei Capitolini, Rome*)
His objective, Vienne: Saint Maurice cathedral nave. (*French Government Tourist Office, London*)
His invasion launching-pad: Tarascon castle. (*Société d'Éditions Publicitaires et Touristiques, Nice*)

XXVI Val d'Aosta, the center of the 'Burgundian' language today:
The valley's finest castle, Fenis. (*Italian State Tourist Office*)

XXVII A traditional costume (inset, a sample of the language). (*Italian State Tourist Office, London*)
Works of the fifteenth-century Duchy of Burgundy:
Beaune, Hôtel-Dieu. (*French Government Tourist Office, London*)

XXVIII The Hercules tapestry, showing Philip the Good and Charles the Bold. (*Burrell Collection, Glasgow Art Gallery and Museum*)

between pages 224 and 225

XXIX Scenes from Charles the Bold's career:
Estavayer: contemporary battlements. (*Swiss National Tourist Office, London*)
Grandson: the battlefield today. (*Swiss National Tourist Office London*)

XXX Late Burgundian sculpture and wood carvings:
Auxerre, Saint Étienne cathedral: the stoning of Saint Stephen. (*Éditions Arthaud, Paris*)
Bourg-en-Bresse, church of Brou: 'Drunkenness'. (*French Government Tourist Office, London*)
Bourg-en-Bresse, church of Brou: 'the Chastisement'. (*French Government Tourist Office*)

XXXI Dukes of Savoy, portraits:
Amadeus, VIII. (*Musées d'Art et d'Histoire, Chambéry*)
Emmanuel Philibert. (*Musées d'Art et d'Histoire, Chambéry*)
Charles Emmanuel I, as young Burgundian dreamer. (*Musées d'Art et d'Histoire, Chambéry*)
Charles Emmanuel I, as mature Italian statesman. (*Musées d'Art et d'Histoire, Chambéry*)

[13]

XXXII Charles Emmanuel's defeat by Geneva, the Escalade:
Geneva's annual celebration: the procession. (*Swiss National Tourist Office, London*)
Geneva's annual celebration: 'la Mère Royaume'. (*Swiss National Tourist Office, London*)
Geneva's annual celebration: a horseman with Geneva's arms. (*Swiss National Tourist Office, London*)
A Geneva house which witnessed the Escalade. (*Swiss National Tourist Office, London*)

Maps

 1 South through Burgundy   18
 2 The Rhône-Saône Basin   20
 3 Charlemagne's Europe and our own   22
 4 Charles the Bold's territories and the award of 1473   30
 5 The Burgundians' migrations   37
 6 The Burgundians' Homeland   40
 7 The First Kingdom   44
 8 Merovingian kingdoms   48
 9 Carolingian kingdoms 843   60
10 Burgundy re-emerges late 9th century   63
11 The First and Second Kingdoms compared   65
12 Burgundian Romanesque   82
13 Franco-Provençal ('Burgundian') and its neighbors   95
14 Europe's frontiers, constant and changing   105
15 Richard I's lands and prospects   111
16 Burgundy's four regions   121
17 'Burgundy Proper'   122
18 Charles of Anjou in the West   133
19 The Arelate 1250–1450: languages and principal states   141
20 Savoy from c. 1270   150
21 Amadeus VIII of Savoy   155
22 Charles the Bold   163
23 Charles Emmanuel of Savoy   192
24 Romance language groups in the Middle Ages   207
25 Franco-Provençal today   210
26 France's frontiers   220

Acknowledgements

I have visited virtually every place mentioned in the book, many of them several times; and I am familiar with every extant church or abbey named here. Obviously I am in the debt of people all over the area who for reasons of space cannot be mentioned, not least the hospitable clergy who have shown me round their buildings and treasures.

Many names, however, cannot be overlooked. My specially cordial thanks go to the Société de Lecture and University Library of Geneva, and the Cabinet des Estampes and Musée des Beaux-Arts of that city, for supplying me with material on which I based the comprehensive history of the Kingdom of Burgundy of which this work is a compression; Monsieur Armand Decour, the historian of Bettant in the ancient land of Savoy, who first brought to life for me the language of old Burgundy which is dying in France; three gentlemen who showed me how much vitality it still has in north-west Italy, Professors Omezzoli and Colliard of Aosta, and Monsieur Henri Armand of the Center for Franco-Provençal Studies at Saint Nicolas, Val d'Aosta; and my Burgundian brother-in-law Jean Millot who established for me to what extent the language has survived in the Swiss Valais. (He also provided me with the genealogies in Appendix VIII.)

Professor Jonas Kristjansson, curator of Iceland's Manuscripts Museum, gave me invaluable advice on the Burgundian origins of northern Europe's epic when I visited him in Reykjavik. I am greatly indebted to Doctor Helmut Trnek of the Kunsthistorisches Museum in Vienna for our long and detailed correspondence about the regalia of the ancient Kingdom, notably the Holy Lance of Saint Maurice; to Doctor Claudio Bertolotto (Soprintendente per i Beni Artistici i Storici del Piemonte in Turin) and Monsieur P. Dumas (of the Musées d'Art et d'Histoire of Chambéry) for information on various matters to do with the Dukes of Savoy (e.g. their regalia and their possession of the Holy Shroud); Professor Noel Coulet of the University of Provence for a long letter about the Angevins' preparations for war in 1281–2; Mr Peter Chablais for his guidance on the Trier agreement of 1473; and Monsieur Charles Bonnet for

[16]

his books about the recent extraordinary fifth and sixth-century archaeological finds in Geneva for which he is responsible. In one way or another I am also beholden to Signor Prola, Soprintendente per i Monumenti della Valle d'Aosta; to Professors Deuchler and Bouffard of Geneva, Quarré of Dijon, Giura of Naples and Zanotto of Turin; to Doctor W. Ryan and Mr J. Perkins of the Warburg Institute, London University; and to Jean Liniger, the author of the latest work on Philippe de Commynes.

The manuscript or parts of it have been through many hands. I was particularly fortunate to receive detailed comments from Doctor Jane Martindale of the University of East Anglia, Doctor Unity Nelson of London University and William Macmillan of the famous publishing family. My debt to them is enormous, as it is also to Lucia Withers whose advice from the viewpoint of the general reader was immensely valuable. Among others who read the manuscript Mr Christopher Sinclair-Stevenson, Philip Ziegler and Madame Thérèse de Saint Phalle of Flammarion (a Burgundian) gave me more general but no less useful counsel. Unless, however, I attribute them to others, the views expressed are my own responsibility.

I wish there were space to do justice to the many relations and friends in Switzerland, France, the Netherlands, United States and England who have given me help and encouragement, notably an 'Allemannic Burgundian', Melchior Borsinger; to Hugh Paget, Gordon Brook-Shepherd, Toby Buchan, Jean-Louis Millot, Galia and Geneviève Millot, Suzanne Hunter, Helen McSweeney, Joan Marmont and Jennifer Burke, and particularly in the earlier years Helen Cope, Gillian Towner and Alistair Maclean; to Al Hart of New York, who must be the most wonderful Literary Agent in the world; to John McLaughlin of Campbell Thomson and McLaughlin, Allen Klots of Dodd, Mead, and Ben Glazebrook, Richard Tomkins and Miles Huddleston at Constable, for believing enough in the book to take it on; to Neil Hyslop for bringing a skilled professional hand to the maps and genealogies; to my wife for her unending patience and support; and last, but very far from least, to my chief collaborator, Christine Noble, who amongst many other things produced a typescript which was as elegant as it was faultless. Fortunately she is blessed with enough perseverance for two; but for that the book would long since have been abandoned.

C.L.S.C.
Chelsea, February 1986

[17]

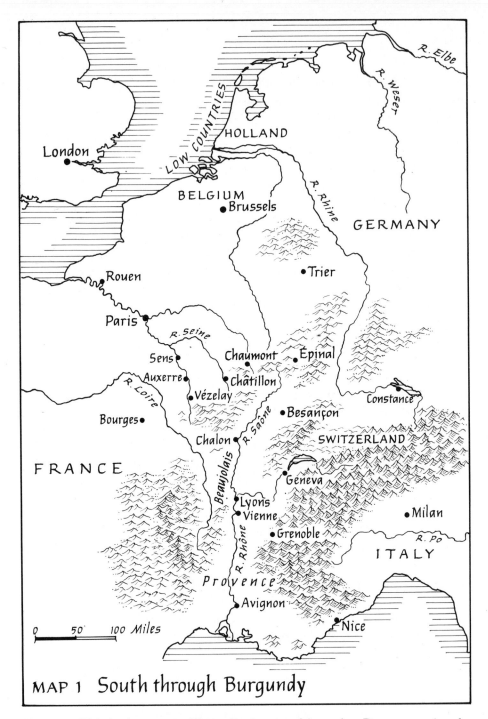

MAP 1 South through Burgundy

Map no. 1 With the department of Yonne forming part of the modern Bourgogne region, the traveler may regard himself as in Burgundy before he reaches Sens (long known as Sens-en-Bourgogne). He will be in the border country of the *Kingdom* of Burgundy from Chalon s/Saône onwards (the Saône was its frontier for many centuries), and he will not leave the territory of the old kingdom until he passes Nice and enters Italy.

Preface:

A Kingdom Discovered

'Burgundy'. Since the holidays of childhood we had been in no doubt where and what it was. It was the land where the vines began and the waters parted: at Auxerre, Châtillon and Chaumont, on the threshold of Burgundy, the streams flowed northwards, back to the gray and the damp, whereas ahead, where the waters would now lead us, were the Mediterranean and the sun. Before long, however, Burgundy was more to us than just the Gateway to the South. It came to mean the pleasures of the wayside, architecture, and living history; and, as our Peugeot bore us down the N6, we used to make-believe we were Caesar's legions marching victorious from Bibracte,* or Richard Lionheart's knights descending from Vézelay to ride along the banks of the Saône and Rhône towards the glitter of Provence, Sicily and the Holy Land.

But we were still as sure as ever that, as we passed the rolling vineyards of Beaujolais – in turn Juliénas, Fleurie and Morgon – it was time to turn and wave goodbye to Burgundy; and long before Avignon, where we would watch the Rhône flow past the broken bridge and we would strike up the well-known song, we knew that we were deep into another land, Provence, the heart of the Midi.

Thirty years later I was sent to work in Geneva, a hundred miles from Burgundy, or so I still believed. Odd discoveries aroused my curiosity but, because they seemed to have no connecting link, it was some time before my eyes were opened. I learnt for instance that a village festival was known as a '*vogue*' in Savoy, to the south of us, and in parts of the Vosges far to the north, whereas '*fête*' was in general use in the lands between. Was this connected, I wondered, with the ability of elderly peasants as distant as those of the Val d'Aosta and Forez, Jura and the hills beyond Grenoble (in English terms, as distant as London and Liverpool, Hull and Exeter) to understand each other's patois, whereas their speech was quite incomprehensible only a few miles further on? (See Map no. 2) Was it only a strange coincidence that the same

* Today Mont Beuvray, between Chalon and Vézelay.

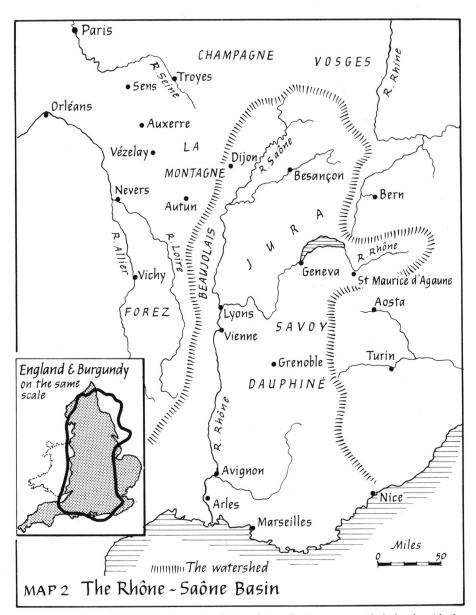

Paris

CHAMPAGNE   VOSGES

R. Seine

•Troyes

•Sens

Orléans

•Auxerre

LA

Vézelay•   MONTAGNE   Dijon   R. Saône

•Besançon

Nevers   •Bern

Autun   J U R A

R. Allier   R. Loire   BEAUJOLAIS

R. Rhône

•Vichy   Geneva   St Maurice d'Agaune

FOREZ   •Aosta

Lyons   SAVOY

Vienne   Turin

•Grenoble

DAUPHINÉ

R. Rhône

Avignon

•Arles   •Nice

Marseilles

England & Burgundy
on the same
scale

Miles

0   50

||||||||||The watershed

MAP 2 The Rhône ‑ Saône Basin

Map no. 2 The watershed enclosing the Rhône‑Saône Basin corresponded closely with the
frontier of the Kingdom of Burgundy. It was least of a barrier in the north, and the Franks
(French) had little difficulty in crossing 'La Montagne', the high ground from which the Seine
and its tributaries flow north and west towards the English Channel.

breed of cattle prevailed throughout this same region and was not to be found outside it until its exportation in recent times?

It did not dawn on me that these patois, these cattle, had anything to do with 'Burgundy', until one day I read that the area they occupied was the homeland which the early Burgundians, who were probably cousins of the Goths, had settled after their menfolk were put to the sword by the Huns in 436 – an event which was immortalized in Bavaria in the Nibelungenlied and in Iceland in the Sagas. So 'Burgundy' had once been more extensive than the great wine-growing area between Champagne and Beaujolais, and it had included Geneva, the center of the Burgundians' homeland and their first capital, and also Besançon and Grenoble?

Another 'discovery' had struck me long before this, but here again I was slow to see a link. There seemed to be a region in eastern France and western Switzerland where the bells in the more ancient parish churches were normally placed above the crossing, a feature which distinguished them from the churches of Italy, Germany and also, generally speaking, the rest of France. Eventually I observed that this region corresponded roughly to the sum of the Burgundy of the wine and the Burgundians' 'homeland'. But no sooner had I become accustomed to the idea of a Burgundy stretching from Auxerre not only to Beaujolais but beyond lake Geneva and Grenoble than I was reminded that Shakespeare spoke in *King Lear* of the wine of France and *milk* of Burgundy since for him and his contemporaries Burgundy was the *Low Countries*; so that it was no great surprise to read that the name 'Kingdom of Burgundy' was to be given to *Belgium* when the Emperor offered it to the Elector of Bavaria in 1784. It was, however, more perplexing to learn that, when Pope John XXIII was deposed by the Council of Constance in the year of Agincourt (1415) and he fled to what is now *German Switzerland*, the contemporary annalist called it 'Burgundia'; that the archbishops of Trier in *north-west Germany* held the title 'Archchancellor of the Kingdom of Burgundy' until the seventeenth century; and that, when Frederick Barbarossa was crowned King of Burgundy in 1178, the ceremony was held at Arles in *Provence*, hundreds of miles from Trier, let alone Belgium.

I was naturally left wondering just how large 'Burgundy' had been, but above all what was this 'kingdom'? How could it disappear from history so completely that it is scarcely mentioned in any general work? And, when it is, the reader is left with the impression that Burgundy was hardly less a chimera, a medieval fantasy, than the licorne or the philosopher's stone?

I already knew that the heartland of the nascent Europe which Charlemagne

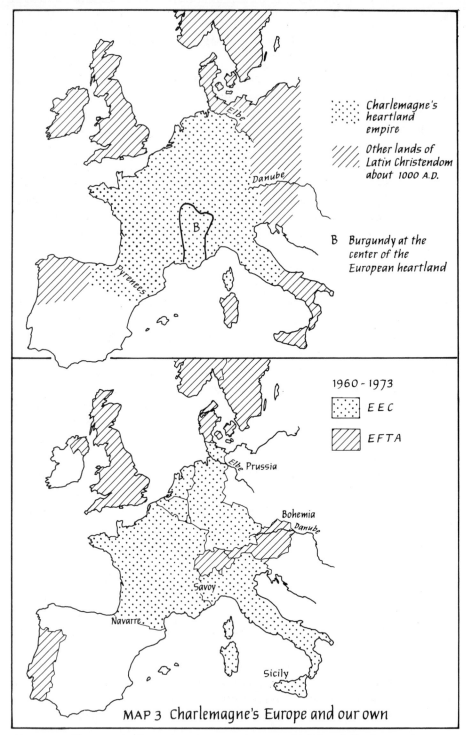

Charlemagne's
heartland
empire

Other lands of
Latin Christendom
about 1000 A.D.

B Burgundy at the
center of the
European heartland

1960 - 1973

EEC

EFTA

MAP 3 Charlemagne's Europe and our own

Map no. 3 The remarkable similarity between the original EEC and Charlemagne's empire, and between the original EFTA and the rest of Latin Christendom, is of no special significance in our story. More relevant is Burgundy's position at the center.

made into his empire became the three kingdoms of Germany, France and Italy.* What I now learnt was that for the greater part of the fifteen centuries which separate us today from the barbarian invasions there was a fourth kingdom, Burgundy. Sooner or later, of course, there would be other Christian kingdoms outside this European heartland: on the periphery, Sicily,** Navarre and Bohemia; in the British Isles and the Iberian and Scandinavian peninsulas; and in the great spaces opening towards Russia and the east Mediterranean lands of the crusades. But in the main body of Western Europe, between the Elbe and the Pyrenees, there were only these four kingdoms, Germany, France, Italy and Burgundy, from the time of Charlemagne onwards; and there were no new creations until the promotion of Prussia (1701)*** and Savoy-Sardinia (1720).

By those dates the Kingdom of Burgundy had disappeared; but only a few decades before that history had seen the last of the attempts to raise it from the ashes – a Dodo**** which was so nearly a Phoenix! Dating from about AD 400, it could claim to be the most ancient kingdom of all Europe. It was as large as England, corresponding in fact remarkably closely with a vast natural feature, the Rhône-Saône basin.***** As children we had watched the waters flow through the broken bridge at Avignon, without thinking that they had come not only, as we had, from the wine country beyond Dijon, but also from Geneva, our future home, and the Alpine mass four hundred miles upstream, not to speak of the rivers of the Vosges, Jura, Lyonnais, Savoy and Dauphiné.

For the millennium when it was more substance than shadow the Kingdom of Burgundy was a match for England in the numbers and the brilliance of its people. Yet today it is forgotten and unknown, for very little trace of it has survived. The Burgundy we took for granted as children, Everyman's Burgundy, the region so renowned for its wine, in fact lay for half of the Kingdom's life outside its borders, and before that it was no more than one of its frontier provinces. It is true that in a sense 'Burgundy' has been perpetuated in the form of successor states – Belgium, the Netherlands, Switzerland and even

* Map no. 3 shows how similar in area Charlemagne's heartland empire was to Europe's heartland of today, i.e. the original EEC, in which once again Germany, France and Italy have been the most prominent countries. Note also 'outer Europe' in both cases.
** Sicily and South Italy formed one state for a long period.
*** 'Germany' was to become several kingdoms: Prussia, Bavaria, Saxony and Württemberg, quite apart from Austria.
**** One can say that the Kingdom of Burgundy and the dodo suffered the same fate around the same time, the latter becoming extinct soon after 1681.
***** See Map no. 2.

Italy. But if the reader expects to find an area where something distinctive like a native language still prevails, the most that can conceivably be claimed for Burgundy relates to an Italian province the size of a small English county!

So deeply has the Kingdom of Burgundy disappeared into oblivion that there is still no comprehensive history about it, at any rate in French or English.* The present work aims only to tell briefly of its triumphs and disaster, and the attempts to restore it. A study so selective and compressed can do little to fill the gap. The historian who takes up the challenge will perhaps agree that Burgundy's case has gone by default and there is here a lost but worthy cause to which justice still needs to be done. History can be a blinkered muse and is too often the tale told by a victor. Burgundy was not Europe's only might-have-been, albeit probably the most fascinating; and a future historian of the lost Burgundy may wish to bring out how different the map of Europe could have looked today if regions with ancient traditions and cultures like Burgundy, Brittany and Provence had survived no less than Switzerland, Belgium and Luxemburg; and particularly if, as would not have been unreasonable, frontiers had been more closely related to languages. In this brief work we shall be concerned with the languages of the area, but we can do no more than touch on such general questions as the relationship between 'language', 'race', 'people', 'nation', 'country' and 'state'. And what indeed of the 'nation state'? For are states always made by nations and nations never by states?

These questions arise with special interest in the territories between the Rhine and Alps and the Pyrenees. Whatever the claims of France's rulers, for most of the period with which we shall be chiefly involved (400–1500) France was effectively limited to the provinces where old French was spoken. It did not even comprise all the territories north of the Loire, and it formed barely one quarter of the modern state of France. In stressing such facts I have tried not so much to see things from a 'Burgundian' point of view as to strike a balance with the conventional standpoint of French historians who often seem to assume that France was predestined to extend to the Rhine, Alps and Pyrenees. I hope the reader will not mistake my attempt to be objective for anti-French prejudice, since for sixty years the land across the Channel has hardly been less dear to me than my own. My aim has been to do justice to Burgundy without being unfair to France.

C.L.S.C.

Geneva and Holme Hale, Norfolk.

* See Appendix IV.

PROLOGUE – TRIER, AUTUMN 1473

Charles the Bold demands the Crown of Burgundy

On 30 September 1473 Charles Duke of Burgundy rode into Trier to meet the Emperor. His bearing declared his certainty of complete success. Mounted on a black horse in battle harness covered with cloth of gold and violet, he was arrayed in polished steel armor and a short cloak glittering with rubies, diamonds and other gems. Frederick III wore a long golden robe bordered with pearls and, behind him, his son Maximilian Hapsburg made a striking figure in silver and crimson. Like the Duke, the Emperor was attended by a brilliant retinue of nobles and clergy, but Frederick was sadly outshone by his feudatory. Charles, on meeting his overlord, might make to kneel before him, might refuse for half an hour before yielding to Frederick's repeated invitation to ride abreast with him, but he knew that the sumptuousness of his entourage showed where lay the real substance of power. The Emperor, whose treasury could ill afford the expense of this meeting with his haughty vassal, could not fail to be reminded of how few territories he could truly call his own when he observed the fourteen Burgundian heralds-at-arms, one for each of Charles's lands, move in procession with one hundred handsome youths and a band of trumpeters.

The splendor of the pageantry maintained throughout the conference is attested by many eye-witnesses. This was not a State Visit lasting the two or three days of modern times; for two months, with Charles technically the guest disporting himself rather as royal host, the banquets and tournaments kept the city in a fever of excitement. As the days and then the weeks passed by, there was ever increasing speculation about the outcome. Only now, after some ten years of diplomatic exchanges, were there elements of an agreement for the principals to discuss. It was Pope Pius II, better known as Aeneas Sylvius Piccolomini, who had brought the imperial and Burgundian courts to negotiate an alliance. Like many contemporaries Pius was tormented by the prospect of Christendom collapsing before the Turks, who barely a decade after capturing

Constantinople (1453) had overrun Bosnia, only a few days' march from either Italy or Austria. He recognized that the Empire under its feeble Hapsburg sovereign desperately needed buttressing by alliance with an ascendant dynasty; and so now, as everyone knew, agreement was to be sealed in Trier by the betrothal of Frederick's son Maximilian to Charles's daughter Mary.

We know today that there was no difficulty in agreeing on the marriage, and that the delay arose from Charles's insistence that his extensive dominions should be elevated to a kingdom – a concession by Frederick which, given Burgundy's wealth and power, would merely give form to undeniable fact. That some crown should be awarded to the duke must have been conceded early in the conference for work was set in hand in the abbey church of Saint Maximin to erect two thrones, for Emperor and king-designate. Builders were busy setting up scaffolding for the benches from which the two courts would watch the ceremony, and it became known in the city that skilled artisans were fashioning a royal crown and scepter. In 1447 Frederick had proposed to Charles's father, Philip the Good, raising the Duchy of Brabant to a kingdom and making him its sovereign, but Philip, who once said 'I want everyone to know that if I wished I would be a king', turned the offer down as inadequate: had history ever known a Kingdom of Brabant? In the course of October Frederick pressed Charles to accept some lesser title than King of Burgundy which, he remembered, previous emperors had feared to assign, but he finally gave way and on 4 November, five weeks after he and Charles had come together, a settlement was reached.

The Kingdom of Burgundy reconstituted for Charles the Bold

First, in a magnificent ceremony during which Charles vowed to lead a crusade to drive the Turks from Europe, Frederick invested him with his latest acquisition, the Duchy of Guelders in the east of the modern Netherlands. It was not lost on observers that, although Charles went through the motions of paying homage to Frederick, the ceremony was conducted at Charles's and not Frederick's headquarters, in a great hall hung with tapestries portraying the conquests of the duke's hero and model, Alexander the Great. It was as though Charles were holding court in one of his palaces in Flanders. But there was a second and even more important piece of business on that day of pageantry, for the ministers of Emperor and duke signed an agreement which opened with this passage:

[28]

The most serene Lord the Emperor will with immediate effect restore and set up the Kingdom of Burgundy for the most illustrious Lord the Duke of Burgundy for himself and for whatever heirs or successors he may have, male or female,* with all the dignities, rights and prerogatives which belong in any way to the said Kingdom of Burgundy.[1]**

There was no need for the text to spell out the 'dignities, rights and prerogatives' of the Kingdom of Burgundy, since both courts knew that they embraced all the lands from the County of Burgundy southwards to the Mediterranean, including western and central Switzerland, Savoy, Dauphiné and Provence (Map no. 4). The agreement stipulated as well that Charles was to be king in the rich territories which the Duke of Savoy held in north Italy, and in other areas which had never been part of the Kingdom of Burgundy stretching from Holland and Friesland as far as the southern limits of Alsace.

In brief a vast band of irregular width stretching from the northern tip of the present-day Netherlands to the Italian Riviera which, as Charles must have been aware, corresponded roughly with the kingdom awarded to Lothar at Verdun in 843 – the ephemeral Middle Kingdom between Germany and France which still awaited its creator.

It was not in the Emperor's power to make Charles king in the ancient heart of his lands, the Duchy of Burgundy, since there Louis XI of France was still nominally king even if Charles did no homage to him; but Charles expected to have little difficulty in eventually gaining recognition that the Duchy and the other lands technically held from Louis were no longer to be comprised in France but were once again part of the Kingdom of Burgundy.

For Charles the agreement was quite literally a crowning glory, for now his power was to be capped with authority. Savoy, already his satellite, would now be his subject. The Swiss might defy him, as also the French in Dauphiné, but if so they would be rebels; for what would previously have been aggression by an alien duke would now be no more than the assertion of their king's sanctified right. Finally, it would be easier to hold 'Good King René'*** to his promise of the succession to Provence, which like Savoy, Dauphiné and most of Switzerland, formed part of the old Burgundian kingdom.

* While still hoping for a son, Charles made ready for Mary to be his heir. She did in fact succeed him.
** See Notes in Appendix V, p. 260.
*** René, Duke of Anjou, Lorraine and Bar, Count of Provence, and titular King of Naples and Sicily (b. 1409, d. 1480). He was the father of Margaret who married Henry VI of England in 1445.

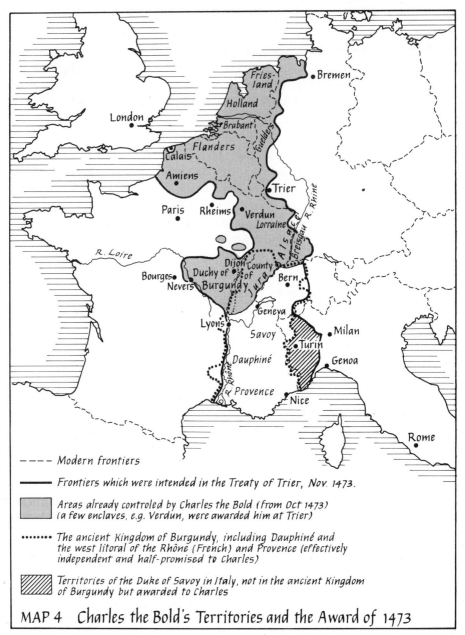

Modern frontiers

Frontiers which were intended in the Treaty of Trier, Nov. 1473.

Areas already controled by Charles the Bold (from Oct 1473) (a few enclaves, e.g. Verdun, were awarded him at Trier)

The ancient Kingdom of Burgundy, including Dauphiné and the west litoral of the Rhône (French) and Provence (effectively independent and half-promised to Charles)

Territories of the Duke of Savoy in Italy, not in the ancient Kingdom of Burgundy but awarded to Charles

MAP 4 Charles the Bold's Territories and the Award of 1473

Map no. 4 The straggling lines running north and south mark out the area of the kingdom described as Charles's in the treaty of Trier of November 1473. All that lay north of the Jura mountains – i.e. the greater part – was already his. Of the rest, Savoy was his satellite and Provence was promised to him; the French controled Dauphiné, but the main resistance would come from the Swiss led by the citizens of Bern.

So, if there had been doubts before about the ability of Charles, whom many considered the finest captain of his age, to impose his will not only from the North Sea to the Jura but down to the Mediterranean, his new royal dignity would dispel them. His father and he had made a solid and efficient state out of their northern provinces, and now it was for him and his successors to extend their dominion from sea to sea. It would be a formidable task but no more daunting than that soon to face the French kings in their equally disparate and wide-spread territories.

Shortly after the signature of the agreement on 4 November Frederick named 25 November as the day, and Trier was in ferment as the great event approached and the new sovereign's crown, scepter, cloak and banner were put on public view. Rulers of many lands had their agents in Trier reporting to them on developments, and in the last days of November a detailed account of Charles's coronation circulated in Germany, Italy and Switzerland. The Swiss had been particularly concerned to follow events since they saw themselves, and rightly, as the first victims of this alliance between the Hapsburgs and Burgundy. They had survived the onslaughts of the Hapsburgs, who had also failed to reduce the free cities of the Rhineland; but the Burgundians had subjected the city states of Flanders and were a much more dangerous threat. The report of the coronation which reached Bern, the most powerful of the cantons, said that Charles was crowned on 24 November king of all the lands he already held in the Empire, and of Milan and other imperial fiefs, and sovereign also over Savoy and all states and cities lying south and east of the Jura which had formed the Kingdom of Burgundy. The Bernese did not question the report, and in good faith they passed it on to their confederates without further ado on 29 November. It was, after all, no more than they had expected.

II

PHOENIX ON THE WING

———

Nibelungs and Merovings:
The First Kingdom of Burgundy

'The skin of our teeth'

The Kingdom of Burgundy which Frederick III had conferred on Charles the Bold had its origins more than one thousand years before, and could claim to be the most ancient of Europe's kingdoms, since it was established on the Rhine by King Gunther* in 413, three years after the sack of Rome by the Goths, the event which the author long believed marked the collapse of the civilized world of the Roman Empire in the terror and chaos of the Dark Ages. He had not heard of the Burgundians, let alone of the shadowy figure of Gunther; but he had a picture of Goths, Vandals and Huns, Franks, Angles and Saxons, sweeping over Gaul, Italy and Britain in hordes, putting their civilized and Christian peoples to the sword, and leveling to the ground everything that, unlike the Colosseum and the Pont du Gard, was not massive enough to withstand them.

For many years the term 'Dark Age Europe' meant to him indeed a wasteland in which public buildings, churches and schools were overtaken by fire, rapine and dark night; and there was no government or law, let alone libraries, art or architecture. He had read somewhere how for long generations Christianity only survived by clinging on to places like Skellig Michael, a rock in the Atlantic many miles from the coast of Ireland.[1] In such remote fastnesses Christian monks took refuge from the barbarian flood, and from there in due course, he had read, they returned to bring the cross and civilization once again to the benighted peoples of Europe. In this manner we were saved by the skin of our teeth from the fate which overtook other civilizations, such as those of Inca and Indus. The author pictured Europe, in sum, as engulfed in a dark age for centuries until the coming of new men like Charlemagne and Alfred, and in this he suspects he was in the company of an overwhelming majority.

* For a chronological list of events, and the names and dates of Burgundy's kings, see Appendices VI and VII.

[35]

It must swiftly be admitted that this 'scenario' is not far from the truth so far as Roman Britain is concerned.[2] It is indicative of the darkness which fell on our island that we should know so little about the era we have peopled with Arthur of Camelot and the Knights of the Round Table, indeed about the two centuries which separate the withdrawal of the legions and the coming of Saint Augustine in 596 – and with him the beginning of a cultural influence from the Continent far more important than that from Britain's Celtic fringe, let alone the west coast of Ireland.

However, the picture of chaos, desolation and ignorance is false for large areas of the Continent. In the early sixth century, when it is reasonable to believe that a prototype for the legendary Arthur was performing deeds of valor, in Italy and elsewhere less wraith-like figures were leaving us evidence of a relatively high civilization which was certainly not being matched in Britain, Celtic or Anglo-Saxon. Travelers who know the early Christian churches of Ravenna and Rome, with their priceless mosaics, will need no telling that Italy continued to enjoy a respectable level of civilization in the fifth and sixth centuries. It is less well known that this was also the case in Spain where the Goths established a kingdom, as they did in Italy; and in the Rhône valley, which came under Burgundian rule in the generation after Gunther,* as we shall see, was defeated and slain by the Huns.

After the 'Disaster of the Nibelungs' the Burgundians settle the Homeland (413–58)

The early Burgundians were probably the most Romanized of the 'barbarians' even before their settlement within the Empire.[3] They were cousins of the Goths and like them came most probably from southern Norway or Sweden, by way of Bornholm (the island between Sweden and Pomerania known a few centuries ago as Burgundarholm), to settle first in Poland and eventually in south Germany.** The Burgundians, or more properly their ruling clan, were also known as 'Nibelungs', the Sons of Nifils, the god of the northern mists.*** For most readers the 'Nibelungs' are the dwarfs whose king Alberich stole the

* Variously Gunthiar(us), Gunnar.
** Map no. 5 shows the Burgundians' migrations; areas of settlement in 443 and 458; and expansion after 458.
*** Also known as Gjukings or (as in Wagner) Gibichungs. The Old Norse Snorra Edda tells of 'the Gjukings who are also called Niflungs'. In the words of the Nibelungenlied, the Nibelungs' 'country was called Burgundy. They lived with their people at Worms on the banks of the Rhine'.

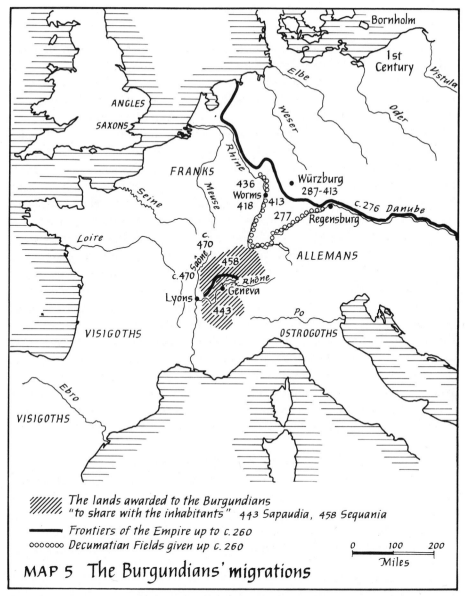

The lands awarded to the Burgundians
"to share with the inhabitants" 443 Sapaudia, 458 Sequania
Frontiers of the Empire up to c. 260
ooooooo Decumatian Fields given up c. 260

0   100   200
Miles

MAP 5 The Burgundians' migrations

Map no. 5 From Poland onwards the Burgundians' migrations fall into five main moves: in 276–7 (into the orbit of Rome); *c.* 413 (to the Rhine around Worms, the 'Kingdom of Worms'); in 443 (to Savoy); in 458 (to the later County of Burgundy); and over the next two decades filling in pockets up to the Saône and spreading thinly beyond it.

In 257–60 the Roman army was withdrawn from Württemberg. The Burgundians were admitted there by Emperor Probus *c.* 277 apparently charged with its defence as Roman 'Federates' against the Allemans. This was the basis of the Burgundians' proud claim later on that they were Romans. However they were expelled from there by the Allemans in 287 and spent more than 100 years in the triangle Würzburg-Eichstätt-Regensburg on the edge of the Romanized area. (See also note 3 on p. 260.) Before they settled in their final homes they had thus been in a partly Romanized area for a century and a half, and for half a century in a thoroughly Romanized province.

Some Burgundians were settled by Probus in Britain, where they helped put down a revolt.

Rhine gold in the Wagnerian operatic cycle *The Ring of the Nibelung*; but some will recall from the Nibelungenlied and the Saga of the Volsungs, the Bavarian and Icelandic epics from the Middle Ages, that 'Nibelung' denoted the ancient dynasty of Burgundy, and in this book it is applied to the family which led the Burgundians to their ultimate home in Gaul and founded their kingdom.[4]

Around 413 we find the Burgundians on the middle Rhine with their capital at Worms. They had now been under Roman influence at close range for nearly 150 years, and had long regarded themselves as 'Romans'.* They were among the first barbarians to be converted, admittedly as Arians and not Catholics, but this did not hold up their Romanization. They were probably the only Teutonic migrant race not to have been any sort of a threat to the Empire, a reputation they put at risk in 436,** however, when they started moving westwards into Gaul, causing such concern to Aetius, the imperial governor of Gaul, that he called on to the Huns to stop them. The Huns would be described about 500 by Jordanes, the historian of the Goths, as 'a foul, stunted, misshapen tribe, scarcely human, with a fearful swarthy aspect, shapeless lumps for heads, pin-holes for eyes, and the cruelty of wild animals'. They were the terror of Roman and Teuton alike, and the battle which followed ended in the massacre of the Burgundians. Their losses were not as numerous as the 30,000 of legend, but certainly included King Gunther; and no defeat in history has made a greater impact on European legend, as we must tell in Appendix I. Yet within twenty years the Burgundians had recovered sufficiently to settle an area as large as Wales and in twenty more they ruled over a kingdom of the size of England.

In 443 and 458 they were given territories which were to be their final homeland: first Sapaudia,*** from which name comes 'Savoy', but which then included also the land between the Jura and lake Geneva as well as the north of Dauphiné; and fifteen years later Sequania, which became the County of Burgundy and is now called Franche Comté (Maps nos 2 and 6). Gunther's son Gundioc**** established his court in the little Roman town of

---

* See comment on Map no. 5.
** Or 437. An example of early dates over which authorities differ.
*** 'The land of the silver pine or fir'. Fir in Latin, *sapinus*; in French, *le sapin*.
**** Gundioc (437–*c.* 470) had as ally one Riothamus described by Jordanes as 'King of the Britons', who were by that time settling in Brittany as well as still holding most of Britain. Jordanes wrote that Riothamus came at the request of the Emperor Anthemius (467–72) to assist him against the Visigoths with an army 'from over the sea'. He took Bourges in the heart of Gaul. He there received a letter from Sidonius Apollinaris (pp. 45 and 50 below), probably in 469. Defeated by the Goths near Chateauroux, according to Jordanes Riothamus 'fled to the

Geneva, and here his minstrels began to immortalize the legend of the Disaster of the Nibelungs. Soon after the accession of Gundioc's son Gundobad in 474 the authority of the Nibelung dynasty stretched from Champagne to the Mediterranean, and from the river Reuss in eastern Switzerland to the Forez mountains, deep into modern France; their main centers had become the much more substantial cities of Vienne and Lyons; and some of their subjects had begun to move outside the donated territories of Sapaudia and Sequania and establish settlements west of the river Saône, on the Côte d'Or and on the high ground beyond.

Like many builders of states Gundobad displayed enlightenment and ruthlessness in almost equal measure. Whilst serving his uncle Ricimer, then effectively the chief minister of Italy, Gundobad apparently decapitated the Emperor Anthemius with his own hands; and he was later to dispose of his own brothers Chilperic and Godegisel with no greater show of mercy in his bid for complete control of Burgundy. But his years at the center of imperial affairs in Italy – he succeeded Ricimer as Patrician in 472 – prepared him for his role as the greatest law-giver of all the 'barbarian' kings. The First Kingdom of Burgundy is usually dated from 443, or even from 413, but its effective consolidation belongs to the 42 years of Gundobad's reign. Unfortunately for his successors, however, Burgundy was militarily no match for the Kingdom which Clovis the Frank was simultaneously building up in north-east Gaul with the aid of his Burgundian queen, Clotilda.

Clotilda is best known to us as the saint who converted Clovis and his people to Christianity. Saints have often been important to history less for their saintliness than for their courage and resourcefulness, and in this respect even Saint Joan gave no more to France than this young princess. She was the daughter of Gundobad's brother Chilperic, whom Gundobad murdered with his wife, sending Clotilda and her sister to a nunnery in Geneva. It is not surprising that she took with her a consuming ambition to destroy the ruling house of Burgundy.

In the nunnery a messenger disguised as a beggar came to her from Clovis

---

Burgundians, who were allies of the Romans' (probably in 470). We hear no more of him. He is given this footnote because Geoffrey Ashe (in *The Discovery of King Arthur*, 1985) suggests that Riothamus is simply 'British' for 'king'; that he was in fact King Arthur; and that Avalon, where Arthur (in history as well as legend?) went to his death, is in Burgundy. (Probably not Avallon. There is unfortunately no space here to discuss any of this, e.g. whether Arthur, if he ever existed, was not after rather than before 500; but were Gundioc and Arthur the precursors of the later age-long British-Burgundian alliance?!)

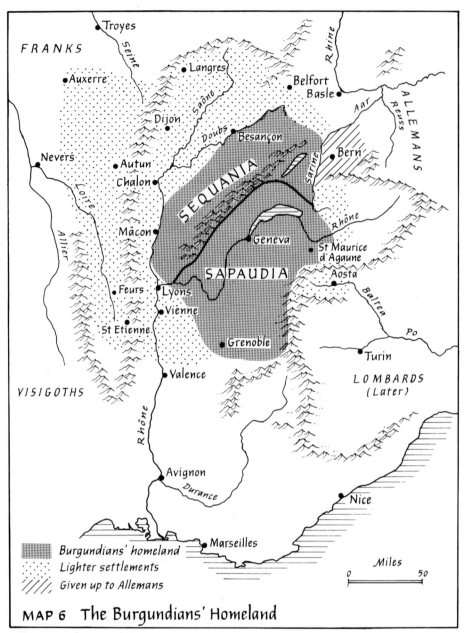

MAP 6 The Burgundians' Homeland

Burgundians' homeland
Lighter settlements
Given up to Allemans

Map no. 6 The Burgundians could be expected to make the deepest impression in the areas shaded heavily: these areas were officially awarded to them, the land being shared out between them and the Gallo-Roman inhabitants (who seem anyway not to have been thick on the ground). What is striking (and not easy to explain) is that the main evidence of their presence, the survival of the Franco-Provençal language, was to be found until recently in large areas to the west and east of the heavy shading, in areas in fact where there were few Burgundians. See Map no. 13, p. 95.

with an offer of marriage. Clotilda accepted joyfully and contrived a romantic and hazardous escape from Geneva. She eluded Gundobad's pursuers by abandoning the coach which carried her baggage and jumping on a horse. When the Burgundian troops overtook the coach she was already safely over the border at Bar-sur-Seine riding hard towards her royal fiancé. The sons she gave Clovis learnt from their implacable mother that filial duty required them to avenge her parents, invade Burgundy and crush their cousins. When they succeeded Clovis in 511, they did not fail her, albeit after a long and bitter war. Gundobad's son Sigismund and his wife and children were thrown into a well near Orleans in 523, and after staunch resistance Godomar, the last of the Nibelung kings, was overwhelmed at Autun in 534.

King Sigismund's qualities and behavior were hardly more saintly than Gundobad's but he was canonized because as crown prince he had had the good sense to renounce the Arian heresy of his dynasty and become a Catholic. A good friend of the Church, he was probably responsible for some of the buildings emerging today from beneath Geneva cathedral. One of his early acts as king was to call together the first of many councils of Burgundian bishops to be held in the next century and a half; and before that he had already founded a monastery at Agaune at the west end of the Swiss Valais just where Saint Maurice had been martyred. Maurice had been the commander of the Theban legion which had been massacred by other troops of the Emperor Diocletian late in the third century for refusing to persecute the Christians.

Almost every history of early Europe writes Finis to the First Kingdom of Burgundy with the defeat of Godomar in 534. The fact that Maurice came to be the protector and patron saint of Burgundy, and what were believed to be his lance, signet ring and sword* became in due course the regalia of the Kingdom, indicated that Burgundy lived on in men's hearts and aspirations. But that is not all, for the Merovings, as Clovis's dynasty is called, preserved intact the kingdom which the Nibelungs had created, and this helped to fix it almost ineradicably on the map of Europe for a thousand years.

---

* For the crown of Burgundy and Holy Lance of Saint Maurice see p. 69 below. Maurice's supposed remains were at Saint-Maurice-d'Agaune (Swiss Valais) and at Vienne, Burgundy's holy city and often its capital (especially 879–1034). The saint's supposed ring was given by the monks of Agaune to the counts of Savoy in the thirteenth century and became part of their enthronement insignia.

*The Merovingian Franks keep the Kingdom of Burgundy
separate and intact (534–726)*

In 534 when the Merovings conquered Burgundy they were already masters
from the Pyrenees to the river Weser, deep into Germany. Aquitaine had been
won from the Burgundians' Visigothic cousins and divided between Clovis's
sons, as was also 'Francia', the Frankish territories which became known as
Austrasia and Neustria; and it was to be expected that they would now break up
Burgundy too, not least because only part of it was truly Burgundian.

It will be important to bear in mind throughout our story that there were *two*
Kingdoms of Burgundy, one enclosing the other. The larger area was initially
not a kingdom or strictly a *Burgundian* state but rather a group of six Roman
provinces* of which Gundioc, the Burgundians' king, was made Magister
Militum or imperial viceroy.[5] It was this greater state, however, to which the
name First Kingdom of Burgundy has been given by historians; and Gundobad
and Sigismund were truly 'kings', their recognition of the emperor being only
nominal.

Before Gundobad, the real creator of the First Kingdom, had disposed
ruthlessly of his brothers, one of them, Godegisel, was ruler of the smaller state
which comprised Sapaudia and Sequania; this, by contrast with the larger, the
imperial authorities had given the Burgundians to settle and make their own
(Map no. 6 on p. 40). For this lesser or mini-kingdom of Burgundy we shall
often use the term Burgundian *Homeland*, because here alone were the
Burgundians relatively thick on the ground and the only significant 'barbarian'
inhabitants, certainly to be numbered in tens of thousands.** Provence had
virtually no Burgundian settlers (and not many Goths)*** and the former had
been there as overlords only briefly; in the east of the Kingdom, in present-day
Switzerland, there were Allemans as well as Burgundians;**** and, more im-

---

* The provinces disappeared, to be replaced by counties, smaller administrative units,
(headed by a *comes*), generally a Roman city with the land around. There were about 300 in Gaul.

** Jerome estimated them in 373, when they were still in Bavaria, at 80,000 souls altogether.
More modern estimates for their settlement in the Homeland three generations later: Jahn
263,700 (!); Chaume 10,000; Salin under 50,000. Perronot's studies[6] suggest to me that
Jerome's figure, allowing for gains and losses in the meantime, might after all be closest. The
areas granted to the Burgundians were probably thinly populated.

*** The Burgundian kings reigned only very briefly south of the Durance before the
Ostrogoths and after them the Franks took over.

**** The Allemans were later to push the Burgundians west of the river Sarine, the linguistic
frontier even today.

portantly for the Merovings, there were perhaps more Franks than Burgundians on 'La Montagne', as the high ground in the north-west of the kingdom is known (Map no. 7). Provence and these Frankish and Allemannic areas will retain an identity of their own throughout our story.

The regions where the Burgundians settled, spilling to some extent over the limits of Sapaudia and Sequania, are known to us from their cemeteries and from place names. The Homeland in which they formed a very significant minority comprised western Switzerland, Savoy, south Franche Comté and north Dauphiné; but their remains are to be found also fairly plentifully in the rest of Dauphiné and in north Franche Comté, west of the Saône both north and south of Lyons, and around Dijon and beyond it on 'La Montagne'.* (It must also be of significance that the breeds of cattle which the Burgundians brought with them in their long trek from Poland should still have been spread over these areas a century ago, before the introduction of other breeds.)[7] The region which the Burgundians settled may be said therefore to stretch from the line Auxerre-Langres-Belfort to one a little to the south of Saint Etienne-Grenoble. For the Burgundian historian Maurice Chaume this was the 'true' Burgundy, or *'Burgundy proper'*, an entity intermediate between the large kingdom and the small, to which later pages must occasionally refer (Map no. 6).

In the mid-sixth century all these territories had become subject to the Franks. It would have been natural for them to destroy the Nibelungs' kingdom to ensure that the Burgundians were no longer any threat; and the obvious course was to break up the viceroyalty given to Gundioc, to detach the Provençal, Allemannic and Frankish regions, and to leave only the mini-kingdom of Burgundy, the Homeland which was an area comparable with Wales.** Moreover the large kingdom the Nibelungs had made out of their six Roman provinces lay near the center of the Merovings' dominions and so was the most obvious territory to be shared out in any partition. The extraordinary fact is that, even though the Merovingian empire was divided between brothers for 188 years out of 217, the Kingdom of Burgundy – an area as large as England – was left intact virtually all of the time. The two parts of Francia,

---

* Page 38 and Map no. 6.

** In *La Provence du premier au douzième siècle* Manteyer wrote (p. 76) not only of 'Provençal Burgundy', 'Allemannic Burgundy' and 'Frankish Burgundy' but also, with more logic than elegance, of 'Burgundian Burgundy'. We shall see below that this was the area in which the Burgundians' Romance language took root, i.e. the Homeland in which Godegisel had been king, plus Lyonnais and Forez to its west and the valleys of Aosta and Susa to the east (Map no. 7).

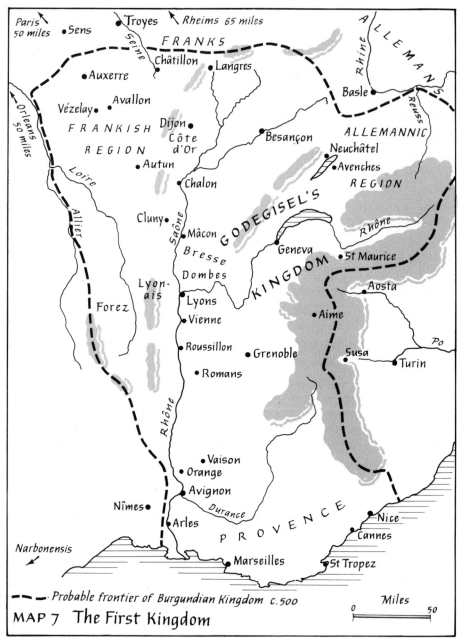

Paris
50 miles

•Sens

•Troyes

↗ Rheims 65 miles

F R A N K S

•Châtillon

•Langres

•Auxerre

Orleans
50 miles

Vézelay•

•Avallon

F R A N K I S H

Dijon•

Côte
d'Or

•Besançon

A L L E M A N N I C

Basle•

Neuchâtel•

R E G I O N

•Autun

Chalon•

Avenches•

R E G I O N

Loire

Allier

Cluny•

Mâcon•

B r e s s e

Geneva•

•St Maurice

Dombes

•Aosta

Lyon-
ais

Forez

Lyons•

•Aime

Vienne•

Rhône

Po

•Roussillon

•Grenoble

•Susa

•Turin

•Romans

Rhône

•Vaison

•Orange

Avignon•

Durance

Nîmes•

Arles•

P R O V E N C E

•Nice

•Cannes

Narbonensis

•Marseilles

•St Tropez

G O D E G I S E L ' S

K I N G D O M

Miles

— — — Probable frontier of Burgundian Kingdom c.500

0   50

MAP 7 The First Kingdom

Map no. 7   Provence was briefly Ostrogothic, Aosta and Susa were annexed in 576.

Austrasia and Neustria, continued to be partitioned just as was Aquitaine, but Burgundy was seemingly a state which it was thought right to preserve; and, unlike the Franks' other subject territories in Aquitaine, Allemania and in due course Italy, Burgundy was not required to pay tribute.

One need not look far for the reasons for Burgundy's survival separate and intact. It is possible that it weighed with the Merovingian kings that Burgundy's frontiers more or less followed the watershed which encloses the Rhône-Saône basin (Map no. 2 on p. 20). But it is probably of greater significance that Burgundy was the most advanced and best organized of the Merovings' territories. Even though Sidonius Apollinaris found the Burgundians un-couth,* no 'barbarians' had been quicker to accept the higher civilization they saw around them or readier to mix with the older inhabitants. In Gaul only Narbonensis, which their Gothic cousins had taken over, could match the level of civic, economic or cultural development of the Rhône valley.

Above all Burgundy had enjoyed a relatively advanced administration for four generations of Nibelung kings. Her laws showed the same amalgam of primitive custom and enlightenment to be found in emergent states throughout history. The Burgundians practised ordeal by battle; and they punished adultery in their women by drowning them in the bogs around their pastures in Poland – a barbarous penalty which needless to say did not apply to the men. But in the legal codes they enacted the Burgundian kings were more concerned that the Burgundians and the Gallo-Roman majority should integrate peace-fully. Thus Gundobad issued one code of law for all his subjects from the Marne to the Mediterranean, whether they were Burgundian or Gallo-Roman,** as well as separate codes for each people. This common code, the Lex Gambetta, went further than any other 'barbarian' attempt at codification and it was outstanding for its time in making Burgundians and Gallo-Romans equal before the law. Intermarriage seems to have been permitted from the beginning, whereas it was forbidden in the Visigoth kingdom in Spain until late in the sixth century, and today the Franks' laws would be condemned as racist. Burgundians and Gallo-Romans served alongside each other in the Burgundian army, whereas in the other 'barbarian' kingdoms the earlier inhabitants were kept separate and subject. The Burgundian Lex Gambetta was greatly

---

* Sidonius Apollinaris, *Carmina xii*. They moved into Lyonnais and the area to the north of it between 459 and 480. Sidonius was Bishop of Lyons till *c.* 488.
** In essentials it lasted six centuries.

influenced by Roman law, the Franks' codes hardly at all, and so they remained comparatively primitive.*

However, the greatest single force for unity in Burgundy in these centuries was probably not the crown (Nibelung or Meroving) but the Burgundian 'national' church. The Burgundian bishops' practice of meeting to evolve uniform policies for their dioceses and to discuss the problems of the realm had begun with the synod called in 517 by King Sigismund and Avitus, Archbishop of Vienne. In 570 Nicetius, Archbishop of Lyons, effectively declared himself Primate of Burgundy; he was later to be canonized for his skill in exorcizing unclean spirits. From 585, thanks to his successor Priscus, councils of the Burgundian clergy seem to have been held every three years. In this way Burgundy was given a corpus of ecclesiastical law – which up to the Renaissance was in many ways as significant in men's lives as secular law – so that in its ecclesiastical system Burgundy became distinguished from Francia and other countries no less than in its secular law and customs.**

*Queen Brunhild, prototype of the Wagnerian heroine (550–613)****

These differences between Francia and Burgundy were not yet pronounced when Clotar I,**** the last son of Clovis, died in 561, having been sole king since 558, and his lands were divided between his sons. (See Map no. 8) Sigebert gained Austrasia and Chilperic west Neustria; probably for the reasons given above Guntram received Burgundy intact and, as his Frankish portion, the territory of Orleans or east Neustria, which meant that he ruled from Paris to the Mediterranean. Guntram's lands were known as the Regnum (Kingdom)

---

* Under the Franks' law, if a free man squeezed the finger of a free woman, he was fined 15 solidi; if her arm, 30! The famous prohibition on women inheriting land, which was invoked by the Valois against Edward III of England's claims to the French crown, appeared in an unimportant section of the Franks' Salic Law.

** The Franks practised the Roman liturgy, the Burgundians the Gallican which had eastern origins; this may have been due to Burgundy's specially close relations with Constantinople.[8] Gallican practices long survived as a form of resistance to the Franks just as the Celtic Church and Irish Catholicism were later to spell opposition to the Roman Church and defiance of the English. See also Appendix V, 'Ashes' note 1.

*** Several writers regard her as prototype, e.g. Drapeyron, Ludovic, *La Reine Brunehilde et la crise sociale du VIe siècle*, Besançon 1867.

**** Clotar (or Chlotar) is the same name as Lothar. It is usual to use the former for Merovings, the latter for Carolings. See Appendix VII.

Burgundiae. It became so normal for east Neustria to be regarded as part of Burgundy that cities where Burgundians can have settled in only the smallest numbers came to be called Burgundian: many centuries later men still spoke of Sens-en-Bourgogne* and Troyes-en-Bourgogne, so strong was the memory of their inclusion in Merovingian Burgundy, in the same manner as a place in the Ile de France, now made famous by Paris's Charles de Gaulle airport, is still called Roissy-en-France. Burgundy formed the bulk of Guntram's lands and its most advanced and richest part; he established his capital in a Burgundian city, Chalon, and with the aid of the Burgundian bishops set about making Burgundy a prosperous land, independent of Francia. Guntram, whom Burgundians honored as a saint, was succeeded in 592 by his nephew Childebert II but the effective ruler of Burgundy until 613 was Childebert's mother, Brunehaut or Brunhild.

Brunhild was a remarkable girl who grew into an astounding woman. She was born about 550 and since she and her sister, Galswintha, were daughters of the Visigothic king of Spain, Athanagild, they had been brought up at one of the most brilliant courts of the day. About 570 she married Guntram's brother, King Sigebert of Austrasia; and not long after this Chilperic King of Neustria married her sister Galswintha, but the latter was strangled in circumstances highly incriminating to Chilperic and Fredegund, his low-born mistress, whom he then married. There can be little doubt that the events which followed provided the inspiration for much of the Siegfried-Brunnhilde legend which is contained in the Nibelungenlied, the Scandinavian saga of the Volsungs and Wagner's *Ring*.** For instance the feud between Queen Brunhild, determined to avenge her sister, and Fredegund, which locked the Merovingian kingdoms in war for forty years (573–613), may have inspired the story of the legendary Brunnhilde's*** quarrel with Gudrun, and the murder of her husband Sigebert in 575 may be the counterpart of Siegfried's murder. However, the Brunnhilde of history, far from throwing herself on her hero's funeral pyre, pursued his killers relentlessly. Unlike the Brunnhilde of legend she did not lose her seemingly superhuman powers with her virginity. The courage with which the queen fought on alone after her husband's murder was indeed worthy of an epic; soon afterwards we find her in Paris, now a beautiful woman of about

---

* Common usage in 16th cent., acc. to Chaume, *Le sentiment national bourguignon*, p. 235 n.

** Furthermore Burgundy's King Sigismund may be the prototype for Siegfried's father, Sigmund.

*** Brynhild in the Sagas.

[47]

BRITONS

ANGLES
AND
SAXONS

Dunwich

SAXONS

Elbe

Rhine

NEUSTRIA

Meuse

AUSTRASIA

Paris
Seine

ALLEMANS

Danube

BRITONS

Tours

Loire

BURGUNDY

Saône

Rhône

Rhône

Po

LOM-
BARDS

B
Y
Z
A
N
T
I
N
E

AQUITAINE

NARBONENSIS

Ebro

VISIGOTHS

Rome

E
M
P
I
R
E

Merovingian kingdoms c.561 – c.714

0   100   200
Miles

MAP 8 The Merovingian Kingdoms

Map no. 8 Apart from the variations noted at Map no. 7, Burgundy's frontiers were pretty constant. Those of the other Merovingian kingdoms, Austrasia, Neustria and Aquitaine, were not.

twenty-five, guarding her dead hero's treasure. (In both Wagner's opera and the Sagas she is guardian of the Ring for a while.)

Here fact and legend part company, but the truth is hardly the less eventful. Falling into her enemies' hands, Brunhild was forcibly married to Chilperic's son Merovech but, since he was her nephew by marriage, the Church annulled the union as incestuous; yet this did not deter Merovech's brother from trying to wed her too, which so incensed his stepmother Fredegund that she had him assassinated.

It was at this stage that her brother-in-law Guntram made her son Childebert heir to Burgundy. This restored her fortunes but the young prince reigned there only briefly (592–5), leaving Brunhild to be regent in Austrasia and Burgundy for his infant sons. Her thirty years' domination of Austrasia ended when she was expelled by the nobles in 599 but she continued in control of Burgundy (592–613), surviving her grandson Theodoric and ruling also for his baby son. She may have been the only queen-greatgrandmother of history; she was certainly one of the most striking figures of her age. She formed an alliance with the east Roman emperor, Justin II, to make war on the Lombards who had ravaged Burgundy in 569 and 574 and in 575 devastated Italy; and in 576 she secured the Lombards' cession of the valleys of Aosta and Susa (Map no. 7), an important event since in one sense they form the main residue of 'Burgundy' today, as we shall see.

Brunhild was in close relations with Pope Gregory the Great (590–604) and at his request assisted Augustine on his way to take the faith to the pagan Jutes, Angles and Saxons of Britain; and the establishment of this link between the two countries must have been at least partly responsible for the despatch of Felix, whom the Venerable Bede described as 'having been born and ordained in Burgundy',[9] to convert the Angles of Norfolk and Suffolk a few years after the queen's death. His see was at Dunwich, later a substantial town which is now below the North Sea. Thus it was thanks in part to the Burgundians that Britain re-entered the stream of European history, in contrast with Burgundy which had hardly left the center of it.

Brunhild was a generous patron of the Church, but she believed in handling her bishops and abbots firmly. She had the Archbishop of Vienne assassinated; and it is no wonder that neither history nor legend accord her the gentler qualities. However, the terror was not all one way: Protade, her 'mayor of the palace' (or chief minister), was murdered by her foes while playing draughts with the court doctor; and her own end was brutally dramatic. In 613, when she was about sixty-three, she was overwhelmed and captured by the Franks in a battle on the shores of Lake Neuchatel in north-west Switzerland. She was tortured for three days and set on a camel as a mark of derision; there cannot have been many in Christian Europe in those days. Then she was tied by her flowing white hair and by an arm and a foot to the tail of a vicious stallion which her captors lashed to fury until her limbs were torn from her body. With the passing of this queen of Burgundy, heroic, legendary and larger-than-life, we take one more step into the gloom that accompanied the disintegration of the classical world.

The sub-Roman Kingdom of Burgundy

The decline and fall of Roman civilization in most parts of the western Empire was not a sudden onset of darkness but rather a gradual passage from bright day to twilight by way of a strikingly long sunset.[10] The arts continued a decline which had begun long before the Empire was taken over by the barbarians, but in Visigothic Aquitaine and in Burgundy, for instance, men of letters like Sidonius Apollinaris and Avitus still wrote verse and prose of distinction at least until the time of Sigismund; the Romans' building techniques were preserved in many areas for several generations more; and in their own very obvious interests the rulers of the successor kingdoms (Ostrogoths in Italy, Visigoths in Spain and Aquitaine, and Nibelungs and Merovings in Burgundy) took over the machinery of government so far as possible intact, and they retained some imperial taxes to pay for their churches, roads and other public works, and the schools which supplied their officials. Relatively few of the Gallo-Romans had been dispossessed to make room for the Burgundian settlers, and the letters which Sidonius wrote at the time (452–79) do not convey the impression of disruption, let alone destruction or chaos. For the vast majority of the population of south-east Gaul life probably changed only slowly between 400 and 700, far less in any case than it did for the Burgundian immigrants. Under King Sigismund (516–23) most Burgundians renounced Arianism and became Catholics like the Gallo-Romans around them. By then they had already gone some way in switching to the manner of life of the older inhabitants, to their weights and measures, paper, script, foodstuffs, art forms, adopting also their social classes and the private ownership of land. In due course they were to start speaking their language, but, as we shall see, with distinctive changes.

The countryside, where most people of both races lived, saw few changes.

[50]

Urban life decayed, yet for several generations Burgundy's chief towns maintained the currency and the municipal organization of Roman times. There is still rich evidence today of the city life of Lyons, Vienne, Autun and Avenches and even more at centers in 'Lower Burgundy', as Provence was often called, like Arles, Orange and Vaison la Romaine. Their communities were often terrorized by the local representatives of the Merovings, and standards of living, public order and culture were steadily declining, even if imperceptibly. But the economic life of the Rhône basin had only been temporarily disrupted by the invasions and hardly affected at all by the settlement of the Burgundians. The Roman roads were intact and the mails ran; internal trade flowed very much as before, and the wine of Vienne, much prized in Rome under the Empire, continued to be exported together with olives and oil, corn, wool and textiles, metals both crude and finished, timber, pottery and glass; and since we know that around 600 there were groups of Levantine merchants resident as far north in Burgundy as Orleans, we can be sure they operated actively in Provence and the Rhône valley well into the seventh century.

It is commonplace that learning survived during the 'Dark Ages' largely because of the spread of monasteries. In this respect no country in western Christendom played as important a role as Burgundy, at any rate if we take account of the whole medieval period, say from 400 to 1300. As though to prepare the ground for Cluny and the Cistercians, Saint Honoratus founded the first important monastery of the western world on the Lérins islands near Cannes at the beginning of the fifth century, and Saint Benedict's foundations in Italy at Monte Cassino and Subiaco are matched in antiquity by that of Caesarius (c. 470–543) at Arles, the most ancient Roman colony in Gaul (45 BC) and its capital for a while under the later Empire.* The Burgundians were proud to gain possession of the remains of Saint Anthony (c. 250–c. 350), whose ascetic existence in the Egyptian desert was perhaps the sublimest of all models for western monasticism, and they established them at Vienne which came to be their holy city. For several centuries it was also the capital and, as we shall see, Burgundy was one day to be called the Kingdom of Arles and Vienne.

Burgundy was notable for church-building in these early centuries. Between 350 and 650 many churches were built in the six Roman provinces which became the First Kingdom of Burgundy, and under Sigismund, for example, there were no less than 27 dioceses. Many, like St Peter's of Geneva, were

* Ausonius called it the 'Rome of the Gauls'.

initially of wood, and most of them disappeared under later stone churches or other buildings; and we shall probably never know how many were erected in any particular period. There is not much hard evidence left today. But one can still see traces of the church of Saint Martin at Aime in the Tarentaise which probably dates from Gundobad's reign (*c.* 500); the foundations of Sigismund's church at Saint Maurice d'Agaune (*c.* 516); and the crypt of Saint Lawrence of Grenoble from a century or so later. In the meantime Queen Brunhild had built Saint Martin of Ainay at Lyons (*c.* 600); the lower part of the tower still remains from her church.

Sidonius wrote when Bishop of Lyons that one basilican church which was erected in his city, probably after the Burgundians had gained control of it (459), had no less than 120 columns. This would have made it comparable in size with San Paolo fuori le Mura, or at least Santa Maria Maggiore, magnificent churches built in the preceding half-century and still two of Rome's finest monuments.* It is far more likely that this and other churches raised by the Burgundian kings and their Merovingian successors were on the scale of the three recently excavated in Geneva,[11] which would have made them no larger than the smallest of the early Christian basilicas still left to us in the eternal city. The ground plans in Geneva are similar, for instance, to that of Sant' Agnese fuori le Mura;** but it is already evident that their workmanship and decoration were crude by comparison. Only the goldsmith's art flourished in Burgundy in those days.

Next to the 'double cathedral'*** and baptistery in Geneva stood a royal palace decorated with mosaics and equipped with Roman baths and heating system. The Burgundian rulers evidently aimed, and with some success, to become Roman patricians. They had poets and rhetoricians at their court, and Geneva, only a small town under the Romans, was now greatly enlarged, though it would still not rival Lyons, Vienne, Autun, Arles or Nîmes,**** and it doubtless soon followed them into decline.

The schools at which young men were trained at public expense for government service were preserved longer in the Rhône valley than anywhere

---

* San Paolo was rebuilt in the nineteenth century.

** They were probably of one storey as against Sant' Agnese's two.

*** Gundobad and Sigismund rebuilt wooden St Peter's in stone. The third church excavated is the Madeleine. A fourth church in Geneva of this period was St Victor's, a nunnery founded by Sedeleuba, St Clotilda's sister.

**** Nîmes was 320 hectares (*c.* 800 acres) in extent, more populous than in 1500 when (like Arles) it had under 10,000 people.

else in the West,*[12] and Greek was still taught and spoken there until well into the sixth century. Their decline was hardly offset, unhappily, by the teaching in cathedrals and monasteries which was enjoyed only by the clergy. Under Brunhild, whose reign extended into the seventh century, the church schools were still teaching the Latin classics as well as the scriptures, and indeed the Archbishop of Vienne was rebuked by the formidable Pope Gregory (c. 540–604) for corrupting the young men of his city by instructing them in the Latin poets!**

Thanks to the priests education of a sort penetrated to the remotest valleys. The church of Burgundy, organized on a 'national' basis from the sixth century, encouraged the veneration of ancient heroes and martyrs, so as to promote the Christian life by way of example. This gave the Gallo-Romans and Burgundians a common heritage and a sense of loyalty not only to their church but to the society to which they both now belonged. For all but a tiny handful the stories of the country's saints and martyrs, heard from the pulpit on Sundays, were the main educational fare of the peoples of Burgundy; it may be too much to say that this played the same part in fostering a Burgundian national awareness that the idolization of Joan of Arc and Alfred the Great was to play in the teaching of the young of France and England, but at the very least it fostered local pride and a sense of shared identity.

Twilight over Burgundy

If there was any time when twilight could be said to have fallen on Burgundy it was probably in the generation or two after the murder of Brunhild (613). Except perhaps for Dagobert (d. 639) she was probably the last ruler of the First Kingdom of whom it may fairly be said that she succeeded in maintaining what was still left of the imperial administration, notably the taxation system, and she rebuilt roads and kept up public works so far as possible as they were under the Empire.[13] Within only a few decades the Merovingian system was to break up, and western Europe to suffer a setback unparalleled before or since.

However, enough has been said here to demonstrate that, despite its violence

---

* It is tempting to argue that the need lasted longer, i.e. Roman-style administration continued longer. This tertiary education (the schools of Rhetoric), following the Roman Empire's primary and secondary (or Grammar) schools, may loosely be compared with the medieval university.

** Virgil, like Sallust and Cicero, was staple fare. Perhaps they were also given Ovid and Catullus.

[53]

and its lawlessness, this was no primitive or savage society. Nor has our story been one of destruction and desolation, as seems to have been the case with Britain, but rather of remorseless and apparently irreversible torpor and decay. Henri Pirenne, in one of the best descriptions[14] of these kingdoms, which were still more Roman than Germanic, wrote that 'Down to the time of the Merovingian decadence the financial resources of the Barbarian kings were very much greater than those of any other Western State would be until the close of the 13th century', by which time Westminster Abbey and La Sainte Chapelle had been built and the mighty Charles of Anjou had failed in his bid to restore the kingdom of the Nibelungs. It would be interesting to debate whether Charles's officers were very much more cultivated than Gundobad's or his men-at-arms better off than Brunhild's; and the cities of Burgundy in the sixth and even seventh centuries could probably be compared with those of thirteenth-century England in terms of numbers, size and the standard of living of common folk, even if the civic buildings surviving from Roman times, let alone Burgundy's little churches, could not match England's Gothic cathedrals in scale or beauty.

In the mid-seventh century there was a sharper downturn in cultural and intellectual life. Towns had become depopulated, and now perhaps only Lyons, Marseilles and Arles still maintained a respectable level of trade.[15] Moreover the standards and influence of the Church itself declined, particularly from the middle of the century. In as many as eleven of the sees of Provence, Burgundy's most civilized area, there are no bishops listed for long periods (in some cases for 150 and 200 years!) and these periods almost all began between 670 and 690. The bishop was a civic as much as a pastoral leader and on him largely depended the peace, order, administration and prosperity of the city and its region, and so those two decades probably witnessed a sharp quickening of Burgundy's twilight. Even the great archbishopric of Arles was apparently vacant from 683 to 794, and Geneva, the Burgundians' old capital, had no bishop from 650 to 833.[16]

Despite this one can say that Burgundy lost its grip on Graeco-Roman culture more slowly than most other western lands. The old structure of society there did not, as in Italy and Spain, suffer from the invasions of the unromanized Lombards (from 568) and the infidel Moors (from 711), and it is with these two countries that Burgundy must be compared, rather than with France,* let alone England.[17] From the outset the Burgundians seem to have

* It will be some time before 'Francia' extends south of the line of Frank settlement, say Bourges-Épinal (Map no. 1, p. 18).

been marked out as northerners turned southern, as were their kinsmen the Goths, and in these centuries Burgundy belonged chiefly to the Mediterranean world. Until Charlemagne gained north and central Italy in 774 Burgundy, largely because it included Provence, was the most civilized of the Franks' kingdoms; and for some seven hundred years from the first contact between their cultures in the fifth century it was the Burgundians who influenced the Franks rather than the other way round.*

Burgundy is still separate until the triumph of Charles Martel (737)

Brunhild's death left the field to Clotar II, the son of her great enemy Fredegund, who now became sole King of the Franks. However, he promptly (614) recognized that Burgundy should remain separate, and more often than not this was its fortune during the century or so of the so-called 'rois fainéants'. These were the puppet Merovings who were ultimately replaced (751) by the Carolings, the dynasty of Charles Martel, whom we meet in the next section.

The most famous of Burgundian leaders in the seventh century was Leodegar, Bishop of Autun, known to us as Saint Léger (616–79), a hard and intolerant man who according to his biographer was 'never softened by the joys of the flesh'. He also obliged the Franks, then under the mayor of the palace Ebroin, to accept that Burgundy was a separate kingdom with its own laws and customs; but Ebroin dishonored his pledge and, in seeking to bring Burgundy under his yoke, besieged Leodegar in Autun (675). To save his beloved city from pillage and murder the bishop agreed to walk out and surrender alone. Ebroin had him blinded and four years later put to death.

A life of Saint Léger was written in verse towards the middle of the tenth century. The author is believed to have been a Burgundian; that his sympathies were certainly Burgundian is clear from his portrayal of Léger as hero and Ebroin as villain. The poem – one of the oldest surviving in the vernacular of Burgundy or anywhere else – tells how after Léger's eyes were put out and his tongue and lips cut off, he was miraculously healed and, when Ebroin in a fury had him beheaded, the saint's body remained standing (*lo corps estera sempre sus*) until his feet were hacked away too.[18]

* The reader may now be satisfied that Burgundy was a separate and distinctive country, which continued to be relatively civilized during the so-called Dark Ages. If he is not specially interested in its decline and then its re-emergence in the Second Kingdom in the next centuries, he might prefer to skip or skim the following sections and move swiftly to page 68.

Ebroin was assassinated in 681. A story current in Lyons shortly afterwards may be a pointer to what Burgundians felt about the Franks. A man whose eyes Ebroin had put out, as he had Léger's, and who had taken refuge at Ile Barbe on the Saône north of Lyons, heard some boatmen rowing against the current of the river. He hailed them to ask where they went. 'We are going to hell,' came back the reply, 'we are taking Ebroin there so he can pay for his crimes.' Ebroin, he believed, was still very much alive, and it was only later that he realized that the oarsmen were not of this world. Some days passed before he learnt that it was in that very hour that the scourge of Burgundy met his end.

Carolings and Rudolfians:
The Second Kingdom Founded

The Moors and Charles Martel

The death of Ebroin in 681 marked the end of effective Merovingian rule in Burgundy. For the next fifty years the country was controled not by the Frank mayors of the palace but by its own free-spirited nobility, and but for the terrible peril which was now to strike Christendom Burgundy might reasonably have expected to regain her full independence, for in the quarter millennium which we have surveyed (c. 450–700) only Visigothic Spain displayed a better record than Burgundy for stability and permanence.

Spain collapsed before the Moorish torrent and for several years it looked as though the same fate would overtake Aquitaine and Burgundy (726–32). Everywhere the menfolk were massacred, the women and children herded southwards into slavery; those who could escaped to the mountains and forests away from the old Roman roads and the river valleys, and only castles perched high on crags survived unscathed. The ancient city of Autun was largely razed to the ground, and the church at Langres in Burgundy's extreme north suffered such damage that it was still unrepaired at the time of Charlemagne's death eighty-three years later.

In Saint Boniface's view the peoples of Spain and Burgundy received no more than their deserts since, as he wrote to Ethelbald, Offa's predecessor as ruler of the English kingdom of Mercia (716–57), their populations 'like the Sodomites had come to despise the laws of marriage and had fallen into luxury and adultery. So far had they departed from God by their fornications that finally the all-powerful Judge allowed the Saracens to come and chastise them by their devastations for forsaking and forgetting his Law.' Indeed the Saracens were halted only at the gates of Sens-en-Bourgogne where the bishop, Saint Ebbo, a figure more martial than holy, defeated and turned them back (731). For the next year, based on Lyonnais, the Saracens devastated Dauphiné, Dombes, Bresse and Forez, until they were routed at Tours in 732 by Charles Martel, son of a mayor of the palace of Austrasia, master of Francia and future founder of the Carolingian dynasty (Maps nos 7 and 8).

When the conqueror turned to Burgundy and marched down the Saône, the Burgundians wondered whether to welcome the Christian neighbors who had ruled them with a light rein for two centuries but now seemed bent on subjugating them, or the infidel who had brought them ineffable misery for the past seven years. Those that preferred their brothers in Christ soon had cause to regret it for Charles Martel was less concerned with liberating the Burgundians from the Saracens than with imposing his own iron grip. His conquest was followed by revolt and reconquest; cities were destroyed for admitting the Moslems, others lest they might do so; so that the Provençalers, now convinced that the Franks' terror was at least as fearful as the Saracens', were provoked into inviting the Mohammedans to return, the gates of Avignon were opened to them, and in parts of the Rhône valley they were welcomed back as deliverers.

It was probably after he had finally gained control (737) that Charles Martel instituted the Carolingian practice of administering Burgundy in the four parts which were identified above, Frankish, Allemannic, Provençal and more truly Burgundian; but it was rarely effective except under Charlemagne (771–814) in the face of Burgundian truculence and rebellion. There were important differences which helped to set the Burgundians and Franks against each other. The former had swiftly been absorbed into the Gallo-Roman population; the Franks, at least to the north of a rough line Bourges-Epinal (Map no. 1), had been numerous enough to retain their identity and to impose their personality, as they notably did on the local Latin speech.[19] French is very different from, for instance, Provençal, which is relatively close to Latin. Under the Merovings the Frankish and Burgundian ways of life had come no closer together and the distinctions between them had emerged ever more strongly: distinctions of race, custom and history, different degrees of Romanization, and contrasting ecclesiastical and secular law and religious and administrative practice. Under the Carolings' oppression sharpening language differences set the two peoples even further apart,* and the heroes of Burgundian legend (Guerin, Gerard of Roussillon, Ganelon and Isembard), who were to be described as traitors in the French *chansons de geste*, played for Burgundy the role of England's Harold son of Godwin and Hereward the Wake in fighting against absorption by a foreign power.

---

* It is not yet time to introduce the language evolved by the Burgundians from the rustic Latin around them. Known as 'Franco-Provençal' (or, in French, 'francoprovençal'), it is discussed on p. 94 and in Appendix II.

Gerard of Roussillon

The greatest of these champions was as resolute as Alfred of England and as fabled as Arthur. Gerard of Roussillon was born to one Leuthard about 800, the year of Charlemagne's coronation as Emperor, probably near Avallon in Frankish Burgundy. He rose to prominence under Charlemagne's son Louis the Pious and was chief minister to Louis's heir Lothar I, who is best known to us as the emperor who had to accept the partition of Verdun in 843, dividing Latin Christendom into what became Germany and France with 'the Middle Kingdom' between them (Map no. 9). Gerard played an active part in Lothar's expedition against the Saracens who were attacking Rome. Up to this point he was a loyal member of the Carolingian 'establishment'. However, from 853 to 870, as Count of Lyons and Vienne and then regent for Lothar's epileptic son Charles, Gerard was effectively ruler of southern Burgundy and often also of the northern part over which reigned Charles's brother, Lothar II; and so he became ever more closely concerned with Burgundy's interests. Burgundy faced danger from two quarters, the West Franks under Charles the Bald and the Vikings, fearless, well-organized and pagan warriors from Scandinavia* who had learned at the end of the eighth century that the coasts of Britain and Francia lay open to easy plunder. By the middle of the ninth their raids had become invasions, and in the terrible years 856–8 they sacked Paris, Orleans, Tours, Blois, Bayeux and Chartres so that Charles the Bald was driven to make peace with Gerard of Burgundy and enlist his help. When in 859 the Vikings sailed round Spain and into the Mediterranean to attack Provence, Gerard was ready for them and his victory, while not as decisive as that of Alfred of England near Chippenham nineteen years later (878), must rank as the Vikings' first serious reverse in Gaul.

Unhappily, with the Viking threat temporarily removed, Charles the Bald was free to attack Burgundy again. As was recorded in the *chanson de geste* of three hundred years later, Gerard pursued Charles to Avallon and defeated him near Vézelay (868, see Map no. 7); but in the next year his ally King Lothar II died and Gerard, now an old man of seventy, was left alone to withstand the Franks. The end was inevitable: he and his heroic wife Bertha finally surrendered Vienne in 871; and he was stripped of all his power and died at Avignon sometime before 879.

Although Gerard's main strength lay in Lyonnais, his authority extended

---

* I generally use 'Vikings' whatever their provenance in Scandinavia.

[59]

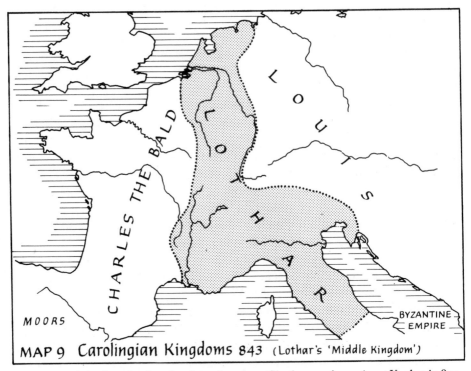

MAP 9 Carolingian Kingdoms 843 (Lothar's 'Middle Kingdom')

Map no. 9 shows how the three brothers shared out Charlemagne's empire at Verdun in 843. This is the origin of the Middle Kingdom mentioned often in these pages.

west of the Saône and over La Montagne, and in 858 he and Bertha founded a monastery on the northern slopes of the latter which was to become one of the most renowned in Christendom, Saint Mary Magdalene of Vézelay, which according to popular belief housed the holy courtesan's remains. In 860 the Vikings sacked it, but after they had also attacked the abbey of Saint Bernard at Romans far to the south, Gerard caught them and put them to flight. He set to work in 863 to re-establish the monastery at Vézelay on a more easily defensible site, on the hill from which the great church dominates the countryside today. Also in 863 he and Bertha founded the less well known abbey of Pothières near Châtillon-sur-Seine; and Saint Peter's of Auxerre and Saint Lazarus' of Avallon and many other monasteries are attributed to them (Map no. 7).

In legend Gerard became more Burgundian than he ever was in life – a national hero comparable to Roland in France and the Cid in Spain, and miracles were wrought in his name. Not only were two *chansons de geste* and a Life written about him between 1100 and 1200, but he was a source of great national pride in the mid-fifteenth century when his biography was written by Wauquelin. There are such close parallels between the *chansons* and the Tristan poems, which are later, that Gerard and Bertha are probably the prototypes of Tristan and Isolde just as Wagner's Brunnhilde and Gunther also seem to be modeled on figures in Burgundian history.[20]

Boso and the Rudolfs restore the Kingdom

Gerard's struggle to maintain Burgundy's integrity and restore its independence bore fruit when a separate Kingdom of Burgundy was the first of the new states to emerge from the crumbling system of the Carolings (Map no. 10 on p. 63). The collapse of the empire first created by Clovis (and to be restored only by Napoleon and Hitler) was due in great measure to the Vikings' onslaughts. Burgundy suffered only relatively less than Neustria (France), as an eye-witness account from Thibaud, a Burgundian monk, tells us. The Danes' 'atrocities had emptied Rouen, Evreux, Bayeux and all the cities of Neustria of their people. Then came the turn of Beauvais, Chartres, Meaux and Melun which these monsters razed to the ground . . . When there was nothing left to destroy in Neustria, indeed in Francia, they reckoned their work to be of no account if they did not also turn the ferocious cruelty of their arms on Burgundy. One can judge what their coming to our country meant: murder, rape, arson, all their usual exploits renewed with the most savage intensity.'

Bèze, Thibaud's monastery near Dijon, Troyes and many other Burgundian centers were put to fire and sword in the next twelve years (886–98), which were described as the worst in Burgundy's history. Thibaud did not record that the Emperor Charles the Fat had bought off the Danes by giving them formal 'authority' to pillage Burgundy and by offering them free passage across Neustria. Burgundy's rape was France's reprieve, but not however Charles's, for he was deposed in the following year (887).

After 887 we can speak more correctly of the separate kingdoms of France, Germany and Italy. By then the Kingdom of Burgundy, more often called Provence at that time, had already been re-established by Boso, Gerard's successor as Count of Vienne and governor of Burgundy, in 879; and some fifty years later it regained the extent it had enjoyed under Gundobad. These two important events must be briefly explained.

Boso's wife Ermingard had been betrothed to the Byzantine emperor and, even more to the point, as daughter of the Carolingian emperor Louis* she regarded herself as sovereign of Burgundy and Italy in her own right, and she persuaded Pope John VIII that it was not fitting for her to remain married to a mere count. It was his duty, she said, to make Boso a king. However, although all six of Burgundy's archbishops and twenty-one bishops were in attendance at Boso and Ermingard's coronation near Vienne, the new king's writ did not run in all parts of the ancient kingdom. Indeed there were two other Burgundies, both of which were separate for a while.

The second Burgundy lay to the north-east; here chief power rested with Boso's brother-in-law, Rudolf Guelf, who in 888 persuaded the Emperor Arnulf to make a separate kingdom of his lands. Called 'Transjuran Burgundy' Rudolf's kingdom comprised most of the Burgundians' Homeland and the Allemannic area, or in modern terms most of Savoy, Franche Comté and Switzerland (Map no. 10 on p. 63); it therefore represented a rather more extensive restoration of the fifth-century 'inner kingdom' of Godegisel (Map no. 7 on p. 44).**

The third Burgundy stretched to the north-west. It came into existence through Boso's appointment of his brother Richard as Count of Autun shortly after his accession. By 890 Richard, who came to be known as the Justiciar, was master also of Sens, Auxerre and Troyes. This area, which can be recognized as

---

* Genealogical table A in Appendix VIII shows most of the personalities mentioned in these pages. See p. 281.

** It would once again have a separate existence in a later age.

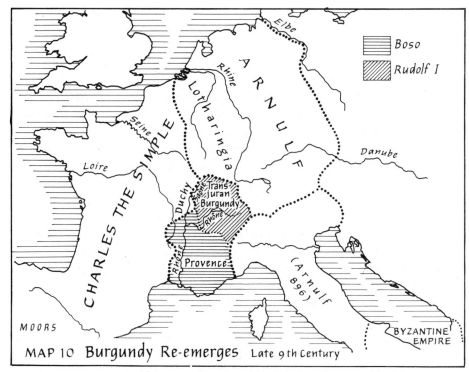

MAP 10 **Burgundy Re-emerges** Late 9th Century

Map no. 10 shows Lothar's Middle Kingdom soon broken into three: Lotharingia, Burgundy and Italy (Charlemagne never gained *south* Italy). It also shows the two 'Burgundies' which came together in the Second Kingdom in 933, the third (the Duchy) being excluded.

the Frankish region of Burgundy, became the Duchy of Burgundy, soon splitting away from the Kingdom and eventually accepting instead the suzerainty of the Capetian kings of France. By contrast, as we must now see, Rudolf's territories in the north-east were soon to be reunited with the southern kingdom of Boso's son Louis.

We shall find the lure of Italy responsible for momentous twists in Burgundy's fortunes. On the first occasion with which we must be concerned the outcome was happier for Burgundy than on those that followed. Ermingard had played a great part in making Boso a king; their son Louis she made King of Italy as well as of Burgundy and Provence, and Emperor too. But in Italy as in Gaul the Burgundians found themselves confronted by their ancient enemies, and at Verona in 905 Louis fell into the hands of his Frankish rival for the Italian throne, only being released after his eyes had been put out. Since his wife Egida, sister of King Athelstan of England, bore him no sons, his power passed inevitably to his regent, Hugh Count of Arles. Count Hugh continued the struggle for control of Italy with the son of Rudolf Guelf, Rudolf II (912–37), the new rival. Suddenly however these two Burgundian contestants, the one in Provence, the other in present-day Switzerland, became involved in an issue much greater than even the mastery of Italy.

Our civilization has never been in greater danger than in the latter years of the ninth century and the opening decades of the tenth, and it might well have been extinguished, as was the brilliant culture of Ireland. The threat from the Vikings was at its peak and for many regions, including Burgundy, the Saracens were hardly less menacing than they had ever been; and now, as though that were not enough, the Magyars descended like a blazing meteor on southern Germany and the Rhineland. The ogres of Europe's fairy tales, horrifying perversions of the human form, are to be recognized in the Ongres or Hongrois, as the Magyars came to be called. In 919 they ravaged large areas of Rudolf's Burgundy, and in 924 they reached the Rhône and threatened both Hugh's lands in Provence and Rudolf's in Lombardy. The result was miraculous: Hugh and Rudolf sank their differences and joined forces to drive off the invaders; and nine years later a momentous bargain was struck under which Hugh gained Italy and Rudolf southern Burgundy. Thus the year 933 can be taken as the culmination of the process of restoring the ancient Kingdom which had started before 800 with the Burgundians' resistance to Charlemagne; and it is of significance to the student of Burgundian history that the frontiers of the Second, or Rudolfian, Kingdom as it is often called, closely approximated to those of the Burgundy of the Nibelungs and Merovings (Map no. 11, page 65).

(Above) A Burgundian vineyard: Duchess Mary of Burgundy's château de Couches near Chalon-sur-Saône. *(Below)* Pont Saint-Bénézet, Avignon. (See page 19)

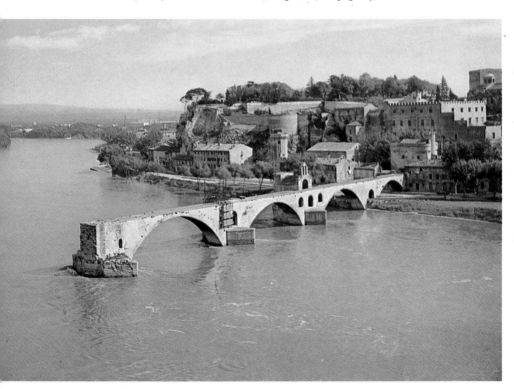

I

(Above) A mosaic of the same period found there. (Below) A

Geneva cathedral: the excavations of 1082–6 revealed

The chalice found at Gourdon west of Tournus, probably made by a sixth-century Burgundian goldsmith. (p. 52)

(Above and below) Tournus, Saint Philibert, mostly *c*.1000. Rebuilt after its sack by Magyars, 937. (pp. 64, 247)

Chapaize, 1020–40, tower *c*.1050; strong influence of Cluny II. Burgundy proper has *c*.500 Romanesque churches, *c*.50 of them pre-Cluny III. (p. 80)

IV

Cluny III, 1088–1109, consecrated 1095. (pp. 80, 248)

V

Paray-le-Monial, mostly *c.*1100–10, consecrated 1104; façade and west
towers before 1050: a scaled-down Cluny, probably the oldest extant church
with pointed vaults and pointed arches. (pp. 80, 249)

The martyrdom of Saint Vincent, in the little church of Berzé-la-Ville where
Abbot Hugh retired. Painted *c.* 1110 by a Cluniac monk or monks. (p. 83)

(*Above*) Vézelay nave, probably 1120–45, (*Below*) Vézelay abbey, on the site chosen by Gerard. Consecrated in 1104, but largely rebuilt after the fire of 1120. (pp. 61, 81, 249)

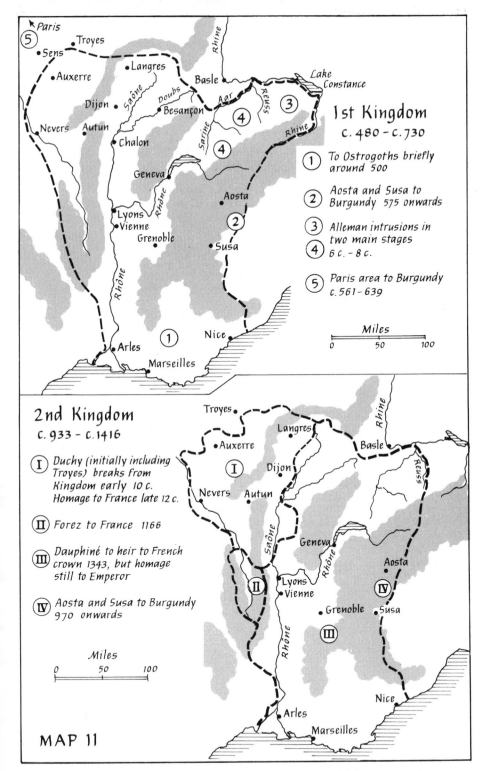

1st Kingdom
c. 480 – c. 730

① To Ostrogoths briefly around 500

② Aosta and Susa to Burgundy 575 onwards

③ Alleman intrusions in two main stages 6 c. – 8 c.

④

⑤ Paris area to Burgundy c. 561 – 639

Miles
0   50   100

2nd Kingdom
c. 933 – c. 1416

Ⅰ Duchy (initially including Troyes) breaks from Kingdom early 10 c. Homage to France late 12 c.

Ⅱ Forez to France 1166

Ⅲ Dauphiné to heir to French crown 1343, but homage still to Emperor

Ⅳ Aosta and Susa to Burgundy 970 onwards

Miles
0   50   100

MAP 11

Map no. 11 shows (with all the qualifications that must be made) how amazingly constant Burgundy's frontiers were, from *c.* 480 to *c.* 1416. See also Map no. 14.

There was however one important omission. We noted that Boso's brother Richard the Justiciar became master of Autun, Sens, Auxerre and Troyes, and so created the future *Duchy* of Burgundy* out of what we have called the Frankish area, the area which belonged ethnically to the Franks rather than to the Burgundians; or, as one can now say, to France rather than to Burgundy. For in the tenth century it becomes right to speak of 'France' and 'French' rather than 'Francia', 'Franks' and 'Frankish', though it will be two or three ceturies before 'France' bears much resemblance to the extensive nation state of today, and even longer before 'France' and 'Burgundy' cease to be distinct.**

We shall see shortly how in the next century Richard's lands passed to the cadet branch of the dynasty reigning in Paris. What must be stressed here is that, although the cultural links remained strong, the future Duchy no longer formed part of the Kingdom of Burgundy.

Conrad the Peaceful (937–93)

The reunited Kingdom of Burgundy passed in 937 to young King Conrad. His reign began sadly. In that year the Magyars made their most terrible attack on Burgundy, devastating the regions of Sens, Troyes, Langres and Lyons; and the destruction at Bèze abbey was so extensive that it was not restored for

---

* It is usually accepted that the separation of the Duchy and the Kingdom of Burgundy dated from the Partition of Verdun in 843, when Gerard of Roussillon's sovereign Lothar I was forced by his brothers to share their grandfather Charlemagne's empire with them; but in *Nouvelle Histoire de Lyon* (p. 140 and accompanying maps) Steyert argues quite plausibly that Verdun and the partitions later in the ninth century left Burgundy with frontiers like those of 500 (i.e. back to those of the Nibelung kingdom, Map no. 7, and omitting Merovingian additions such as Orleans, Paris etc.). Whatever the date of its initiation, the political separation of the Kingdom and Duchy can now be seen to have been firm from the mid-tenth century. But the frontier does not seem to have stabilized until the eleventh century (perhaps with the Capetians' defeat of Otto William in 1015, see below); e.g. Cluny was in the Kingdom of Burgundy at least until 994 when Rudolf III installed Odilo as abbot.

** For the most part the Burgundians have become French in recent centuries, and the people of Burgundy do not today distinguish themselves from the French; but does the present narrative need terms (other than 'France' and 'French') to denote the state which grew up with Paris as its capital and the people which it ruled? 'West Franks' will do no longer. Nor will 'North French' do, though even today some people see France as made up of Franks in the north and Gauls in the south. (To non-French in the Middle Ages Gallia, as distinct from Francia, meant Burgundy – and perhaps Aquitaine.) We can use 'Paris' or a similar euphemism; Germans have spoken of 'Parisismus' for Paris's policy of subjecting the regions. But by and large 'French' will have to be

fifty-one years. The Saracens, based in the area above Saint Tropez known today as Les Maures (the Moors), raided the Rhône valley and the plain of Lombardy for nearly eighty years. In 920 they wiped out a group of English pilgrims on their way to Rome. The Archbishop of Aix-en-Provence withdrew to Rheims as no place closer seemed safe enough for the fulfilment of his pastoral duties.

Conrad of Burgundy was named the Peaceful but in 954 he gained victory over the Saracens and Magyars in a coup which may be unique in military history. When he learnt that forces of both Magyars and Saracens were on the warpath, he sent envoys to tell the Magyars that the Saracens lay in wait for them and that if they would join forces with the Burgundians they would together destroy the Saracens. He then warned the Saracens of the Magyars' approach and similarly promised them his help. Both invading armies were successfully deceived; they engaged each other in battle just as the Burgundian army, with a perfect sense of timing, appeared on the field, and Conrad continued to tell each side that he would shortly come to its assistance. When he judged that the two hostile forces had sufficiently weakened each other, the Burgundians were launched against them and both were brilliantly destroyed.

It was the Emperor Otto I who finally checked the Magyars, by his victory at Lechfeld in the following year (955), and the Abbot of Cluny, where the famous monastery had been founded in 910, who was largely responsible for the expulsion of the Saracens from Provence. Majolus had been taken prisoner by them in 972 and bade his monks pay one thousand pounds' weight of silver for his ransom – no wonder, as the Cluniac monk Rudolf Glaber (c. 1000–1050) records, they were reduced to tears. To be avenged on the infidel Majolus launched a holy war which led to the extermination, expulsion or forced conversion of the Saracens. This success not only inaugurated an age of peace in Burgundy which was to bring prosperity and a remarkable outburst of cultural activity; it may also be said to mark the beginning of the crusading movement, rather than the First Crusade of 1095.

---

used to make the distinction from 'Burgundian', even though the former today embraces the latter.

The 'Kingdom of France' like the 'Kingdom of the West Franks' stretched theoretically to the Pyrenees. But for a long time only part of it was 'French', in the sense of being controled by the King of France or of speaking the language which became French, and it should be clear from the context when 'France' and 'French' refer to this more limited sense, viz. to little more than the royal domain (the Ile de France – the Paris basin) together with Champagne.

The Fall of the Phoenix

Conrad seems to have had no part in this important episode and indeed there is little more to be said which is directly to the credit of the Rudolfian dynasty. Throughout the tenth century Burgundy lay exposed to external threat, first from the West Franks, and even more from the Kingdom of the East Franks, ruled from 936 by the powerful and energetic Ottonians of Saxony. The disaster which overtook Rudolfian Burgundy was not sudden extinction but progressive self-destruction as inadequacy became impotence, and dependence on the Ottonian emperors became vassaldom; but the end was not to come without valiant struggles by two Burgundian princes which, if either had been successful, would have given the history of Burgundy a different course.

Conrad was succeeded as King of Burgundy in 993 by his son Rudolf III. In 1006 the Emperor Henry II seized Basle and extracted a promise from Rudolf to name him his heir. Rudolf was childless and Henry was his oldest nephew;* however the prospect was anathema in Burgundy to high and low alike, and when Otto William, the most powerful lord in the Kingdom, raised the standard of revolt in 1016, many rallied to him; few Burgundians wished to be ruled by the alien Germans. But Otto William was more than a folk hero, he was a man of high ambition. A contemporary wrote of him: 'Though nominally a vassal of the King of Burgundy, Otto William was resolved to be sovereign master of his own territories.'

Otto William, whose mother was Burgundian, was the son and grandson of the last 'national' kings of Italy,** now ousted by the Ottonian emperors. He was initially Count of Mâcon and Count of Burgundy, which means he held the lands north and west of the Jura known today as Franche Comté. In 1002 he was chosen by the bishops and barons of the area to succeed his stepfather as Duke of Burgundy, but he was expelled from the Duchy after a long conflict by the King of France, Robert Capet. The latter's younger son, also Robert, became Duke of Burgundy, founding the junior branch of the Capetian dynasty. This ruled in Dijon*** for three centuries, coincidentally about as long as the senior branch in Paris, a story to which we shall return.

* See Genealogical table A, p. 281.
** In effect north Italy; the south was largely Byzantine or Saracen. Historians such as Chaume and Z. N. Brooke (*Hist. Europe* 911–1198, p. 33) speak of the fortunes of Burgundy and Italy at this period being 'inextricably mixed'.
*** It was a few years after this that Dijon became the regular capital of the Duchy of Burgundy. See Genealogical table B, p. 282.

Unhappily Otto William divided his efforts between his ambitions in Italy and in Burgundy and he was defeated in both – perhaps the first case of a Burgundian prince failing in Burgundy because of involvement in Italy. But he and his allies continued to defy Rudolf and to challenge Henry's claims to the succession. Their efforts seemed rewarded when Henry died in 1024, for his successor Conrad, the first Franconian emperor, had only a very distant claim of blood to the Burgundian throne. However, he had married one of Rudolf's nieces and in 1026 Otto William died, and so Rudolf set aside the rights of his nephew and heir Odo of Blois and on his death-bed in 1032 he sent Burgundy's regalia* to Conrad.

The Emperor was far off fighting the Poles and for a year or so fortune swung Odo's way. He was Count of Champagne and could call on support in several quarters. He soon occupied western Switzerland, and the Archbishop of Lyons, Count of Genevois and many others recognized him as king. On his way to Vienne, the capital of the Kingdom, he was given a rapturous welcome in Lyons. It was only after Conrad had won to his side Humbert White Hands, Count of Maurienne and founder of the Savoy dynasty, that the German cause prospered; and though Conrad had the upper hand from 1034, final victory was denied him until Odo perished in battle at Bar in 1037.

There is an interesting parallel with a northern kingdom of comparable size but lesser antiquity, which accepted foreign conquest no more willingly some thirty years later. Edward, King of England, known to us as the Confessor, fell under the influence of a neighboring power, just as Rudolf III did, and similarly promised the crown to its ruler, William of Normandy. Harold, Earl of Wessex, who was cast in the role of Odo of Blois, was likewise killed in battle, and in both cases the foreign claimant was able to install an alien rule. In terms of political

---

* Most works mention the *Holy Lance of Saint Maurice* (p. 41 above) in this connection as well as the crown, but the Lance was already in the emperor's possession. Its origins and history are obscure and its association with Maurice extremely improbable. Gregory of Tours reports that in 585 Guntram designated Brunhild's son Childebert as heir to Burgundy 'by placing the Lance in his hand' (p. 47). In 921/2 we find the Lance (the same?) in the hands of Rudolf I, then King of Italy and Burgundy. Henry I (the Fowler) extracted it from him in 926 first by threatening to devastate Burgundy and then by ceding lands to him as well as much gold. His son Otto's victory at Lechfeld (p. 67) was attributed to the invincibility afforded by the Lance. (For a recent English work stressing the importance of the Holy Lance and such relics, see Leyser, K. J., *Medieval Germany and its neighbours 900–1250* (1982) p. 215 f. For the best piece in English on the Lance itself, see Adelson, H. L., in the *Art Bulletin* Vol. 48, No. 2, 1966).

The Lance is now in Vienna's Kunsthistorisches Museum. This museum also holds the Holy Roman Empire crown. Until comparatively recently it was believed (wrongly) that it had previously been the *crown of Burgundy* assigned by Rudolf III to the Emperor Conrad.

identity both countries had been reduced to ashes, phoenixes whose weakness may perhaps be equated with self-destruction.

The parallel must not be carried too far. England became herself again, having after some two hundred years absorbed her Norman conquerors;* she re-emerged as one of Europe's nation states and went on to be for a while the foremost power in the world. After the same two centuries the emperors' control had become so slight that Burgundy too was ripe for rule by sovereigns as homespun as England's Plantagenets had become. But she did not rise from the ashes like England, nor even succeed as did the two other kingdoms of the Holy Roman Empire in achieving belated unity and independence in recent times.

Yet in a very important sense Burgundy emerged from the two centuries of alien rule with her identity more intact than England's. The military opposition of the English was brief, but more significantly they offered even less resistance to the culture which the Normans brought. By contrast, as we see in the next chapter, Burgundian culture was already so vigorous that over these two centuries it gave little ground to its invaders and, on the contrary, spread its striking art forms and techniques all over western Christendom. With her identity so robust in this vital respect, there was a good prospect of Burgundy rising from the ashes. The rest of this book is mostly concerned with her attempts, successes and final frustration.

---

* The loss of their homeland in Normandy at the beginning of the thirteenth century (1204) hastened the metamorphosis of Normans into Englishmen. From 1066 to 1204 England can be said to be under alien rule; after 1327 (the outbreak of the Hundred Years' War) the rulers are effectively English kings. Before 1204 the literature of the rulers is in a Langue d'Oil dialect usually known as Anglo-Norman; after 1327 (or soon after) it is in English. We can therefore speak of *Norman* rule ceasing in England between 1204 and 1327, say around 1265 as a mid-point. As will become clearer below, one can speak of the Franconian etc. rule in Burgundy lasting from 1038 and 1254, so that for the purposes of this analogy it seems fair to think of alien rule in England and in Burgundy covering very roughly the same period, *c.* 1050 to *c.* 1250.

III

THE PARAGON OF EXCELLENCE AND BEAUTY

Burgundy born again

Burgundy's loss of independence coincided with the beginning of her finest hour. This is not such a paradox as it might seem. When the Normans conquered England they replaced the vast bulk of its ruling class, cleric or secular, with their own men. The Franconians* were Franks, and so were perhaps to be feared in Burgundy as greatly as Clovis, Charles Martel or Charles the Bald; but in fact when they took power they hardly touched the fabric of Burgundy's administration. Historians argue to what extent the structure in England was rebuilt, but they agree that Burgundy was not even given a new façade. Thus whereas the flowering of England may chiefly be attributed to the Normans, in Burgundy the credit goes to the Burgundians themselves.**

The years 1050–1250, in England roughly the Norman period, were Burgundy's golden age, and indeed it was Europe's great era of medieval civilization. For both Burgundy and Europe the previous hundred years 950–1050 were a crucial formative period as the terror of the invasions of Saracens, Vikings and Magyars receded. Few countries had suffered more than Burgundy, and few were now to recover more swiftly. Burgundy lay at the hub, between Germany and Iberia, France and Italy; it was at the heart of the new Europe and in the center of its new renaissance. We need hardly recall its ancient possession of Latin culture or the aptitude of its barbarian settlers. Its position on the trade routes ensured that it was open to ideas from Christian regions as distant as Armenia and Ireland and from the Moslem world of Syria and Spain; and the revival of commerce brought life again to towns like

* The four great German duchies were Franconia, Saxony, Swabia and Bavaria, and were based on races – Franconia on the east Franks, Swabia on the Allemans. Saxons, Franconians (= Salians) and Swabians (i.e. Hohenstaufen) all gave dynasties to the Empire.

** Trevor Rowley's *The Norman Heritage* is an excellent recent (1982) survey of the Normans' impact on England, notably on its administration. By 1090 only one of the sixteen English bishoprics was held by an Englishman, and only half a dozen of the 180 greater landlords or tenants-in-chief were English. Forty new towns were established by 1130, forty-nine more in 1191–1230. The Franconians made very few such changes in Burgundy.

Marseilles, Lyons, Arles, Valence, Vienne and Avignon, a few of which still retained something of the municipal paraphernalia of Roman cities.

In the countryside of Burgundy the changes may have been even more important. From this time onwards armed violence played a much smaller part in life than is commonly supposed, and there was no pestilence such as had hit the western world in the third century or would come again in the fourteenth. The climate had gradually become more temperate so that even in England the vine became widespread, and under these gentler conditions both population and land under tillage expanded greatly between 950 and 1250. In Burgundy the forests on the banks of the Saône and the Beaujolais hills were cleared from the middle of the tenth century, and in Dauphiné from the eleventh; and there was now a vast extension of vine-growing all over Burgundy as elsewhere. Indeed, in the eleventh and twelfth centuries the economy of western Europe, based chiefly on the activities of ploughman, herd and smith, underwent a revolution hardly less significant than the industrial one of the eighteenth and nineteenth, for the breaking of new land was accompanied by improved farming techniques, bringing great increases in yields. Perhaps no single innovation was more important than the use of the horse for plough and cart – so much more speedy and efficient than oxen.

Far from bringing the end of the world, as some feared,* the millennium was marked in Christendom, and notably in Burgundy, by rising confidence and growing prosperity; and in no way was this more evident than in their new churches.

> About the year one thousand and in the first three years of this century, one saw in almost all the world, above all in Italy and the Gauls, the rebuilding of holy basilicas from top to bottom even though there was often no need. There was rivalry throughout Christendom as to who would have the most beautiful ones. It could have been said that the world was shedding its rags to deck itself out again in a white robe of churches. The faithful thus renovated almost every cathedral and also the monasteries of the many saints and the little parish churches.

This often quoted passage comes from the history written by the Burgundian Rudolf Glaber, a witness of the part played by Cluny in Burgundy's renaissance. Ineffectual as they were as rulers the Rudolfians at least were active

---

* Probably fewer than it used to be thought.

patrons of this great monastic order, founded in 910; and when Burgundy ceased to have kings of its own, it gained instead a line of churchmen of far greater stature and significance, culminating in Saint Bernard of Clairvaux. Bernard died in 1153 when Burgundy's influence in Christendom was at its height. Its golden age had begun a century before, very shortly after the passing of its kings, and had opened with the long and brilliant reign of Saint Hugh, Abbot of Cluny (1049–1109).

Romanesque and Gothic Art

The mighty Order of Cluny

Hugh of Chameliac, who came from a noble family of Brionnais in the west of the Kingdom of Burgundy, was raised to the abbacy at the tender age of 25 and became one of the greatest statesmen and builders that the Church ever produced. The Church was in those days the main driving force of European society, for it alone had authority throughout western Christendom. Moreover it was the most highly organized institution until the emergence of the Renaissance kingdom-state. Equipped with the best trained staff of the age it did not suffer, as did lay institutions, from breaks in authority caused by death or deposition. The bishops were not only the rulers of men's souls but were often given the secular and administrative authority of counts or barons, and the archbishops of Lyons and Besançon, for instance, were amongst the most powerful of the nobles of Burgundy. The Church's great and ever-growing possessions made it a state within a state, frequently able to defy a king by appealing over his head to the Pope as chief of all Christendom. It towered like a noble Romanesque abbey church above the hovels of the ignorant faithful. But more than that, for it was not merely a question of scale, of power, of permanence: without the Church there would have been total illiteracy and technological stagnation. The Church provided virtually everyone who could read or write; the administrators from governor to petty clerk; the scientist, philosopher, doctor, teacher. It was 'the establishment', and in no country was its role more significant than in Burgundy, its influence there growing steadily as the Order of Cluny gained in power with the passage of the tenth and eleventh centuries. Three Cluniac monks were elevated to the holy see, but from the time of Majolus, head of the Order between 954 and 994, the abbot's power rivaled that of the Pope and indeed the Emperor, let alone the King of Burgundy or King of France. Moreover Cluny's influence was powerful at all levels, not only on pontiffs and monarchs, but on millions of common folk. By Hugh's death in 1109 it controled 1100 monasteries, later in the century 1450;

in an age when government was so primitive and weak, a few intelligent men under instructions from an autocratic center could work their will over thousands.

Cluny's and Burgundy's part in the recovery of the West

Most American and English students of history are aware of western Christendom's remarkable recovery and advance in the eleventh to thirteenth centuries: how in the tenth Spain was almost lost, Rome itself threatened, and every Catholic land the prey for Saracens, Vikings or Magyars, and how by the thirteenth century the foe had been cleared from Provence, Portugal, most of Spain, southern Italy and Sicily. By then control of the Mediterranean had passed largely to the navies of Genoa and Venice, and Christian states had been established in the enemy's homeland in the Levant. Not only had the Magyars and the western Slavs been converted, but the Teutonic Knights had carried the cross as far as Lithuania.

It is general knowledge that this huge expansion of Europe resulted largely from the Church's giving direction to Christendom's growing energy and power. It is less well known that, although in later times the French, Normans and Germans played a more prominent role in the extension of Christendom's frontiers, no one did more than the Burgundians to set this great advance in motion. When the former Cluniac monk Urban II passed through Cluny in 1095 to launch the First Crusade, he did homage at the tomb of Abbot Majolus, largely because he had organized the first holy war against the Saracens: their expulsion from Provence late in the tenth century* was the turn of the tide.

Moreover Burgundians, some in armor, some in the black robes of Cluny, took the lead in helping the princes of Iberia to get rid of the Saracens; the crusades in the west started before those in the east and were to have far more significant and permanent results. Raymond of Burgundy** was charged by his father-in-law Alfonzo VI of Leon-Castile (1072–1109) with the reconstruction of Salamanca, Avila and Segovia, desolated by the wars with the Moors, and the walls of Avila look today very much as they were left by Raymond and his Burgundian engineers and masons nine hundred years ago. Alfonzo made his other Burgundian son-in-law, Henry,** Count of Portugal; soon to become

---

* Page 67 above.
** Raymond and Henry were not blood relations. The former was the great-grandson of Otto William, *Count* of Burgundy; the latter grandson of the younger Robert (effectively the first Capetian *Duke*) mentioned on p. 68. Genealogical tables B and C on pp. 282–3.

independent sovereigns, Henry's descendants held the Portuguese crown until 1580.

The Cistercian Order

Perhaps the cutting edge of every movement is destined to become blunted by success. In any case Cluny's idealism was tempered from an early stage with Burgundian realism and moderation; and the easy-going and convivial habits which crept over the movement in the eleventh century seem more in keeping with the Burgundians' character than the zealous austerities of either of the other monastic movements that they produced, the Cistercian and Carthusian. Only the Cistercian can feature here.* The order was started at Cîteaux in 1098 by Robert, Abbot of Molesme, but the real founder was his successor Stephen Harding (1110), with the result that the first Cistercians were a mixture of Burgundians and English. It was Stephen the Englishman who laid down the order's constitution and rules of life (1119), banning from the Cistercian monasteries such Cluniac luxuries as gold and silver ornaments, stained glass and bells. His successor, Saint Bernard, a native of Dijonnais, was of a tough and unforgiving spirit alien to his Burgundy, for he abominated laughter and his best-loved text was from Saint Jerome, 'A monk's duty is to mourn, not to teach'. Bernard's crusade against the arts of Cluny could not prevent the Cistercians from leaving us wonderful treasures in stone. There may be no Cistercian sculpture and painting but Cistercian architecture is even more lovely than Cluny's.

As we shall see shortly, what the Cluniacs did in spreading Romanesque over Europe the Cistercians did for early Gothic. Both had a significant effect on the thought and behavior of Christians of every rank and country; and if the abbots of Cluny probably exercised more power and influence in high places than the Cistercian leaders (apart from the outspoken and domineering Bernard himself) – in brief, they meant more in political terms – there is no doubt that the Cistercians counted for much more in economic life because of their development and dispersion of technology. At their height they had no less than 3000 monasteries.

The monastic life had begun as a refuge from an anarchic and unhappy world after the fashion of Saint Anthony, but now the hermit had become the

---

* Nor can we deal with non-Burgundian monastic centers such as Gorze and Prémontré.

agronomist and engineer, and the world a place to be improved by science as much as by prayer. The time which the Cluniac spent illuminating his manuscripts the Cistercian devoted to agriculture and the crafts. No section of society was more responsible than the Cistercians for the rising standard of living in an age which witnessed improvements in the plough and the invention of the spinning wheel; the repair and upkeep of the ancient Roman roads; the development of the vine; and the conversion of forest and marsh and, in the Low Countries, even the sea-bed into farmland.

The economy of England, for example, benefited immensely through the efforts of what initially was only a handful of dedicated and intelligent men, most of them Burgundians who in many cases came from Bernard's monastery at Clairvaux. They gave a great impetus to horse and sheep breeding: desolate moors became vast pasturelands; Fountains abbey alone managed some 18,000 sheep in the thirteenth century[1] and like other Cistercian houses sold the wool to merchants in France, the Low Countries and Italy. The later wealth and greatness of England, which were based largely on her wool trade, can thus in some measure be attributed to the Cistercians of the twelfth and thirteenth centuries.

The magnificent architecture of Cluny

There are few people familiar with European history who do not know of the glorious era of the dukes of Burgundy in the fifteenth century, but how many know of the other golden age of Burgundy, mentioned briefly above, which lasted from about 1050 to 1250? Or if they do, will they perhaps think of it as French rather than Burgundian? After all, for art historians 'France' naturally embraces 'Burgundy'. In the Romanesque period and later, however, France and Burgundy were distinct. The dukes of Burgundy did homage to the French kings only from 1194; and the rest of Burgundy had even slighter links with France. It was only from about 1200, with the remarkable successes of Philip Augustus (1180–1223), that France became a great power in medieval terms and extended significantly beyond the Ile de France – the Paris basin.*

1050–1250 is the period in which the great monastic orders of Burgundy did so much to lead and fashion Christian society, and the age may be termed golden chiefly because of the magnificent achievements of the Cluniac order in

* See footnote to page 66.

the arts generally and of the Cistercians in their noble architecture.* The merit and significance of these achievements may still not be properly recognized, partly because all three successive churches at Cluny have disappeared (except for a lone transept of 'Cluny III'), as have largely the Cistercian mother houses, Cîteaux and Clairvaux; and the triumphs of French engineers and craftsmen in developing Gothic after the middle of the twelfth century have obscured what their Burgundian predecessors did to prepare the way for them. Only a little can be said in a chapter of this length to do justice to Burgundy on these points and to demonstrate how vastly important was its influence on European art during this formative period.**

Due largely to the leadership of the energetic abbots of Cluny the Burgundians made an important contribution to the development of the new architecture of the West which is known as First Romanesque. 'Cluny II', built by Abbot Majolus and consecrated in 985, was for instance not only the chief model for the churches of the period over a vast area, the best examples which have survived being at Romainmotier in the Suisse Romande and at Chapaize and Uchizy in Brionnais, north-west of Lyons; it was also the inspiration, perhaps at one remove, for many of the churches built by the Normans both in their French duchy and in their new English kingdom, not least the magnificent cathedral of Durham.***

In the tenth and eleventh centuries Burgundy was no more than just one of the cradles of the First Romanesque (Map no. 12), outpaced by Lombardy – the style is often called 'Lombard'; by Catalonia which raised vaults (the element so typical of the style) some decades earlier than Burgundy;**** and by the Rhineland, where the might of the Empire was reflected in great cathedrals such as those at Trier (1017–47) and Speyer (1030–61). However, by 1100, thanks to the monks who under Saint Hugh's direction were then completing the third church at Cluny, Burgundy was leaving her First Romanesque

---

* Some readers may consider that I give too much credit to the Cluniacs and Cistercians of Burgundy, and too little to the builders of the Ile de France, Champagne and Picardy. I recommend them to the works of Kingsley Porter, Evans, Conant, Puig i Cadafalch and Lasteyrie mentioned in Appendix IV (Art and Architecture), and I hope they will conclude that I have been fair.

** Readers who would be satisfied with a very brief summary of Burgundy's cultural achievements in the Middle Ages could now turn on to page 98, 'The Power and the Glory'. Suggestions for further reading are in Appendix IV.

*** See Appendix III, note B, on p. 249.

**** Or Provence which was closely related, but which is usually regarded as a separate school of Romanesque.

partners behind, and fifty years later she had done more than any country to evolve the architectural elements which are regarded as distinguishing Gothic.*

Cluny III was bought for its stone by a shrewd businessman soon after the French Revolution, and it was demolished over a space of thirteen years without serious protest. Thus the remains, which are not far from the main road to the Riviera some fifty miles north of Lyons, fail to convey that this was the greatest of all medieval churches, unchallenged for five hundred years until the raising of new Saint Peter's in Rome. Its scale may however be gauged if one imagines Paray-le-Monial – a 'must' for the visitor to Burgundy – as being considerably larger in all three dimensions than Durham cathedral, the greatest Romanesque church of England.

Cluny's sculpture and painting

Only a little of the sculpture which once embellished the great church is preserved for us in the museum at Cluny, but fortunately stonework of equal quality is still in its place at Vézelay, Burgundy's finest Romanesque church; at Autun, its noblest 'half-Gothic' one;** and in many less well-known. The Burgundians are famous for their doorways – for instance the Christs-in-Majesty at Vézelay and Charlieu, and that at Autun which is attributed to Gislebertus (Gilbert), probably the greatest artist in Europe before Giotto.*** Yet it is not to their treatment of religious subjects that we should look for the most interesting Burgundian work, but rather at the human and animal figures on doorways and capitals in the Cluniac churches. The enchanting nude of Eve the seductress at Autun, which was probably carved by Gilbert, may be the best-known example, but one should not miss the contrasting portrayals of the Flight into Egypt at Saulieu and at Autun, or of Samson grappling with the lion at Anzy-le-Duc and at Vienne; nor the griffins and the three charming naked children at Geneva, the cythar player in the museum at Cluny, Balaam and his ass at Saulieu, or Saint George slaying the dragon at Saint Martin d'Ainay's at Lyons. If there is any single area on which the admirer of Burgundian sculpture should concentrate, it is the Brionnais for here there are a dozen ancient

* Appendix III, B on p. 248.
** Appendix III, B.
*** He served his apprenticeship at Cluny up to c. 1120. (Beckwith, J., *Early Medieval Art*, p. 252.)

[81]

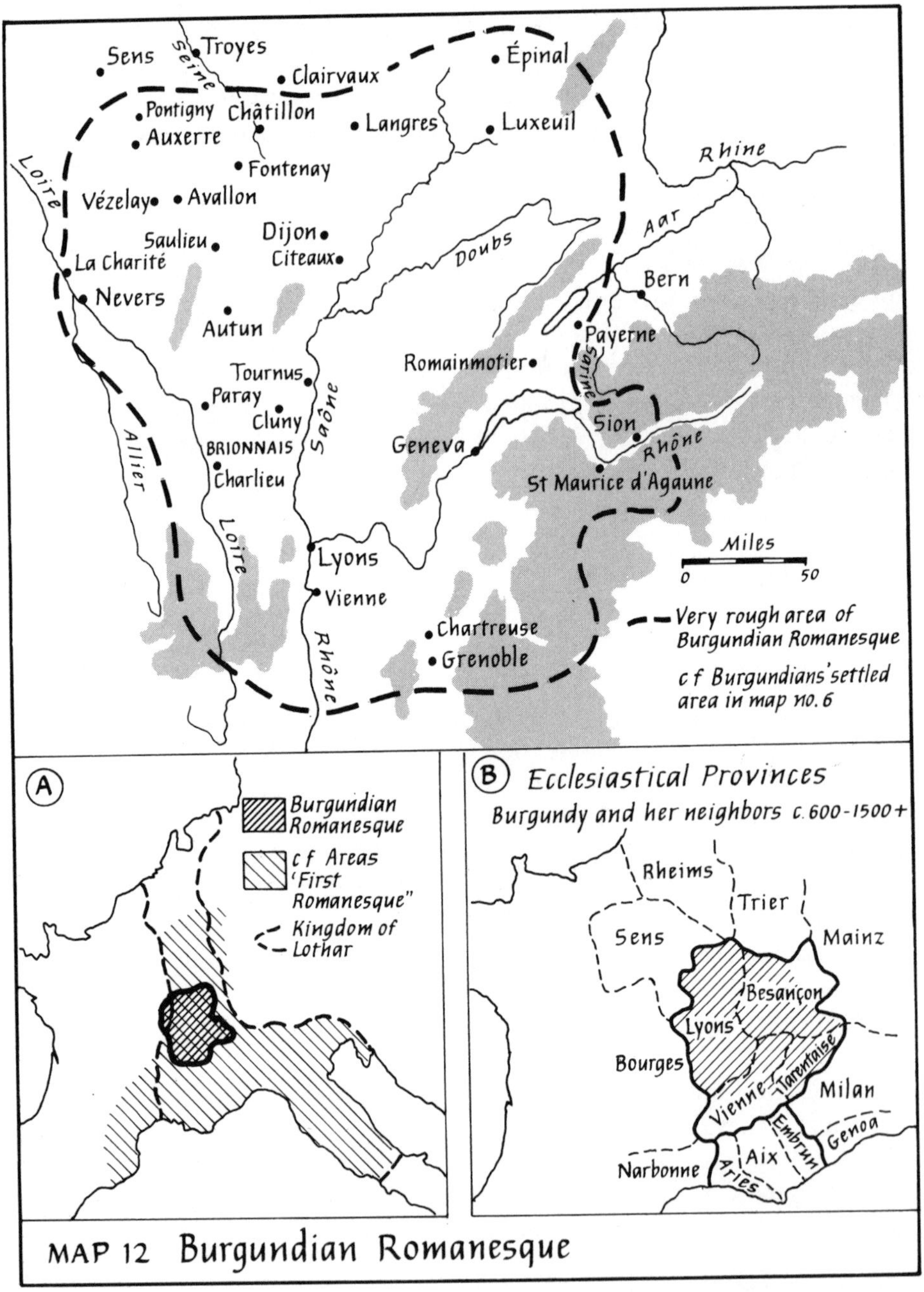
Sens
Troyes
Seine
Clairvaux
Épinal
Pontigny
Châtillon
Auxerre
Langres
Luxeuil
Loire
Fontenay
Rhine
Vézelay
Avallon
Saulieu
Dijon
Aar
La Charité
Citeaux
Doubs
Nevers
Bern
Autun
Payerne
Tournus
Romainmotier
Paray
Saône
Sarine
Cluny
Sion
Allier
BRIONNAIS
Geneva
Rhône
Charlieu
St Maurice d'Agaune
Loire
Lyons
Miles
0
50
Vienne
Very rough area of Burgundian Romanesque
Rhône
Chartreuse
Grenoble
cf Burgundians' settled area in map no. 6
A
Burgundian Romanesque
cf Areas 'First Romanesque"
Kingdom of Lothar
B
Ecclesiastical Provinces
Burgundy and her neighbors c. 600-1500+
Rheims
Trier
Sens
Mainz
Besançon
Lyons
Bourges
Tarentaise
Milan
Vienne
Embrun
Genoa
Aix
Narbonne
Arles
MAP 12 Burgundian Romanesque

Map no. 12 The 'very rough' area shown in the main map appears with an unbroken line in inset A, and as the hatched part of inset B, where it is seen to correspond very closely with the four Burgundian ecclesiastical provinces (as distinct from those of Provence): Lyons, Vienne, Besançon and Tarentaise.

churches outstanding for their capitals and tympana, and it was in the Brionnais, notably at Anzy and Charlieu, that this superb art first appeared even before Saint Hugh began rebuilding Cluny and founded its great school of sculptors and painters.

Burgundy's sculpture is remarkable for its fecund invention, its imaginative adaptation of ideas taken from Gallo-roman art, and its realistic and earthy blending of religious and everyday subjects; and its most endearing qualities are its humanity and humor.

We shall never know how many of western Europe's frescos from the eleventh and twelfth centuries have been lost, but it is generally accepted that, whereas Romanesque France produced very little painting of any kind, at that time Burgundy and Aquitaine could match any region of western Europe. There was an abundance of painting in Burgundy from the middle of the eleventh century and the ceiling of the chapel of Saint-Chef in the department of Isère dates from 1070 or soon after. Other examples from this period are to be found at Anzy-le-Duc and in the crypt of the cathedral at Auxerre; and there is a large fragment from the Burgundian abbey of Charlieu in the Musée de Cluny – for long the Paris residence of the abbots – showing Boso, the restorer of the Kingdom of Burgundy in the ninth century, offering the abbey, which he had founded, to a rather uninterested Saint Stephen.

The typical blue backgrounds of the school of Cluny and its painted Christs in Majesty were to be found all over south-eastern Gaul, in Dauphiné and the lower Rhône valley as well as in Burgundy proper. An impression of the lost frescos in the apse of Cluny III may be gained from the apse of Paray-le-Monial and better still, perhaps, from the Christ in Majesty and the Martyrdom of Saint Vincent in the little church of Berzé-la-Ville, between Cluny and Mâcon; they were almost certainly executed by monks from Cluny between 1100 and 1110 for Abbot Hugh who retired there in his later years.

In one form of painting the Burgundians particularly excelled: their illuminated manuscripts. Those from Cluny have tragically been lost, but they were probably of the same fine quality as the ones left to us from Stephen Harding's reign at Citeaux; Oursel comments that these manuscripts rendered by Burgundian monks and their English brethren belong 'in the first rank of the treasures of the Middle Ages'.[2]

Medieval Burgundy's most precious legacy

Language makes frontiers,* art transcends them. Yet there have been art styles which distinguished regions and countries. Art historians** generally accept that there is such an area where the churches of the Romanesque period are distinctively 'Burgundian', which not surprisingly comprises the four ancient ecclesiastical provinces of the Frankish and more truly Burgundian regions: Lyons, Vienne, Besançon and Tarentaise. Thus the area of Burgundian Romanesque corresponds to Burgundy proper: the area which the Burgundians settled more or less densely in the fifth century, as distinct from the two regions, Allemannic and Provençal, which were Burgundian not in character but only by conquest. (See Maps nos 12 and 7.)

Obviously there are variations, but very many of Burgundy's village churches are cruciform in shape with a cupola and often a tower over the crossing and a triple apse. The method of vaulting and the porches are also peculiar to Burgundy. However, there are other reasons for giving special attention to Burgundy's ecclesiastical architecture. It may possess few great Gothic cathedrals to match those of France or of England, and other countries can boast of Romanesque cathedrals or abbeys to compare with Payerne or Vézelay. Nor is Burgundy unique even in its remarkable abundance of Romanesque parish churches – five hundred dotted over the countryside from Châtillon-sur-Seine to Sion in the Swiss Valais – although there can be few regions in Europe which can rival the single department of Saône-et-Loire where there are no less than two hundred. But what is of supreme interest about the parish churches of Burgundy is, first, that many of them have sculpture which very often outshines that of the greatest cathedrals elsewhere; and, secondly, most of Burgundy's small churches have not undergone the renovation to which the twelfth-century churches of England were subjected in the fifteenth and nineteenth centuries and those of Italy in the sixteenth and seventeenth. Thanks to this, Burgundy's wealth of unspoilt Romanesque art remains one of Europe's greatest glories; and it was its discovery twenty years ago that first set the author off on his quest for 'Burgundy'.

---

* To what extent is discussed briefly in a later chapter.
** e.g. Lasteyrie, Viollet-le-Duc, Eygun, Valléry-Radot. The area of Burgundian Gothic, discussed below, presents more of a problem, but is generally similar. See Branner, and Appendix III.

Burgundian half-Gothic is spread all over Latin Christendom

Most of Burgundy's churches, small or large, were based on the First Romanesque cruciform design which had a cupola over the crossing surmounted by a tower, a design which had been developed particularly successfully by the Cluniacs; and there are comparatively few churches in Burgundy which were built by the Cistercians – their remarkable abbeys are mostly to be found much further from home. The oldest extant Cistercian church is almost certainly little Bonmont built north of Geneva in 1131, a simply cut but neglected diamond – it has long* been used to store hay and machinery! Fontenay, larger and finished later (1130–46), is a close contemporary of Autun.** Like Autun, Fontenay has pointed arches and pointed vault: the Cistercians took over the Cluniacs' 'Burgundian half-Gothic' in many respects, notably the pointed arch and vault, and they also – for instance at Pontigny (after 1150) – made good use of the pointed 'lancet' window. But at Fontenay and Pontigny there are none of the sculptured creatures which so affronted Saint Bernard, and no colored window glass. Since there are no bells there are no belfries; compare the three gaunt towers of Paray-le-Monial and the unbroken line of Pontigny's roof.

Outside Burgundy the Cluniacs built most of their foundations in France, Aquitaine and Iberia. By contrast, as the American art historian Conant wrote,[3] the Cistercians introduced their 'suave Burgundian architecture' as far afield as Sweden, Portugal, Cyprus and Lebanon. However in *Italy*, stubbornly Roman and Romanesque, neither order made great architectural impact, and Burgundian influences were by and large confined to a few abbeys such as Fossanova and to the cathedrals of Genoa and Siena. They were more successful in Iberia, France, England and even in Germany.

At the time of the Cluniac and Cistercian 'conquest' of Latin Christendom, *Germany* was politically and culturally more powerful than France. Burgundy was part of the Holy Roman Empire and German ideas might have been expected to prevail. However, the two abbey churches at Cluny, II and III, far from being inspired by German models, had a great influence in the Rhineland, Switzerland and beyond; and later on the Cistercians carried their style to the valleys of Germany just as they did elsewhere.

The monks of Cluny provided *Iberia* with no less than thirteen of its bishops

* Most recently visited in 1980.
** Page 81.

[85]

around 1100 and could take chief credit for the building not only of the great church at Compostella (1075 plus) but also of most of the monasteries on the pilgrimage roads running to it from Aquitaine and Burgundy. The Cistercians modeled Poblet abbey (near Tarragona, 1162) on Fontenay and it became the mausoleum of the kings of Aragon, while in Portugal they left us the magnificent complex at Alcobaca.

In no country was the influence of the Burgundian architects, both Cluniac and Cistercian, so great as it was in *France*. After 1150 France (the Ile de France, Champagne and Picardy – the ecclesiastical provinces of Sens and Rheims) led Christendom in the development of architecture; but not long before that date she was one of Europe's most backward lands, architecturally speaking, outstripped by Italy, Spain, Germany, Normandy and England as well as by Burgundy. In 1137, when the rebuilding of Saint Denis was set in hand by Suger, who was abbot there 1122–51, France could boast not one single church to compare with Cluny, Speyer, Santiago de Compostella, San Ambrogio of Milan, Saint Sernin of Toulouse,* Saint Mark of Venice, the duomo at Pisa, or the greatest of the Norman churches on either side of the Channel.[4]

Abbot Suger is often referred to as 'the inventor of Gothic' and Saint Denis as 'the first Gothic church' – claims which will not be challenged here but which must be seen in perspective. The elements Suger introduced at Saint Denis which are regarded as typical of Gothic were already in use. The pointed arch was introduced in Italy about 1066 and in Burgundy in 1088; the pointed vault was common in Cluniac naves from 1100; the lancet window was to be found in Cistercian abbeys in Burgundy shortly after 1130; and the nave walls at Cluny were strengthened with flying buttresses in 1135. However, more than any of these features French art historians like Focillon regard the rib vault as the touchstone of Gothic. If they are right it must be significant that the stage of development reached in the rib-vaulting of Durham's aisles** in 1093 was not attained in the Ile de France until at least thirty years later. Indeed the French hesitated to vault their naves until the middle of the twelfth century, over a hundred years after the vault had become general in Burgundy.

France – the royal domain and Champagne, that is – was thus something of an architectural void before 1150. In filling it so brilliantly there is little doubt

---

* Not under more than nominal French suzerainty until a century later.
** The vaults for Durham's choir and nave also seem to have been projected with ribs at that time; they were actually built with them 1107–30.

that Suger and his imitators drew their inspiration chiefly from the Burgundian monastic orders – from Cluniac and Cistercian abbeys in neighboring Normandy hardly less than those in France itself; and the same sort of links may be found between Burgundian and French sculpture.[5] Throughout the half century between the rebuilding of Cluny and of Saint Denis (1088–1137) there was no sculpture in France to compare with Burgundy's; the capital which displays the acrobat at Saint Martin des Champs (c. 1140), for instance, is no match for the dozens of capitals carved in Burgundy during the previous two generations. Even the famous western portal at Chartres, which dates from after 1140, seems crude by comparison. In any event the better work done at Chartres, which had so wide an influence in the second half of the century, was of Burgundian inspiration. The head sculptor at Chartres was obviously inspired by the tympana at Autun and Vézelay, and notably by the fluttering and graceful draperies at which the Burgundian artists were so skilful. The so-called Master of Etampes, who also worked at Chartres, was even closer in style to the Burgundians and above all to Gilbert. Thus what is generally regarded as the influence of Chartres was in fact largely the influence of Burgundy.

Burgundian Gothic is overtaken by 'le style français'

The differences we recognize between 'Romanesque', 'half-Gothic' and 'Gothic'* would have baffled the architects of Burgundy, France and England of the later twelfth century, but they would have been aware that they had chosen different ways to develop the ideas which had come to them from Cluny and Clairvaux. For their part, when they raised churches which we label as 'Gothic', the Burgundians excelled in their ingenuity and their sense of line and proportion. They did not strive to set their roofs in the clouds but rather to strike a perfect balance between the height of the nave and its width, and to convey by the most skilful illusion the impression of spaciousness, lightness and fragility.** Most significant, perhaps, is that, although the Burgundians soon recovered from the puritanical blight of Saint Bernard's teaching and once again adorned their churches with sculpture, they were long reluctant to follow

---

* Appendix III, B.
** Perhaps their finest example is Notre Dame de Dijon, raised on remarkably slender columns early in the thirteenth century. For Burgundian Gothic, see Appendix III, C.

[87]

the French into the luxuriance of 'Rayonnant' Gothic,* preferring to rebuild Saint Bénigne of Dijon after 1281 in their own restrained and dignified manner.

In brief French and Burgundian ideas developed in parallel in Burgundy throughout the thirteenth century, sometimes competing, sometimes combining. In the end the Burgundian style was overtaken first by the introduction of Rayonnant decoration applied on Burgundian forms, and then by the adoption of Rayonnant designs. It is easy to see from a visit to its churches that Lyons began to fall under French cultural influence in the thirteenth century as northern political forces swept in.

France and Burgundy and the coming of Gothic

The architecture of Burgundy gave way to the 'French style', as it was known,** late in the thirteenth century. Elsewhere, except in Italy where its own Romanesque generally persisted, architects had turned from Burgundy to France for their inspiration after 1200: the cathedral of Lisbon, for instance, had been 'built Burgundian' in the late twelfth century but the work done in the thirteenth was 'French'. Only in England, to which we must turn shortly, did Burgundian Gothic survive. Yet Burgundy's role in the development of medieval art was as important as that of France, and the extent of her influence radiating to the remotest corners of Latin Christendom was undoubtedly greater.

There is unfortunately no room here for more than the briefest comparison of the parts played by Burgundy and France. However, we must remember that, since most of Burgundy is now part of France, it is not strange that credit for its achievements has been given to the French, even though an extreme partisan of Burgundy might declare that it would be equally just to ascribe Scotland's triumphs to the English, and that what was created in Lyons, Avignon or Arles while the Kingdom of Burgundy was still within the Empire could as fairly be called German! In any event, when one is studying the arts of Burgundy and of France, the picture is further confused by wide but mistaken acceptance of the

---

* Roughly equivalent to England's 'Decorated', it reached maturity in the French royal domain c. 1250. From 1186 this included not only Ile de France (see map at endpaper) but also south Picardy where Amiens' Rayonnant is outstanding.

** Or '*opus francigenum*'.

view that the Ile de France led Europe in architecture before 1150 just as it undoubtedly did thereafter until the renaissance of Italy.

No one will ever rob the architects of the Ile de France and Champagne of their claim to have created the finest Gothic cathedrals, and no Burgundian erected Gothic masterpieces to compare with Notre Dame de Paris, Amiens, Bourges or Beauvais. But it was Burgundy's role to make these masterpieces possible by fusing into a coherent architectural style the elements which made up Gothic – a style which was the chrysalis from which High Gothic burst so magnificently at Laon, Noyon, Soissons and Chartres in the late twelfth century.*

'Burgundo-English' Romanesque and Gothic

The influence of Burgundy on the arts of *Normandy* and *England* was as profound as in Iberia or France. In 1002, at the invitation of the Norman duke Richard II, William of Volpiano sent monks from the abbey of Saint Bénigne at Dijon to reform the houses of the Duchy. One result was the Normans' adoption of Burgundian art forms; for instance Norman and English Romanesque churches often have a cupola and tower at the crossing, although the bells are not normally hung there, as in Burgundy, but at the west end. Bernay in Normandy (c. 1050–5) and even Durham in north England (1096–1133) were modeled on Cluny II, and Castle Acre priory in Norfolk, albeit in ruins, is England's outstanding example of Cluniac architecture.

Burgundian influence on England in the Cistercian half-Gothic period, which the English call 'Transitional', was even more important because it was direct and not second-hand by way of Normandy. Daughter houses of Cîteaux and Clairvaux at Waverley in Surrey (c. 1128), Tintern and Rievaulx (both in 1131) were succeeded by Fountains in Yorkshire, where we find not only the half-Gothic of the first Cistercian settlers (1132 plus) but also, notably in the Chapel of the Nine Altars (1210–47), the style which their successors perfected. This may arguably be termed 'Burgundian Gothic' as well as 'Early English'. There is no purpose in debating to what extent Early English,

---

* The first major Gothic cathedral is often said to be Sens (completed c. 1175), 'Sens-en-Bourgogne' on the threshold between Burgundy and France. There is no room here to debate to what extent its style is French or Burgundian. It was the model for the choir at Canterbury (1175–92).

England's first developed style of Gothic*, is Burgundian in inspiration as well as French and homespun, but it is worth observing that the great church that is the quintessence of Early English, Lincoln, was built by a man from Burgundy, Saint Hugh of the Burgundian order of Carthusians (1192 onwards).**

The extraordinarily close links between Burgundy and England in this period involve many other famous names, including four archbishops of Canterbury: Anselm, who came from Aosta, and three who took refuge at Cistercian Pontigny, Thomas à Becket, Stephen Langton and Saint Edmund of Abingdon. Edmund's body was laid to rest there behind the high altar and Pontigny's links with Edmund and with England were recognized in a curious way: whereas the women of Burgundy or other countries were allowed into the abbey church only on the feast of Saint Edmund's translation, women from England were granted admittance at all times.

* The first English church with 'any serious claim to be called Gothic' is Roche abbey in Yorkshire (Cistercian c. 1160) (P. Kidson: *A History of English Architecture*, p. 68). Perhaps Wells' nave (1174 onwards, i.e. contemporary with Canterbury's choir) is the first in a truly English Gothic idiom.

** Lincoln is often described as 'revolutionary' and as 'setting the style for the 13th century'. It draws little on French inspiration, a lot on north-English which was very largely Cistercian. How far Hugh drew also on ideas then current in Burgundy it is impossible to judge. He was born in 1140 on the border of Savoy and Dauphiné. His house in London was the origin of Lincoln's Inn.

For Burgundian influence in England see also Appendix III, C.

Thought and Literature

Reform and heresy

Burgundy's contribution to Europe's thought was far less significant than to its art. Her church schools and universities, for instance at Geneva, Grenoble, Lyons, Autun and Auxerre, never achieved the fame of Paris, Oxford or Bologna; and there were few Burgundian philosophers of importance. Saint Anselm, who became Archbishop of Canterbury and one of the Church's great teachers, was born in 1033 at Aosta just within the confines of the Kingdom of Burgundy, but neither he nor Honorius, who anticipated Renaissance thinkers in teaching at Autun that 'there is no other authority than truth proved by reason', can be regarded as truly Burgundian. Moreover the great age of medieval philosophy corresponds with a period, the thirteenth century, when Burgundy was in decline. Of the fourteen universities existing in Europe in 1300 not one was in Burgundy.

Burgundy's role lay less in philosophical enquiry than in ecclesiastical reform and in debate on the place of the Church in medieval life. The role of the Cluniacs, Cistercians and Carthusians in seeking to correct and purify the Church, and thus they hoped the lives of all men, has been referred to already, and there is no name better known in this respect than Saint Bernard's.* For some thinking men, however, Bernard's attack on the luxury of the monasteries was not enough, for they increasingly found themselves in conflict with the Church's teaching or authority. In the tenth, eleventh and twelfth centuries men had a freedom to believe as they wished which was not to be recovered until the eighteenth century; and it was not until late in the twelfth that the Church felt threatened, first by the Cathars and then by the Valdensians. Neither Cathars nor Valdensians form part of the main stream of medieval philosophy, but in the end they count for more than the Realists and

* The contribution to current thought made by Bernard's contemporary at Cluny (Peter the Venerable, abbot 1122–55) deserves mention too.

[91]

Nominalists who struggled for intellectual supremacy, for their beliefs reached far more people and the long-term influence at least of the Valdensians was much greater.

Valdensianism and Catharism grew up in the regions south of the Loire and Côte d'Or which took a great leap forward in the generations after the Viking, Saracen and Magyar invasions ceased: in fact from around 1000. This civilization embraced most of the Kingdom of Burgundy but it was at its most brilliant in the Toulousain and it is perhaps best known to us for the troubadours and the vernacular lyric poetry which they addressed to the beauties of the Languedoc nobility, but the most striking feature of this southern civilization was a freedom of thought, enquiry and criticism, which was more marked in Provence (and Languedoc) than in Burgundy proper. Here strange beliefs like Catharism and movements of protest such as Valdensianism could flourish most easily. Catharism was not of Burgundian but eastern origin, though it was very strong particularly in the south of the Kingdom of Burgundy; and its main significance for the Kingdom is that the invasion to suppress it, the so-called Albigensian Crusade (1209–44), established French power in south Gaul and was thus highly instrumental in preventing the Burgundian phoenix from rising once more.

The total extinction of Catharism gives the lie to the misplaced belief that all powerful movements of the intellect or the spirit will ultimately live through the fiercest oppression. Valdensianism had a happier fate as well as a different source. Its origins were in Burgundy and it is probably its greatest contribution to the freedom of thought.

The Valdensians

The Valdensians were founded and given their name by Peter Valdez, a rich merchant of Lyons who had little or no Latin and wished to read the scriptures for himself, and so about 1170 he commissioned two priests to translate them into the vernacular, presumably into the Lyonnais dialect.* It soon became clear to him that Christian life had departed a long way from that taught in the Gospels. A manuscript of the fifteenth century, written by a Valdensian and now in England at Cambridge, tells how up to the time of Constantine the heads of the Church had lived in poverty and humility but thereafter the Church was

---

* A version of Franco-Provençal, see p. 94.

corrupted; and how eight hundred years after Constantine, Valdez appeared, sold his goods and distributed the proceeds to the poor and started preaching against the 'heresy' of the Pope.

The Poor of Lyons, as Valdez's followers were first called, believed that the key to life lay in the direct, personal understanding of the message of God in the Bible; and he despatched his disciples in pairs to preach in towns, villages and by the wayside, carrying texts with them in the vernacular so that the scriptures could become better known. The movement spread like wildfire especially in southern Burgundy, notably Dauphiné and Provence, in other parts of the Midi, and in Bohemia where Valdez died in 1217. It was not declared heretical until the Lateran Council of 1215, seven years after Innocent III had called for a crusade against the Cathars. Most of the early Valdensians' beliefs hardly deserved proscription by the Church, since they enjoined the renunciation of private property and fasting three days a week; indeed husbands and wives were required to separate so as to give themselves wholly to God. The simple faith of the Poor amounted, they believed, to little more than a literal application of the teachings of Jesus as set down in the gospels; and so they naturally repudiated indulgences, purgatory and masses for the dead, for which they could find no scriptural authority. Their technique of itinerant preaching, which the Cathars also adopted, was so effective that Innocent was only too ready to use it to counter heresy; against Valdensians and Cathars the Church ranged Dominicans and Franciscans. The Valdensian ministers lived in monastic-type houses when not on the road, and in this and in their asceticism and simple teaching they were precursors of the friars. Had they been founded a generation earlier the Franciscans, like the Poor of Lyons, might have been proscribed by the Papacy – so narrow can the line be between Reform and Revolt – and indeed Innocent only recognized their value to the Church after hesitation and suspicion.

Despite persecution the Valdensians' Church survived until they were absorbed centuries later by Protestantism, the Italian flanks of the Cottian Alps becoming their chief refuge and fortress. Here they were harassed bitterly by the Dukes* of Savoy at intervals from the early fourteenth century onwards; and in the seventeenth Cromwell sent an ambassador to protest, and Milton wrote his immortal tribute, 'Avenge, O Lord, thy slaughtered saints'.**

The Valdensians had an influence out of all proportion to their surviving

---

* Counts until 1416. (See p. 157.)
** Sonnet, *On the late massacre in Piedmont*.

numbers. Their beliefs persisted in Bohemia and contributed greatly to the rise of the Hussite movement; Protestants of the sixteenth century came to honor them as the only Christians to have preserved the pure faith of the early Fathers; and the first Protestant French translation of the bible resulted from meetings of Valdensians and Swiss reformers in the sixteenth century. Whatever their importance for the development of the reformed churches – and Valdez can fairly be called the first of all Protestants – the Valdensians may at least claim to be amongst history's most resolute and tenacious victims of religious persecution.

The everyday use of 'Burgundian'

There is, regrettably, very little space here for the story of the spoken and written word in the Kingdom of Burgundy. Its dialects fell into four groups. Provençal in the south and Schwyzerdütsch in the Allemannic area (now northern and central Switzerland) will be the most familiar to the reader; however, we are not concerned here with them or with the old Langue d'Oïl dialects of present-day Burgundy and Franche Comté, but only with Franco-Provençal.* This was the Romance language spoken wherever the Burgundians had settled relatively densely, western Switzerland, Savoy, northern Dauphiné, and southern Franche Comté. It was, in brief, the language of the Burgundian Homeland, though it was also spoken in Lyonnais and Forez to the west and the valleys of Aosta and Susa to the east (Map no. 13). Appendix II, which is devoted to a brief study of Franco-Provençal, argues that it might better be called 'Burgundian'.

Philologists say that the 'linguistic norm' of Franco-Provençal was to be heard in Lyons. Not surprisingly, the language was used for the written as well as the spoken word whenever Latin was not thought appropriate. Obviously countless examples of written 'Burgundian' have been lost, but enough have survived to demonstrate beyond all doubt that a relatively uniform language was in use throughout the area for judgements and ordinances no less than for wills, agreements, tolls and epitaphs[6] – as uniform, say, as the written word used in the length and breadth of Tudor England. Indeed the Kingdom of Burgundy could boast a tongue which was spoken and written in a larger proportion of its area than French was in the Kingdom of France.

* As British philologists call it. Those who still speak it write 'francoprovençal'.

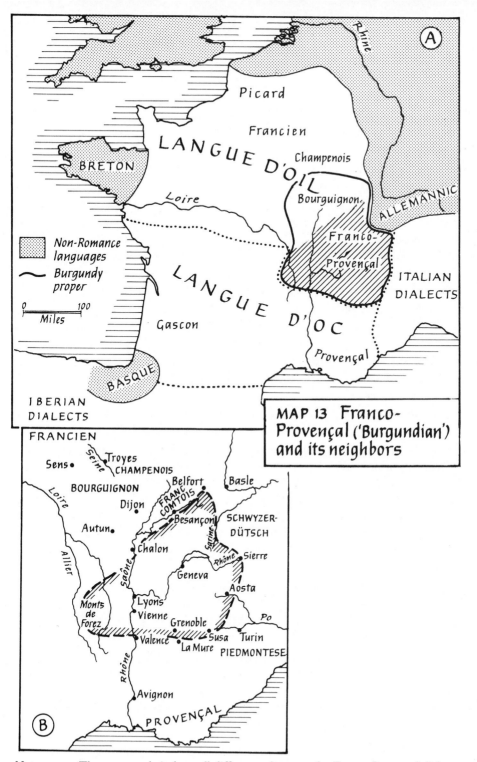

Map A

BRETON

Picard

Francien

Champenois

LANGUE D'OIL

Rhine

ALLEMANNIC

Bourguignon

Franco-Provençal

ITALIAN DIALECTS

Loire

Non-Romance languages

Burgundy proper

0   100
Miles

LANGUE D'OC

Gascon

Provençal

BASQUE

IBERIAN DIALECTS

A

MAP 13 Franco-Provençal ('Burgundian') and its neighbors

Map B

FRANCIEN

Sens •

Troyes
CHAMPENOIS

Seine

BOURGUIGNON

Belfort

Basle

Dijon •

FRANC COMTOIS

Besançon •

SCHWYZER-DÜTSCH

Autun •

Chalon •

Saône

Rhône

Sierre

Loire

Allier

Geneva •

Aosta •

Saône

Monts de Forez

Lyons •

Vienne •

Grenoble •

Po

Valence •

La Mure •

Susa

Turin •

PIEDMONTESE

Rhône

Avignon •

PROVENÇAL

B

Map no. 13 There were relatively small differences between the Franco-Provençal dialects, that of Lyons being regarded by some modern philologists as the norm. The map does not distinguish Bas-Bourguignon or variants of Provençal.

Burgundian literature

There are very few surviving examples of literature in any European vernacular from before 1200, and it is exceedingly difficult even to guess how many works were composed in 'Burgundian'. There is good reason for believing that the Strasbourg Oath of 843, the earliest known text in any vernacular of Gaul, was written in a dialect of the Rhône valley (and Burgundian is more likely than Provençal, given the location of Strasbourg); and we need have little doubt that that is the medium of the Passion of Christ and Life of Saint Léger, the third and fourth oldest texts of Gaul, dating from the tenth century. The *chanson de geste Gérard de Roussillon* (*c.* 1160) may not be in Franco-Provençal (Burgundian), as Elcock[7] maintains, but *Alexander of Macedon* (*c.* 1180) certainly is. This epic about a man who was to be such a great hero to a later Burgundian, Charles the Bold, was written by Alberic of Pisançon, near Vienne; it is a work of considerable merit and Elcock comments: 'In its subject matter, as the first of a series of Romance poems recounting the exploits of Alexander the Great, it breaks new ground; as northern France created the secular epic, and Provence the lyric, so the Franco-Provençal area gave birth to the roman d'antiquité, the source of courtly romance'.

The prose Life of Beatrice of Ornaciu quoted in Appendix II dates from about 1300 and the Legend of Saint Bartholomew, also from Lyonnais, is a little older. Perhaps many others were written which are now lost, but one group of people had good reason to preserve their vernacular writings, the Valdensians, who believed in disseminating the gospel and their protestant teachings in the vulgar tongue. For three hundred years after Valdez of Lyons had the Bible translated into his vernacular (*c.* 1170) his followers wrote dozens of works of which many are extant in what is almost certainly the Lyonnais version of 'Burgundian', such as *La Nobla Leczon*, *La Barca* and *Lo Despreczi del Mont* (scorn of the world).

Even if 'Burgundian literature' had consisted only of the few works referred to here, it may fairly be compared with the medieval vernacular literature of Normandy, Picardy and Champagne. At any rate the output in medieval French (Francien) before 1300 was poorer still, nor was the vernacular literature of Italy, Castile and Portugal at this time any more remarkable. It is only in the fourteenth century that the Romance vernaculars blossomed.*

---

* Chaucer's *Canterbury Tales* (in a fusion of Romance Anglo-Norman and early English) dates from the end of it.

Anzy-le-Duc, mid-eleventh century, generally regarded as the model for
Vézelay. One of many churches in Brionnais which have remarkable sculpture.

The Holy Lance. The silver sheath placed on it by Emperor Henry III (detailed picture) says it is 'confirmation that this is the Nail of the Lord and the Lance of Saint Maurice'. Charles IV added the gold band (top picture) saying 'The Lance and the Nail of the Lord'. (The blade may be no more than a monastery bread knife of *c.* seventh century, and the 'Holy Nail' wired to it, believed to be from the Cross, can only be traced back to the early tenth century.) (p. 69n)

(Left) 'The Musician', one of the remarkable capitals which survive from Cluny III. Carved between 1088 and 1095 and now in the town museum. *(Right)* The Flight into Egypt, Saint Andoche, Saulieu, a church consecrated in 1119 by the Burgundian pope, Calixtus II. (p. 81)

Balaam and his ass, a frequent subject of Cluniac sculpture, this example also at Saulieu. (p. 81)

'Luxury' in the narthex of Charlieu abbey, *c*.1130.

'Eve', the sculpture previously in Autun cathedral, now in the town's Rolin Museum. The work of Gislebertus, *c.* 1140, like the tympanum and much other sculpture in the cathedral. Probably the finest Romanesque nude. (p. 81)

Cluny, before its demolition: an eighteenth-century print. The church was the largest until Saint

La Charité-sur-Loire, 1100–06. Originally the second largest Cluniac
church, but most of the nave has disappeared. In 1080 there were 200 monks.
(p. 250)

(Far left) La
Charité, the abbey
choir. *(Left)*
Paray-le-Monial,
the apse.

(Above) Fontenay abbey, the nave, 1130–47. A Cistercian contemporary of
Autun, more austere and with no sculpture. (p. 85) *(Right)* Autun cathedral,
the nave, 1126–40. Cruciform, with a cupola and small central tower, this is
perhaps the climax of Cluniac architecture.

XV

Vézelay, the façade, finished between 1145 and 1152. The narthex was
consecrated in 1132. The façade was greatly altered in the thirteenth century
and restored by Viollet-le-Duc c.1868.

Language is the truest hallmark of a 'nation', and literature is the most 'national' form of culture. Some peoples may boast that the flame of their national spirit burnt on despite their absorption in an alien state, and the Poles justly look back with pride to Mickiewicz and the Hungarians to Petőfi and Vörösmarty; but there was no similar flowering of national literature under foreign rule in Ireland, Slovakia, Croatia or Serbia. The peoples of the Rhône Basin were more tenacious. In Provence the successors of the troubadours continued to compose their verse in the Langue d'Oc for at least three hundred years after the coming of the French in the thirteenth century. In Burgundy vernacular literature was a younger plant and still tender when French culture began to obtrude in the late twelfth and thirteenth centuries, yet it survived into the nineteenth, producing some respectable verse until about 1650. So, even if Burgundian literature did not thrive as strongly as the fully mature literature of Provence, neither did it perish in its fragile youth as did the Picard and Champenois. Had the region of Paris been exposed to a powerful foreign culture from the late twelfth century onwards such as Burgundy had to endure, can we be sure that there would have been any literature whatever in what could truly be called French?

The Power and the Glory

It is not of every age or country that one can say that excellence and power went hand in hand; too often the glory that has gone with power has lacked taste, and the exquisite has been outshone by the merely magnificent. Happily in the centuries when it had power Burgundy could also glory in excellence; and this, perhaps, was because the power was not political but cultural, its founthead not its secular rulers but its monastic orders, international in their extension and influence, both national and international in their inspiration and complexion.

Paradoxically Burgundy's greatness in this age of the Crusades – roughly the eleventh, twelfth and thirteenth centuries – was reflected in the strength not only of the established Church but also of the revolt against it. It was the age of Valdez as well as of Hugh of Cluny and Bernard of Clairvaux. Burgundy may have contributed little to medieval philosophy, but she yielded to none as regards her spirit of independent thought no less than her part in Church reform. In both respects her influence was important, indeed incalculable in its ultimate effect.

There is no medieval literature of greater importance than that of the Langue d'Oc, and it flowered in Provence ('Lower Burgundy') hardly less than in Périgord and Toulousain. However it belonged less to the Kingdom of Burgundy than to Aquitaine; and for the more truly Burgundian literature, written in Franco-Provençal, we can only claim that seven hundred years ago it had as good prospects as the literature of the Ile de France, Italy, Spain and Portugal; and very few peoples who were overwhelmed by an alien culture, as the Burgundians were subsequently, made any greater contribution to European letters.

There is less doubt about the significance of Burgundy's medieval art. What Hugh's Cluny III was to High Romanesque and proto-Gothic, Majolus's Cluny II was to First Romanesque; and, despite Bernard's rejection of their sculpture and painting, in architecture the Cistercians were the Cluniacs' direct heirs, both of them fusing together the elements of the style we call Gothic. Burgundy was more important to Romanesque than Catalonia, Italy or Germany, let alone

France, Aquitaine, Normandy or England. She was perhaps as important to Gothic as France, in so far as she was its 'inventor' no less than France was its finest developer. In sum no country had as powerful an influence as Burgundy on the artistic development of Latin Christendom between 1050 and 1200 when its styles were extending over Iberia, Ireland, Scandinavia and central Europe, and into the Middle East. Not only had Burgundy's own Romanesque and half-Gothic art and architecture few peers anywhere, but the best buildings in other countries were in many cases erected by Cluniac or Cistercian monks. The extent to which the influence they spread was *Burgundian* can be judged from the fact that almost all of the 694 Cistercian churches built before 1200 were derived from only two or three Burgundian models.

Great architecture often spells great power: in France from the late twelfth century, before her, in Burgundy. Burgundy's influence was exercised through Cluny's 1450 houses, spread mostly over Gaul and Iberia, but the Cistercians' 3000 stretched from Ireland to Lebanon and from Portugal to the Gulf of Finland. These abbeys were the outward and visible sign of an influence far wider and deeper than the field of architecture; the evidence of Burgundy's art all over the lands of Latin Christendom testifies not only to the power of Burgundy's artistic creation but also to the prevalence of ideas and techniques of every kind originating in monasteries in Burgundy or in monasteries founded elsewhere by Burgundian orders. The Cluniac and Cistercian houses were thus centers for a cultural radiation which affected virtually every aspect of life. Both orders influenced the thought and customs of the age; and the Cistercians in particular led Europe in agriculture, animal husbandry, viniculture, land reclamation and irrigation, textiles and metallurgy. From the eleventh to the thirteenth century no country contributed more richly than Burgundy to European civilization, progress and prosperity.

IV

'ASHES'

Under the King-Emperors

The permanence of Burgundy's frontiers

The Holy Roman Empire, whose creation we can attribute to Charlemagne,* was in theory universal but consisted in fact of four kingdoms: Italy, Burgundy, and those of the east and west Franks. When after a peripatetic century the imperial title finally came to rest in 962 with the kings of the east Franks (or Germans), the west Franks (or French) accordingly refused allegiance, which emperors like Henry VI sought to recover. Otto I** regained Italy and from 1038 the Emperor would hold four crowns again – imperial, German, Italian and Burgundian – unless he chose to assign one to a son or other junior partner.

From the outset the Franconian emperors made it clear that, like the Merovings and unlike the Carolings, they would not annex Burgundy to their own Frank kingdom (i.e. Germany) but would rule it separately. As soon as he was in control Conrad II relinquished the Burgundian throne in favor of his son; and, when in the next year, 1039, Conrad died, his heir became Henry III of Germany and Henry I of Burgundy. Both emperors recognized that, as was to be case for many generations, men regarded Burgundy*** as a permanent feature of their world, as identifiable as Germany or France, and more so than Italy; and the frontiers of the Kingdom of Burgundy were in fact amongst the most constant of Europe, changing little between the fifth and fifteenth centuries (see Map no. 14). There was more variation in the first half of these thousand years than in the second: Paris was part of Burgundy for a while under the Merovings; for a half-century there were two kingdoms of Burgundy until Rudolf II reunited them in 933; towards 950 the Duchy of Burgundy was accepted as being politically part of the Kingdom of France, although ecclesiastically it stayed one unit with the Kingdom of Burgundy, since its bishops

---

* Though the term is thirteenth-century.
** See Genealogical tables A and C (pp. 281, 283) for this chapter.
*** From *c.* 1200 more often called the Kingdom of Arles or Arelate (p. 113 below).

remained subject to the archbishop of Lyons; and after a century of belonging to Italy, about 970 the Aosta and Susa valleys were restored to Burgundy. From then until the fifteenth century the only change was the loss in 1166 of the County of Forez which switched its allegiance from the King of Burgundy to the King of France. Lyons remained part of Burgundy despite its seizure by the French in 1312, and to their chagrin the Emperor Sigismund reasserted his rights there during visits in 1415 and 1416. Similarly when the French secured Dauphiné in 1378 they accepted that it remained part of the Arelate, as the Kingdom had come to be called to avoid confusion with the Duchy of Burgundy.

The frontiers during the greater part of this millennium ran from the Mediterranean northwards along the line of the mountains to the west of the Rhône, enclosing Beaujolais in Burgundy; up the Saône almost to its source, then south-eastwards past Belfort and across to the Rhine at Basle; up the Reuss to the mountain-mass where the Rhine and Rhône have their beginnings; across Piedmont to embrace the Aosta and Susa valleys; and down the line of the Alps back once more to the Mediterranean coast. These frontiers, including specifically north-western Piedmont and the County of Burgundy, were defined yet again by the Emperor Charles IV in the instrument of 1378 which made the Dauphin Charles his viceroy in the Arelate.*

Burgundy was therefore a feature on the map of Europe which educated men were accustomed to, and many would not have been surprised to see it take on more substantial form. As time passed and there were only infrequent demonstrations of imperial authority – for instance Sigismund's royal progresses through the Arelate in 1415–16 – people naturally became ever vaguer about the limits of the Kingdom. However, in a speech to the Council of Constance in 1414 Gerson referred to Vienne as being in Burgundy and not as in Dauphiné of France, even though he was the leader of the French king's delegation; in a book written about 1450 Lyons is described as in Burgundy, not France; and a contemporary reference to Pope John XXIII taking flight from the Council of Constance (in the Kingdom of Germany) to what is now German Switzerland calls the latter 'Burgundy'.

When the ministers of the Emperor Frederick III and Charles the Bold drew up the agreement in Trier in 1473 to reconstitute the Kingdom, they mentioned places like Cleves and Toul which lay outside it, and also Savoy since its Italian territories were involved, but they considered it unnecessary to list the

---

* Savoy, although still in the Kingdom, was excluded from the Dauphin's area.

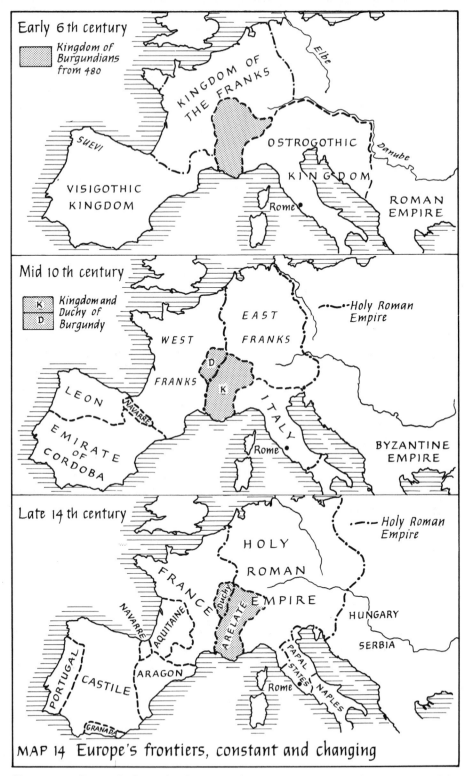

Early 6th century

Kingdom of Burgundians from 480

KINGDOM OF THE FRANKS

SUEVI

VISIGOTHIC KINGDOM

OSTROGOTHIC KINGDOM

Rome

ROMAN EMPIRE

Elbe

Danube

Mid 10th century

K · Kingdom and
D · Duchy of Burgundy

WEST FRANKS

EAST FRANKS

D

K

ITALY

Holy Roman Empire

LEON

NAVARRE

EMIRATE OF CORDOBA

Rome

BYZANTINE EMPIRE

Late 14th century

Holy Roman Empire

FRANCE

HOLY ROMAN EMPIRE

Duchy

ARELATE

NAVARRE

AQUITAINE

PORTUGAL

CASTILE

ARAGON

GRANADA

Rome

PAPAL STATES

NAPLES

HUNGARY

SERBIA

MAP 14 Europe's frontiers, constant and changing

Map no. 14 Burgundy (later, the Arelate) had exceptionally constant frontiers, even if the separation of the Duchy of Burgundy is allowed for (marked 'D').

constituent parts of the Kingdom itself. The consternation of the Swiss showed that they knew that most of their lands were included. Indeed the Hapsburg and Burgundian ministers realized that the frontiers they had in mind were so well known that it sufficed, even in such a detailed and formal document, to speak only of 'all the dignities, rights and prerogatives which belong in any way to the said Kingdom of Burgundy'.

Even when Duke Charles Emmanuel of Savoy set about recreating the Kingdom of Arles around 1600, there was little surprise that he saw it comprising Geneva, the County of Burgundy, Lyonnais, Dauphiné and Provence – all of its old regions in fact except German Switzerland and Valais.

The governing of Burgundy*

In theory the three kingdoms which were united in the person of the Emperor were equal in status, but in practice it was inevitable that Burgundy should rank below Germany and Italy. Burgundy's importance lay largely in the routes which it provided between the Emperor's other kingdoms: if Italy was what India became to a later empire, Burgundy was its Middle East and the Alpine passes its Suez. The King-Emperors never established their authority in Burgundy as for instance the Normans did in England or Sicily, but royal power was more real than in Italy and hardly less so than in France or Germany outside the king's own hereditary lands. However, the nobles of Burgundy maintained resistance to the Holy Roman Emperors from the early eleventh century for several generations, not only from the natural impulse to reject outside control but also from a feeling that they were defending an ancient inheritance. The chronicler Alpert wrote that when the lords of Burgundy defied the Emperor they insisted on their right to choose their own sovereign

---

* The Preface stressed how selective this book is. When it was compressed from a longer work, one section which was very greatly shortened dealt with the centuries following the absorption of the Kingdom of Burgundy into the Holy Roman Empire. In the interests of brevity little of the political history has been retained, except when it concerns the attempts to restore the Kingdom. The result is a lack of balance: e.g. the monastic orders have been treated out of their political context, and so also has medieval Burgundy's contribution to European culture. And there now follows a perhaps unduly long section on Richard I's connection with Burgundy – possibly justified if it offers a new slant.

To get a more balanced picture Boehm, Fournier, Steyert, Richard and Jacob should be referred to. (See the works listed in Appendix IV)

from amongst their own people as was laid down in 'the perpetual law of the Burgundians'. Otto of Freising complained that the Burgundians gave great trouble to his nephew the Emperor Frederick I, known as Barbarossa (1152–90), attributing this to the memory of 'the old days when Burgundy had strong kings of her own' and to 'her appetite for liberty which the Burgundians regard as priceless'.

Since in addition the Emperors found that their widespread responsibilities in Germany and Italy left them little time for their third kingdom, affairs there got easily out of hand. The words of Wipon, the imperial chaplain, to Conrad II could have been addressed to almost all of the King-Emperors of the next four centuries: 'My king, Burgundy calls for you! Rise and come quickly! For if the master is away for long, the loyalty of his subjects wavers. The old saying is profoundly true: out of sight, out of mind. Although Burgundy now enjoys peace, thanks to you, she needs to contemplate in your person the fountain of this peace and refresh her eyes with the sight of her king'. Absence demanded delegation of authority and the King-Emperors generally followed the practice already adopted for Germany and Italy of appointing an Archchancellor and a Chancellor of Burgundy. The Chancellor, usually a bishop, was responsible for official business such as the granting of rights and privileges on behalf of the sovereign. The Archchancellor, a more honorific position, was normally an archbishop (Besançon, Vienne or Lyons) and from about 1250 he was regularly the Archbishop of Trier, who was the Imperial Elector effectively 'representing' Burgundy when a new Emperor was chosen. From that period onwards there were seven Electors, the other six being the archbishops of Mainz and Cologne, as archchancellors of Germany and Italy, and four great nobles of Germany; their duties were confirmed and codified by the Emperor Charles IV in his Golden Bull of 1356, and the Archbishop of Trier continued to bear the title of 'Archchancellor for Gaul[1] and the Arelate' until the seventeenth century.

The problems of the Emperors' three kingdoms called for different political solutions. At no point do the Emperors seem to have planned to give either Germany or Italy its own separate king; in their different ways each was more personal, more important to them than was Burgundy, and neither had enjoyed long periods of rule by an independent dynasty as had Burgundy. Thus they not only appointed Imperial Vicars (viceroys) for Burgundy as often for Lombardy and Tuscany, but frequently they tried to revert in effect to the situation existing before 1034, a separate Burgundy with its own king, a homage-paying junior partner.

Emperor Frederick I (Barbarossa)

The King-Emperor who had the greatest success in extending his dominion over the Kingdom of Burgundy was the Hohenstaufen Frederick I, known as Barbarossa. He paid frequent visits to Lyons and other centers, receiving homage, dispensing justice and granting concessions, and at Arles in June 1178 he had the archbishop crown him King of Burgundy in the fine Romanesque church of Saint Trophîme,* in the presence of the archbishops of Vienne and Aix and several bishops and nobles including the Count of Toulouse. Among the many acts and ceremonies of which we have record, Frederick made Bertrand de Baux Prince of Orange, the town near Avignon; thus originated a title that was to pass to the founders of the Netherlands monarchy, which by a coincidence is (as we shall see) an offspring of the state of Burgundy. Then, moving north, the newly crowned king halted at Valence and Vienne, and at Lyons not only the archbishops of that city and Vienne waited on him with the bishops of Valence and Grenoble but also the Duke of Burgundy. In 1186, four years before his death, Frederick used the occasion of his son Henry's marriage at Milan to Constance, the heiress of the Kingdom of Sicily, to have Henry crowned King of Italy while he himself was recrowned King of Burgundy, on this occasion by the Archbishop of Vienne.

---

* Trophimus of Ephesus, who was converted by St Paul and is mentioned in the New Testament, brought the faith to the Rhône valley *c.* AD 60 and became the first Bishop of Arles.

Richard Lionheart,
William of Baux and the Kingdom

The Emperor promises the crown of Burgundy to Richard I

Henry VI succeeded his father, Frederick Barbarossa, in June 1190 at the age of 25. In his reign of only seven years he came closer than any Emperor before or since to gaining universal recognition as the overlord of all Christendom. He maintained his father's claims to the homage of Denmark, Hungary and Poland. He not only added Sicily as a fourth kingdom held like Germany, Italy and Burgundy directly by the Emperor; he persuaded the kings of Armenia and Cyprus to accept his imperial suzerainty rather than that of Constantinople, which, had he lived to see his schemes brought to fruition in the Fourth Crusade (1204), would also have become his vassal; and he received the homage of the King of England, once a province of the Roman Empire and a glittering jewel hardly less desirable for the imperial crown than France, the only kingdom missing from the four in the Empire as reconstituted by Charlemagne. 'Above all else', wrote Roger Howden,* Henry 'desired to make the Kingdom of France subject to the Roman Empire'.[2]

So wide were Henry's commitments and ambitions that he could give less time to Burgundy than his predecessors. Coronation at Arles or Vienne does not seem to have figured in his plans and he chose instead to make Richard I of England king also of Burgundy, a story which is little known.

Richard Lionheart had been imprisoned by Leopold, Duke of Austria, on his way home from the Third Crusade (December 1192), an outrage against the immunity of a royal crusader which shocked the world but which Henry, even for his times a cold and calculating prince devoid of honor, heart or scruple, saw he could turn to his advantage. He bought Richard's person from Leopold, ignoring pressure from the Pope and some of his magnates to set him free, charged Richard with a string of crimes, and as price for his release demanded an immense ransom and homage for his lands.

* Or Roger of Hoveden, as in the Rolls Series[2].

Richard's case could hardly have been more perilous. In England his brother John was in rebellion to usurp the throne. In league with him was Philip II of France, the royal comrade-in-arms who had sworn an oath to Richard, when he left him in Palestine to soldier on alone against the infidel, not to interfere in his lands or scheme against him (July 1190). Philip so far betrayed his promise as to offer all Richard's continental possessions to John, seize the Vexin (between Paris and Rouen), and prepare to take over several other territories (Map no. 15). From the moment he heard of Richard's capture Philip did his utmost to ensure that he remained out of the way indefinitely; and Henry was naturally happy to oblige him while he was extracting all he could from Richard, not least his promise to raise the ransom.

During the spring of 1193, however, events moved in favor of the royal prisoner. Richard had in the meantime promised homage for England;[3] and he now won much support at the imperial council held at Speyer in Holy Week, defending himself with courage, dignity and candor against the charges brought by Henry and the ambassadors of Philip. Moreover, his cause had been well argued too by the envoy wisely chosen by the English to start negotiations for their king's release. Savaric, Bishop of Bath, had a Burgundian mother and she appears to have been a cousin of Henry's mother, Beatrice, who had brought the County of Burgundy to Frederick I as dowry.[4] He was present at Henry's court from the first weeks of 1193 and for the next four years he played a notable part in the exchanges between the two monarchs.

But Richard benefited above all from Henry's growing concern about the ambitions of Philip, the king rightly named Augustus who was one of the three or four to whom chief credit belongs for the creation of Europe's greatest state. Henry must soon have realized that he was unlikely, to adapt Roger Howden's words, to make the Kingdom of France subject to a German-dominated empire so long as kings like Philip confronted it, and history was indeed not to see that outcome for just on three quarters of a millennium. It was henceforth more often a question of 'Germany' holding France at bay.

The immediate threat was Philip's intention to marry the sister of the King of Denmark, of which Henry considered himself suzerain; but the longer-term French menace was already taking shape against Henry's Kingdom of Burgundy. The lord of Bresse, the rich province east of the Saône, had offered to switch his homage to Philip's father Louis VII in 1160, and the Count of Forez had actually done so in 1166. Henry no doubt considered that none of his Burgundian feudatories was powerful enough to help him meet the French menace; he needed the support of a prince who could pose a direct counter-

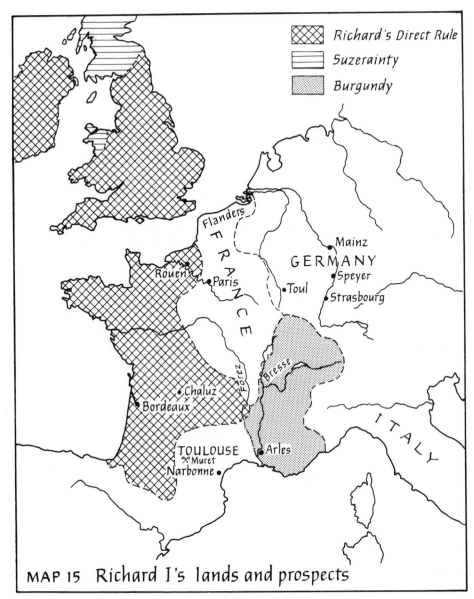

Legend:
- ▨ Richard's Direct Rule
- ☰ Suzerainty
- ⣿ Burgundy

Flanders

FRANCE

GERMANY

Rouen
Paris
Mainz
Speyer
Toul
Strasbourg

Forez

Bresse

Chaluz
Bordeaux

ITALY

TOULOUSE
× Muret
Narbonne

Arles

MAP 15 Richard I's lands and prospects

Map no. 15 Richard I's lands in SE Aquitaine marched with Burgundy and placed him relatively close to Provence and so to Arles.

threat to Philip, and no one met this bill but Richard whose huge domains marched not only with France but with the Kingdom of Burgundy[5] (Map no. 15).

It is therefore not surprising that Henry turned to Richard; and when the latter was brought to the imperial court at Hagenau near Strasbourg on 19 April 1193, he found himself no longer a criminal on a charge but welcomed cordially as a royal brother. Henry was due to meet Philip near Toul in Lorraine, in the Franco-imperial border country, on 25 June; but instead Henry opened a conference with Richard at Worms (on that same date, so as to underline the point), which was attended by Savaric as well as many princes of the Empire. First there was the question of Richard's ransom; with that settled, discussion turned to Henry's plans for Burgundy. If (as is probable) he first suggested that Richard should be Imperial Vicar – his viceroy – we can be sure that Richard held out for the crown itself, and there seems no doubt that Henry agreed to this at Worms subject to his getting his pound of flesh. Howden writes of the payment of Richard's ransom 'in very great part' in the summer and autumn of 1193, and 'after this the Emperor gave to the King of England, establishing it by his charter, the following territories' which, as Howden's list shows, amounted to almost all of the Kingdom of Burgundy together with the County of Toulouse, which was not Henry's to give away.* (The territories omitted were not very substantial, since Richard's new kingdom comprised 33 bishoprics, and the number usually given for Burgundy at different periods was 25.)**

This great news was announced in a letter which the Emperor addressed on 20 December to the English people, in which he said:

> Henry, by the grace of God, Emperor of the Romans, and ever august, to his dearly beloved friends, the archbishops, earls, barons, knights, and all the faithful subjects of Richard, illustrious King of England, his favor and every blessing. We have thought it proper to intimate to all and every one of you that we have appointed a certain day for the liberation of our dearly beloved friend, your lord Richard, the illustrious King of the English: the second day in the fourth week after the Nativity of our Lord (17 January 1194), at Speyer or else at Worms;*** and we have appointed seven days after that (24

* A translation of this passage appears with comments in note 6.
** Compare England's 15 bishoprics (and 2 archbishoprics).
*** Like Mainz, cities on the middle Rhine where the Emperors often held their peripatetic councils.

January) as the day of his coronation as King of Provence, which we have promised to him; and this you are to consider certain and undoubted. For it is our purpose and our will to exalt and most highly honor your aforesaid lord, as being our special friend.[7]

In calling the kingdom 'Provence' Henry's letter to the English reflected the uncertainty of the time as to what it should be called now that, as noted above, 'Burgundy' had come to mean the French duchy for most people. Very soon after this it became usual to refer not to the Kingdom of Burgundy but rather to 'the Kingdom of Arles and Vienne' or, for short, the Kingdom of Arles or the Arelate (*Arelatum*).*

Richard's expectations were obviously high when he wrote on 22 December 1193 from Speyer telling the Archbishop of Canterbury the dates of his release and his coronation as King of Burgundy.[8] His mother, Eleanor of Aquitaine, took ship to the Rhineland to lead a great retinue of bishops and magnates to attend the imperial council at Speyer to witness Richard's release on 17 January. There was general consternation when, without explanation, the Emperor adjourned the council for a fortnight. When it reconvened at Mainz on 2 February Henry adjourned it again, this time admitting to Richard that he was still holding him prisoner because Philip and John had offered him a sum even greater than the English ransom! It was only because the German magnates remembered the promises made at Worms and took Richard's part that the devious Emperor gave way and set him free on 4 February.

It is doubtful what else took place at Mainz that day. It seems that Richard duly 'surrendered' England to the 'Lord of the World', as Howden calls Henry in his account, and received it back from him as a fief; but it is unclear whether more was, or needed to be, done as regards Richard's title to Burgundy. Bryce may be right in asserting that he was invested with the kingdom that day.[9] In any case the place for the coronation was not in the Rhineland but at Arles.[10] Richard obviously gave higher priority to reasserting his rights in England, Normandy and Aquitaine; and, having dealt firmly but generously with

---

* Or even to the Kingdom of Vienne although this implied rather the northern part of the Kingdom of Burgundy, corresponding with the Rudolfian kingdom before it was united in the early tenth century with the then Kingdom of Provence. Since that union Provence had been no more than a county.

As noted above Frederick I was crowned King of Burgundy in 1178 by the Archbishop of Arles, and again in 1186 in Milan – but this time by the Archbishop of Vienne, no doubt to show he was king of both Lower and Upper Burgundy, or King of Arles and Vienne as he would have been called in the thirteenth century.

John, within a few weeks he set about driving Philip from the lands he had usurped.

Richard as 'King of Burgundy'

No doubt Richard planned to be crowned at Arles one day and there must have been exchanges with Henry about this of which we have no record. In the meantime in the summer of 1195 the Emperor sent Richard a 'great golden crown',[11] which can hardly have been for any kingdom but Burgundy. We can reasonably assume that Henry was confirming Richard's title to Burgundy and recognizing that his commitments elsewhere delayed his coronation in the regular manner at Arles; but what is certain is that Savaric, who by agreement between the Emperor and Richard had been made Chancellor of Burgundy, continued in that office until Henry knew he was nearing his end and sent him back to Richard with a message releasing him from his homage for England (1197). It can therefore not have been as vassal-king of England that Richard was bidden to Cologne to take part on 22 February 1198 in the election of Henry's successor; the only position which could make Richard a prince of the Empire was King of Burgundy.[12] He excused himself, since he was still busy recovering territories in France which Philip Augustus had seized; but the delegates he sent were highly successful, for his nephew Otto IV was chosen and he became a stalwart opponent of the French king.

On his release from Germany early in 1194 Richard had sent word to the crusaders in the Holy Land that he would rejoin them as soon as God had granted him peace and vengeance on his enemies. Now, five years later, he could think again about that promise. Slowly but surely he had worsted Philip and restored his authority throughout the Angevin empire. His attempt in March 1199 to get his hands on a treasure he learnt was held in the ill-defended castle of Chaluz not far from Limoges was something of a side-show, and his thoughts were already on leaving Aquitaine for other fields. If, as is probable, he had next turned his face again towards Jerusalem he would soon have come to Provence. Would he have summoned the archbishop to crown him King of Burgundy as he passed through Arles? We shall never know, for it was at Chaluz that, as Richard's biographers tell in detail,[13] the arrow pierced his left shoulder which proved fatal.

As Steyert, the historian of Lyons, remarks,[14] Richard died King of Burgundy without having had the chance to assert his rights there. Richard, who was not quite 42, might have developed a greater interest in Burgundy than he had shown in England; Duke of Aquitaine since he was 15, he was a man of the south as fluent in the Langue d'Oc as in Norman French – and more at home, it seems, than he was in English. However, English readers should not be tempted into speculating that, had Richard lived to the ripe old age of his father Henry II, the pennant of Saint George would have fluttered over Avignon and Lyons as long as it did over Bordeaux;* his brother John would very probably have lost Burgundy as swiftly as he did Normandy. But it is permissible to believe that Richard would probably have succeeded in being crowned at Arles, which would have been an honor of high significance as events turned out, since it was enjoyed by only one prince after Barbarossa, by the last Emperor to reign at all effectively in Burgundy, Charles IV, who was anointed in 1365. At least Richard would probably have received wider allegiance from the lords of Burgundy than did the next man to be invested with the royal prerogative.

Frederick II designates William of Baux as King of Burgundy

The fortunes of the King-Emperors reached their highest peak in Burgundy at the end of the twelfth century; with the beginning of the thirteenth they went into swift decline as the pontificate of Innocent III (1198–1216) prepared the ground for the Empire's crushing defeat by the Papacy. The next Hohenstaufen emperor, Frederick II, the son of Henry VI, was in great difficulties in Germany and Italy throughout his reign (1212–50) and, needing to reduce his burdens in Burgundy, decided to re-establish it as a separate kingdom, thus reviving his father's project of 1193. His choice fell on William of Baux, Prince of Orange,** who in 1215 was offered 'the Kingdom of Vienne which is also called the Kingdom of Arles'. The diploma which Frederick addressed to William declared that he would be crowned king at the same time as Frederick himself was installed as Emperor, and it called on 'all the inhabitants of this kingdom to give to you, William, and to your heirs, the oath of loyalty which they owe to your regal dignity'. Unhappily for William and for Frederick few Burgundians thought much of William's dignity and, although the House of Orange maintained their rights to the throne, Frederick had to turn to other men to represent his cause. In 1216 we find Odo III, Duke of Burgundy,

* i.e., until 19 October 1453.
** See p. 108 above.

described as 'Vicar of King Frederick' in the Kingdom of Arles and Vienne; in 1220 William Marquis of Monteferrato was appointed and in 1238 Bernard de Lorette; but Frederick revived the scheme for a separate kingdom a few years later. His bastard son Manfred was to marry the Duke of Savoy's daughter and become king; the marriage took place in 1248 but not the coronation.

Until the very end Frederick II thought of the Arelate as a separate kingdom. On his death-bed he named his eldest legitimate son Conrad IV as King of Germany, Italy and Sicily, but not King of Arles. Nor after all was Manfred to get the Arelate (he was made Conrad's viceroy in Italy and Sicily); and Frederick left it instead to his other legitimate son, a lad not yet in his teens. This was Henry,* son of Isabella of England and so nephew of Richard Earl of Cornwall who, as we shall see in the next section, was later to be widely accepted as King of Arles. But the boy Henry was never to enjoy his Burgundian inheritance, for he died in 1253.

In the next century and a half almost every emperor sought to delegate power in Burgundy, either by appointing a viceroy or by gaining agreement to the installation of a king who would, at any rate nominally, be his liege man.** But from the mid twelve-hundreds onwards there was to be a third, and to us more interesting, choice: the restoration of the ancient kingdom, independent as well as separate, a goal which was pursued by several princes, notably dukes of Burgundy and counts of Savoy, Provence and Viennois. Apart from Charles the Bold, whose bid was mentioned in the Prologue, at least two came sufficiently close to raising the Burgundian phoenix for their attempts to deserve the telling, Charles Emmanuel of Savoy in the seventeenth century and Charles of Anjou late in the thirteenth.

---

* Not to be confused with the Henry whom Frederick had by his first wife and who died in 1242.

** Examples of the second course: Emperor Rudolf I's second son Hartmann 1278, Charles the Lame of Anjou 1277–82, King Robert of Naples' son 1310, Humbert II Dauphin of Viennois 1334, and several princes of France, e.g. the son of Philip IV. See for example *Cam. Med. Hist.* VIII, p. 320 ff.

PHOENIX RESURGENT

———

The Views from the Crest

The end of the twelfth century, which saw the deaths of the Emperor Henry VI and Richard Lionheart (1197, 1199), was also the mid-point in a story which opened with the First Kingdom of Burgundy in the fifth century (413–1200–1985). This is not of historical significance in itself, but it proved to be both a crest and a parting of the ways. Looking back from the summit, the view was almost as sunlit as any in European history. All countries of Latin Christendom had suffered the terror of Saracen, Viking or Magyar, and had lapsed into chaos and cultural darkness; very few, if any, had enjoyed a civilization higher than Burgundy's if that three-quarter millennium (450–1200), with its rises as well as its dips, is taken overall. Ahead, however, the prospect was more overcast, as the rest of this book will tell. During the thirteenth century Burgundy fell behind her rivals, particularly France; her sovereigns, the Holy Roman Emperors, lost control; and so she found herself faced, albeit unconsciously, with three options: her break-up into her component parts (which have been identified briefly but to which we return below); her take-over by another power (the West Franks, now, instead of the East); and the resurgence of the Phoenix through the restoration of a separate, independent kingdom. Before we describe to what extent Burgundy experienced all three of these options, it will probably be helpful if we recall how the Burgundians, who were first located by Pliny the Elder in AD 59 in the region of the Baltic, came to form the kingdom hundreds of miles away over which the Hohenstaufen Henry VI reigned towards the close of the twelfth century.

In the three centuries which followed Pliny the Burgundians came increasingly under the influence of Rome and showed themselves to be amongst the most apt of her pupils, if not the most advanced of them all. There is little evidence of this until their ruling dynasty, the 'Nibelungs' (443–534), established themselves in Geneva and founded the *First Kingdom*.* It was taken over

---

* Throughout this section the reader should turn as necessary to Maps nos 7, 16 and 17, and to Appendices VI and VII, the lists of events and of rulers.

intact by the Merovingian Franks (534–687) rather as the Kingdom of England was taken over centuries later by the Normans, but Anglo-Saxon England was less successful in preserving its identity.

The Kingdom of Burgundy consisted of four distinct parts, based on its four languages.

I The most truly *Burgundian* region corresponded with the Burgundians' Romance language, known to philologists as Franco-Provençal. It may be sub-divided into three:

the Homeland consisting of Savoy, Suisse Romande (western Switzerland), north Dauphiné and south Franche Comté (County of Burgundy), where the Burgundians had settled relatively densely in the fifth century;

Lyonnais and Forez to the west; and

the valleys of Aosta and Susa to the east.

All four of these little territories also spoke Franco-Provençal even though, by contrast with the Homeland, their settlement by Burgundians was slight.

The other three areas did not speak Franco-Provençal:

II *The Frankish region of Burgundy*, where fewer Burgundians had settled than in the Homeland, and where there were also Frank immigrants who obviously had ties with the Frank kingdoms of Austrasia and Neustria* to the north. This region divided in two:

The *Duchy* of Burgundy, where Bourguignon and Bas-Bourguignon were spoken; and

The *County* of Burgundy where (except for the Franco-Provençal south) Franc-Comtois, a dialect related to Bourguignon, was the speech.

III *The Allemannic region* (central Switzerland), largely peopled by a third barbarian race, the Allemans, where Schwyzerdütsch was universally spoken (and indeed still is).

IV *Provence*, where the few barbarian settlers were largely Goths and where the abiding influence of Rome was strongest. Here the language was what is today often called 'Occitan', but 'Provençal' is more convenient in these pages.

---

* Neustria became France. Austrasia, initially mostly west of the Rhine (i.e. the Lotharingia of the ninth century), expanded eastwards and eventually with Saxony etc. became Germany.

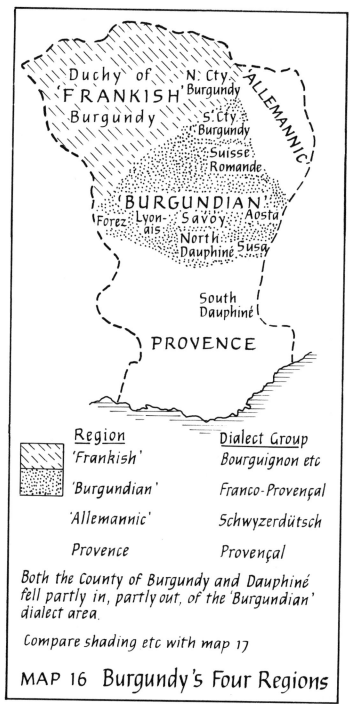

Region	Dialect Group
'Frankish'	Bourguignon etc
'Burgundian'	Franco-Provençal
'Allemannic'	Schwyzerdütsch
Provence	Provençal

Both the County of Burgundy and Dauphiné fell partly in, partly out, of the 'Burgundian' dialect area.

Compare shading etc with map 17

MAP 16 Burgundy's Four Regions

Maps nos. 16 and 17 The shading in 16 and 17 shows the often mentioned correlation between the Homeland and Franco-Provençal. The 'Burgundian' area (Homeland etc) and the 'Frankish' area (Duchy etc), shaded and hatched in 16, together made up Burgundy proper.

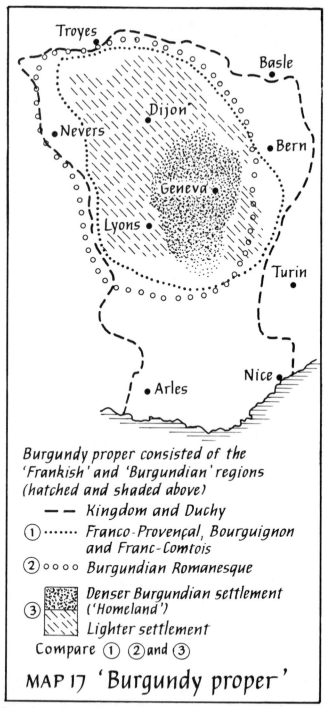

Burgundy proper consisted of the
'Frankish' and 'Burgundian' regions
(hatched and shaded above)

— — Kingdom and Duchy

① ⋯⋯ Franco-Provençal, Bourguignon
　　　 and Franc-Comtois

② ∘∘∘∘ Burgundian Romanesque

③ [shaded] Denser Burgundian settlement
　　　 ('Homeland')
　　 [hatched] Lighter settlement

Compare ① ② and ③

MAP 17 'Burgundy proper'

Map no. 17 shows how closely the areas settled by the Burgundians, corresponded with Burgundy's Romanesque area (and with 'ecclesiastical' Burgundy, see Map no. 12).

Readers will find it useful to identify these regions and areas on Maps 7 and 16, since they all (except Forez) will have a notable part to play in our story. Indeed, after we leave behind the crest of AD 1200, we shall as often be concerned with the 'four Burgundies' ('Burgundian', 'Frankish', etc.) as with the one.

Although its amorphous nature cannot be stressed too strongly, there was another 'Burgundy', which was briefly introduced on page 43. The Allemannic region and Provence had become Burgundian only through the extension of Nibelung and Merovingian power. They never became truly Burgundian in character. Virtually no Burgundians had settled in Provence, and those who had made their home in the Allemannic region had been driven westwards over the Sarine or absorbed by the Allemans at latest by the ninth century. *'Burgundy proper'* was not surprisingly connected with the lands settled by the Burgundians, which stretched roughly from a line south of Saint Etienne-Grenoble to Auxerre-Langres-Belfort (Map no. 6), in other words the Homeland, Lyonnais and the Duchy; and this was approximately Maurice Chaume's 'true Burgundy', which he said enclosed Dijon, Vienne and Saint Maurice d'Agaune. It was a region with the vaguest possible outline, distinguished chiefly perhaps by the emergence, in the 'Frankish' region no less than in the 'Burgundian', in Dijonnais no less than Lyonnais, of Burgundy's remarkable Romanesque art – cultural unity of a sort which thus survived the political separation of the two areas in the tenth century. (Maps 6, 12 and 17 show the rough concurrence between the Burgundians' settlements and their architecture.)

Another distinction, which will be more important after 1200 than before (and one with firmer outlines) is that between the *Greater Burgundy* of the First Kingdom and the *Lesser Burgundy* of the Homeland: under Godegisel, the uncle of Saint Clotilda who converted the pagan Franks *c.* 500, the Homeland briefly formed a little kingdom in the midst of the greater state of his more famous brother Gundobad (Map no. 7); and it will be of special significance after the mid-thirteenth century.

The First Kingdom came to its end with the Moors' invasions early in the eighth century. The *Carolingian Franks* (737–879), who succeeded the Merovings as rulers of Burgundy (as well as of Austrasia and Neustria) were less disposed to preserve its identity; and their repression prompted revolt by men like Gerard of Roussillon whom later ages regarded as Burgundian patriots. The Carolings' decline in the ninth century resulted in the emergence of France, Germany and Italy as separate kingdoms, and of the *Second Kingdom* of Burgundy under its own *Rudolfian* dynasty (879–1032). For a short time, under

[123]

Rudolf I, there was a smaller state which recalled very roughly the old Homeland mini-kingdom of Godegisel, but in 933 it was reunited with Provence, and from then on the Second Kingdom's frontiers were remarkably similar to those of the First. Indeed, as Maps nos 11 and 14 show, the frontiers were extraordinarily constant for a thousand years. The main difference was the detachment of the (Frankish) Duchy of Burgundy which was generally regarded as part of France from the tenth century, although it only did homage to the French king from the late twelfth.

The Rudolfians' kingdom thus comprised the Burgundian, Allemannic and Provençal regions mentioned above. Generally speaking they were no more impotent than most other monarchs of Latin Christendom, the important exception being the Holy Roman Emperor in Germany. However, the Rudolfians collapsed around 1000, and the Franconian emperors took over, some 30 years before the Normans occupied England; but the Second Kingdom continued under these 'Franks', as the First did under the Merovings. (Its frontiers were hardly to change for 300 years.) The 'King-Emperors' were more concerned with their other kingdoms, Germany and Italy, and ruled Burgundy through viceroys ('reign' would be a more fitting verb), and the most interesting experiment they conceived was Henry VI's choice of Richard Lionheart of England to be King of Burgundy – or the Arelate as it came to be called (1193–9).

We have seen how throughout this long period Burgundy was in the forefront of western civilization: during the long post-Roman sunset and twilight of the fifth to eighth centuries (the period of the First Kingdom); and during the recovery of the tenth and early eleventh centuries (corresponding to the Rudolfian Second Kingdom), which led to the great age of Romanesque and early Gothic when the Burgundian Orders of *Cluny* and *Cîteaux* were the powerhouses of artistic, agricultural and economic development, and carried Burgundian art and technology to Ireland and Sweden, Portugal and Palestine (1000–1200). But after the twelfth-century crest the prospect changes. Not only does Burgundy lose the leadership of Latin Christendom; its very survival is in doubt; or at best it seems more likely to break into its four parts – Frankish, Allemannic, Provençal and the Burgundian Homeland – than to be restored as a single entity. But all four regions were to throw up dynasties in the thirteenth century which would seek to raise the Phoenix. The Hapsburgs from the Allemannic region – Hapsburg is between Basle and Zürich, close to Burgundy's eastern border on the Reuss – aimed in the late twelve hundreds to make it a client kingdom of the Empire. The Angevins of Provence came much closer to success both then and in the next two generations. In the Frankish region the Capetian dukes consolidated the Duchy which their Valois successors expanded into the Burgundian state which, although it proved abortive, is the one best known to history.* Finally the counts of Savoy created the most durable 'Burgundy' of all.

---

* The dukes were of the Valois dynasty from the mid-fourteenth century. But their Capetian forebears rose to considerable power in the thirteenth.

The Phoenix Analogy

The phoenix, Webster's Dictionary tells us, was 'a legendary bird . . . living five or six centuries . . . , consumed by fire by its own act, and rising . . . from its ashes . . .'

It gives as a second description 'The paragon of excellence or beauty'.

It need hardly be stressed that the Phoenix Analogy used in these pages has absolutely no historical significance. Here we have, however, a remarkable and happy coincidence, with such a striking artistic symmetry that an author may perhaps be forgiven for employing it as a convenient illustrative device. For our Burgundian phoenix was on the wing for six hundred years, the six centuries between the establishment of the First Kingdom under the Nibelungs and the collapse of the later native dynasty of the Rudolfians (443–1032); or for some five hundred if we discount the century during which its wings were clipped by the Carolings (say from Charles Martel's conquest in 737 to its resurgence under Gerard about 850).

But the analogy should not be pressed too far. Although the Rudolfians brought on disaster by their feebleness, it would be an exaggeration to speak of Burgundy being 'consumed by fire by its own act'; and it did not disappear from history as did Mercia, Northumbria, Aquitaine and Leon, all proud kingdoms in their day. Moreover it was while independent Burgundy was politically speaking 'reduced to ashes' that it was so outstandingly a 'paragon of excellence and beauty'. These two centuries (1032–1250) of political wilderness were culturally a golden age, when the Burgundians influenced their conquerors, and many others, more than the other way round.

Even in a political sense there were embers glowing in the ashes. We have just recalled that the King-Emperors recognized Burgundy's distinctiveness and kept it as a separate state just as the Merovings did the First Kingdom half a millennium earlier, and this time its frontiers were yet more stable than before (Maps nos 11 and 14);* and we observed that

* Pages 65 and 105.

in the thirteenth century dynasties would emerge which would strive to raise the phoenix. Of these the first for us to consider came to power in Provence.

Charles of Anjou:
The First Near-miss

Master of Provence and uncrowned King of Arles

Charles of Anjou was the youngest brother of Louis IX of France, Saint Louis, the last of the great crusaders. He was eventually to be master of most of Italy and Greece, and to bear at one time or another this remarkable string of titles: in the west King of Sicily,* Count of Anjou, Maine and Provence, Imperial Vicar of Tuscany, Podesta of Florence, Senator of Rome, Governor of Bologna and lord of many other Italian cities; and in the east, King of Jerusalem, Epirus and Albania, Prince of Achaia and Lord of Morea (Peloponnese). His high birth and forceful character, let alone the help he was to receive from Louis and the latter's son and successor, Philip III, assured him a great destiny; but of all the lofty goals to which he was to aspire, that of the crown of Burgundy was brought within his reach only by his remarkably successful marriage.

Count Raymond Berenger V of Provence had married three of his four beautiful and cultured daughters most brilliantly, Margaret to Louis IX of France, Eleanor to Henry III of England, and Sanchia to Henry's able brother, Richard of Cornwall.** Raymond Berenger named the youngest, Beatrice, as heiress to his lands, and three weeks after his death in August 1245 the Estates hailed her as Countess of Provence. Beatrice, then about 14, did not lack for suitors. The Emperor Frederick II had just been declared deposed by Innocent IV at a vast council held in Lyons cathedral; in this life and death struggle control of Provence would have greatly restored his position, at least in the western Mediterranean and in north Italy, and he proposed a match with his heir Conrad, sending twenty ships to Provence as a display of strength. Aragonese troops pressing the claims of Prince Alfonso laid siege to her person, but they were driven off by a French force, and it was its captain, Charles of

---

* Included south Italy; later known as the Kingdom of Apulia, or of Naples, or of the Two Sicilies.

** For this chapter see Genealogical tables C and D, pp. 283–4, and Map no. 18 on p. 133.

Castle Acre priory, Norfolk, founded by Burgundian and English Cluniacs
*c.*1090, now a ruin. A reconstruction by Alan Sorrell. The church is early
twelfth century, the great west window fifteenth century, the rest mostly
mid-twelfth except the Prior's quarters in the foreground, which are
fourteenth century. *(Below)* Rievaulx abbey, Yorkshire, founded in 1131 by
Saint Bernard's Secretary and other monks from Clairvaux, and soon
enlarged. This shows the choir, built *c.*1230 when Cistercian architecture had
abandoned its early severity. (p. 89)

(Above) Savoy Palace, London, in 1736. Built *c.* 1240–45 by Peter of Savoy, then living in England as Earl of Richmond. Converted by Henry VII into a poor-house. Nothing remains. *(Below)* Chillon castle, mid-thirteenth century: Peter's favorite residence, its exterior little changed since his time. (p. 152)

Scenes of Charles the Bold's
defeats: Grandson castle,
thirteenth century *(above)* and
(left) Morat, the town walls much
as in Charles's day. (pp. 179–80)

Dijon, the church of Notre Dame, 1230–51. One of the finest examples of
Burgundian Gothic. This unique façade recalls the remarkable inventiveness
of Burgundy's thirteenth-century architects; regrettably the ingenuity with
which they solved structural problems cannot be caught by camera or artist.
(p. 87)

Anjou, who won this glittering prize. Charles was 20, Beatrice 15, when their marriage on 31 January 1246 not only produced the unusual phenomenon of four sisters married to two pairs of brothers, it also united two of the most brilliant and ambitious figures of the century, who were to be the instruments of the final debacle of Frederick's Hohenstaufen dynasty.

Beatrice of Provence's ambition for a crown to make her the equal of Margaret of France and Eleanor of England was sharpened in 1256 by the prospect of her third sister, Sanchia, also becoming a queen through the election of Richard of Cornwall as King of the Romans (that is, of Germany) and thus Emperor-designate; and since Provence was not likely to be made a kingdom once more, her thoughts naturally turned to the Arelate of which Provence formed part. It can hardly have been a coincidence that Richard and Sanchia's coronation as King and Queen of the Romans in Aachen on 17 May 1257 was followed in August by Robert of Baux's cession to Charles of the title to the crown of Arles and Vienne which had been granted to his father William.

We can only guess why Charles did not at once declare himself King of Burgundy or Arles; Frederick II's successor Conrad was dead and the Hohenstaufen claimant, his half-brother Manfred, was confined to Sicily and south Italy, and few people recognised 'Richard of Allemayne' as sovereign also of the Arelate.* The opposition of Charles's brother Louis IX would have counted with him in those early days, but whatever the reason Charles showed that the reconstitution of the Kingdom of Arles had become one of his main objectives[1] by extending his power northwards in the next eight years, up the Rhône and towards the lands of the Dauphin of Viennois and Count of Savoy, confident that his chance would come in due time.

Charles and Beatrice had one especially good reason for confidence: they were soon to have a first-class base. The land to which Beatrice had succeeded in 1245 could compare in civilization with any in Europe. In architecture, it is true, Provence could not match the finest Gothic achievements of Lyonnais or the Duchy of Burgundy, let alone Ile de France, Champagne and England; but in the poetry of the Langue d'Oc, which was already setting the pattern for the vernacular flowering of Italy and elsewhere, the leadership had moved from Limousin, Périgord and Toulousain to the court of Aix-en-Provence. There were few lands which had enjoyed peace and prosperity with so little interruption. Since the end of the tenth century Provence had grown more in population and wealth than almost any other part of Europe.[2] Raymond Berenger

---

* The Count of Savoy and others did later.

bequeathed to Beatrice an administrative machine to be rivaled only by those created by the Normans in England and Sicily; and between 1251, when he returned from Saint Louis's disastrous crusade in Egypt, and 1265, when he began his long sojourn in Italy, Charles disposed of resistance from Provence's independent-minded towns, stamped out its brigandage, gave it security not known since the height of the Roman Empire, and continued steadily to strengthen the administration and enrich the exchequer. Provence had been the base for Caesar's conquest of Gaul thirteen centuries ago; it was now no less well-suited to be the springboard for Charles's and Beatrice's ambitions.

Beatrice's dream of a crown was fulfilled first in Italy. In 1264 the Pope, determined on the destruction of the Hohenstaufen, offered Charles the Kingdom of Sicily; and even before they had set foot in their new domain, Charles and Beatrice were crowned in Rome (1266). Thus she became a queen like Margaret of France, Eleanor of England and Sanchia of Germany (four dazzling sisters who all became queens: when has history come closer to fairy tale?). She and Charles swiftly set about making their kingdom a reality. Charles defeated and slew King Manfred Hohenstaufen at Benevento, north-east of Naples, in a victory which was to give him sixteen years of almost unchallenged pre-eminence in the Italian peninsula; but he merely exclaimed, 'What do you wish me to rejoice at? To a truly valiant man the whole world would not suffice!' Indeed, in the years which followed Charles seemed to have all Christendom, east as well as west, as his goal. He captured Manfred's nephew Conradin, the new King of Sicily, in 1268 and in that year became ruler, direct or indirect, of most of the peninsula.

The reconstitution of the Kingdom of Burgundy 1277–82

For nearly ten years Charles's power in Italy was virtually unchallenged. Then in 1277 Giovanni Orsini became Pope as Nicholas III and swiftly set in hand his scheme for a new order in western Europe. At the time there was a widespread feeling that the day of an elective, universal empire was past and that the future belonged to hereditary, national monarchies of which France was the most striking example, and therefore the Empire should be divided into its component kingdoms. Nicholas's scheme aimed in particular at making the Pope supreme in Italy at least in name. Rudolf Hapsburg, Emperor since 1274, would renounce his claims on Italy in return for agreement that the Kingdom of Germany would be hereditary in his family; and Charles of Anjou, whose power in central Italy Nicholas also succeeded in reducing, would receive as compensation the Kingdom of Arles and Vienne. In this manner would the Burgundian phoenix be raised from the ashes.

Nicholas's negotiations with Rudolf and Charles occupied 1278 and 1279 and were just complete when he died in August 1280. It had been agreed that Charles himself, who was now over 60, should not be crowned King of Arles but rather his heir, Charles the Lame, Prince of Salerno, who in preparation for the high honor was made Count of Provence. However it was assumed that since Salerno would before long become King of Naples as Charles II, the real founder of the new line of Kings of Arles would be his son, Charles Martel; and so the keystone of the settlement was the boy's betrothal to Clementia Hapsburg, Rudolf's daughter. In January 1280 the Pope issued the necessary dispensations; Rudolf and Charles of Anjou gave effect to their agreements in diplomas dated March, April and May 1280; and in 1281 Rudolf secured the approval of the princes of the Empire to the reconstitution of the Kingdom of Arles.[3]

The great scheme moved from planning to execution with the wedding of Charles Martel and Clementia, performed by the new Pope Martin IV at Orvieto in March 1281. The Angevins immediately set military preparations in hand to take over the Rhôneland, and the road before them should now have lain open. There were no other serious contenders for the crown of Arles since the Baux family's claims to it had been surrendered to Charles of Anjou, and since the Emperor Rudolf, in whom sovereignty rested, had now formally agreed to the crowning of Charles's son. Martin IV (1281–5) was no less deeply committed, since he was Charles's choice as pontiff. Moreover Charles's resources in men and money had always largely come from France, and French power was now more decisive in southern Gaul than at any time since Charlemagne, since vast areas of Aquitaine and elsewhere had recently fallen to Saint Louis's successor, Philip III. It seemed only a matter of months before the Archbishop of Arles carried out the coronation ceremony in Saint Trophime's and the Angevin dynasty was installed on the throne of Burgundy.

The obstacle proved to be the resentment which had built up years before between Beatrice and her sister, Margaret, now the widow of Louis and queen-mother of France; for Margaret had never surrendered the rights she believed she had in Provence as their father's eldest child. For months she tried to win Rudolf's or the Pope's support; and when at last her efforts failed, she called several magnates who shared her fear of the Angevins to a conference at Mâcon, north of Lyons, in the autumn of 1281. They decided to assemble at Lyons in May 1282 and, in the words of their agreement, to 'oppose the King of

Vienne' with armed force. Margaret's diplomacy had brought the Angevins many months of delay; she now hoped it might block their road to victory.

The reference however to Charles the Lame, not as Count of Provence nor even as King of Arles but as King of Vienne, which is far deeper into Burgundy, shows in what great measure the Angevins had already won the psychological battle. Even the clergy of Lyons, yet further north, joined with those of Vienne in February 1282 in a statement which spoke of 'the arrival of the King' as though it were a disaster that could no longer be avoided.* Temporal authorities no better disposed to him, such as Count Philip of Savoy, had hardly less cause for anxiety. They would not have forgotten the firmness with which the Angevins had crushed resistance when they took over Provence, still less the ease of their conquest of south Italy and Sicily; moreover, the campaigns which led to Benevento and Tagliacozzo had been conducted several hundreds of miles from the Angevins' base in Provence, and from the main source of their troops, in France – entailing difficulties in sum which would not arise in a campaign up the valley of the Rhône.

At this stage, at the beginning of 1282, the Angevins were still relying more on diplomacy than on force. Two rulers on their route northwards, the dowager Countess of Viennois and the Count of Valentinois who were hostile to Margaret, seem to have fallen in with Charles the Lame; and in the early weeks of the year we find him at Romans, only 35 miles from Vienne, already acting as though he were king, confirming rights and granting privileges (Map no. 18). Meanwhile Margaret was making one last effort to detach the Emperor from the Angevins' coalition, but she failed, and now her own supporters deserted her. Edward I, who had been won to her side by her sister the queen-mother of England, was diverted by a rebellion in Wales,** and Peter of Alençon, Margaret's own son, and the Count of Burgundy abandoned her to join Charles of Anjou in Italy.

For four years, now, the Angevins' diplomacy had been leading them steadily closer to the crown of Arles, and as every month passed the prospect of serious opposition to their advance up the Rhône to Vienne and Lyons became ever less. Whatever forces might rally to Margaret's standard at Lyons in the

---

* A contemporary annalist, Tholomäus of Lucca, wrote of him as King Charles the Younger and of the 'Kingdom of Vienne' as Rudolf's dowry present to the Angevins.
** Edward felt his commitment to his aunt strongly. The best way to be freed from it (though she released him in Feb. 1282) was to prevail on Charles the Lame (his first cousin) to suspend or postpone his invasion. Resmini *Das Arelat nach 1250* (p. 173) tells of their correspondence (Nov. 1281–Feb. 1282).

Inset map labels:

Saône
•Mâcon •Geneva
Lyons SAVOY
•Vienne
VIENNOIS
•Grenoble
Rhône •Romans
VALEN-
TINOIS •Turin
P R O V E N C E
•Orange
•Avignon
•Tarascon
Arles
Nice
Aix
Marseilles

Main map labels:

GERMANY

F R A N C E

Duchy
of
Burgundy

County
of
Burgundy

•Geneva
Lyons
S A V O Y
•Milan
•Venice
Dauphiné
•Turin
Genoa•
Provence
•Aix
Florence•
I T A L Y

Rome• ✗ Tagliacozzo

✗ Benevento

Naples•

KINGDOM

O F

S I C I L Y

Palermo•
•Messina

Legend:

▨ Possessions
▨ Strong influence
---- Kingdom of Burgundy

0   100   200 Miles

MAP 18   Charles of Anjou in the West

Map no. 18 Charles's power in the eastern Mediterranean was extensive but less real than in the west. We are not concerned with it here. His son, Charles the Lame, had extended his authority north of Provence almost to Vienne when disaster overtook the Angevins in Sicily.

spring of 1282 could hardly be a match for the army which the Angevins had long been preparing. Smiths and armorers had been at work from Nîmes to Nice and beyond for over a year, and knights and men-at-arms had assembled from cities and feudatories throughout the land. Repairs had been made to the roads, especially the highway following the Rhône upstream, and boats to carry the army now gathering were moored north and south of Tarascon.* This already very ancient city lay up-river from Arles, almost half-way to Avignon; and its castle, erected in the previous century on the remains of the Roman castrum, was the center of the Angevins' preparations for war.** Here, according to legend, an amphibious monster had once terrorized the town until it was miraculously tamed and caught by Saint Martha; but the new amphibious creature, which was gathering its strength on the banks of the great river, the Angevin army, was to be frustrated by an intervention of providence of a very different nature. It occurred many hundreds of miles away, in one of those incidents which, although trifling in themselves, can set off a chain reaction that alters the course of history.

The Sicilian Vespers

With the death of Manfred at Benevento the mantle of Barbarossa and Frederick II fell on his fourteen-year-old nephew, Conradin, who during his brief reign displayed courage and enterprise worthy of his brilliant forebears. But after only two years (1268) Charles of Anjou took him prisoner at Tagliacozzo, fifty miles east of Rome; put him through a mock trial; and watched his execution, before thousands of his weeping subjects, in the market place of Naples. Mary and Charles Stuart met death with no greater nobility than the last of the mighty Hohenstaufen dynasty. Before he placed his head on the block the boy king threw his glove into the crowd in a last defiant gesture. In this manner (wrote Sismondi) he brought home to his people that it was directly up to them to cast off the hateful yoke of the French 'and to wash their heads clean of the blood of their kings and their compatriots'.[4] When, fourteen years later, this challenge was taken up, it was indeed by the common folk of Conradin's kingdom.

* Tholomäus of Lucca wrote of the armada 'which had been assembled around Tarascon for the invasion of Vienne before the revolt broke out in Sicily', adding 'I saw it myself.'

** The castle, as completed by 'Good King René' (see page 29) nearly two hundred years later, is today one of the finest sights of medieval Provence.

On Easter Monday 1282, when the military preparations in Provence were all but complete, many of the townsfolk of Palermo in far-off Sicily were on their way to the church of the Holy Spirit two miles outside the city walls. The hated French* authorities had banned the carrying of arms, but no such offense was in the minds of the holiday throng which (as the accounts of the episode tell) was happily picking flowers by the roadside and rejoicing noisily in the return of spring.[5] However, a French officer called Drouet swaggered up to a pretty young woman of good family who was nearing the church with her parents and fiancé and, under the pretext of searching her for a weapon, insolently fondled her breasts. The girl swooned in her fiancé's arms and cries of fury broke out around her. 'Death, death to the French!' was taken up on every side while the church bells still pealed for vespers. Drouet was overpowered and struck down with his own sword, and of the French going to the service not a soul escaped. The violence spread like wildfire. In Palermo, that night alone, two or three thousand French – men, women and children – were massacred, in retribution for the judicial murder of Conradin, and for the long years of French atrocity and extortion. All Sicily flared up like tinder; and, but for Messina which held out a little longer, within a few days the island was rid of its oppressors.

On the scaffold Conradin had named the Aragonese as his heirs** and the Sicilians were now quick to call them to their aid; and so Sicily was lost to the Angevins for ever, staying Aragonese, and then Spanish, until modern times.

For the next twenty years the Prince of Salerno, now Charles II of Naples, was too busy saving what he could of his southern kingdom to continue carving one out in south-east Gaul; and his son Charles Martel inherited a crown elsewhere – in Hungary from his mother. But Charles II, who was Count of Provence as well as King of Naples, had by no means forgotten the crown of Arles.

The character of Charles of Anjou

We have outrun the reign of Charles II's father, the mighty Charles I, so as to tell briefly of the consequences of the Sicilian Vespers. Charles of Anjou

---

* The Angevins were (at least largely) French, even if Provence was not; and they used French officials and troops.

** King Peter III of Aragon had married Constance, sister of Conradin's uncle Manfred. He became King Peter I of Sicily.

survived that shattering end to his ambitions by three years (d. 1285). This cynosure of all Europe was not only the most interesting, perhaps, of all the princes who ever aspired to restore the Kingdom of Burgundy, but he was also one of the Middle Ages' outstanding personalities. The most quoted description of Charles is that of the nearly contemporary Florentine chronicler, Giovanni Villani:[6]

> Wise and prudent in council, valiant in arms, severe, dreaded by all the kings of the earth, magnanimous and of a nobility of thought to match the greatest of undertakings, resolute in adversity, steadfast and true to all his promises, talking little but doing much, laughing rarely, as grave as a monk, a zealous Catholic, harsh in meting out justice, fierce in aspect. He was tall and muscular, his complexion olive, his nose long. He looked more fitted than any other prince for the majesty of kings. He slept hardly at all, saying that sleep was a waste of time. He was lavish in arming his knights but greedy to acquire land, signories and money from anywhere to finance his enterprises. He never found pleasure in actors, troubadours or courtiers.*

By others Charles was more hated than admired. His execution of Conradin was not soon forgotten, nor his refusal to let King Manfred be buried in holy ground. Manfred's wife, sister and children were cast into prison and died there, and his principal supporters were put to death with a ruthlessness remarkable for that or any age. After Charles's victory outside its walls Benevento offered him no resistance at all, but he allowed it to be pillaged for no less than eight days, as an example to any city rash enough to oppose him. Its inhabitants were butchered, women, children and aged, and it became, in Sismondi's words, a town of deserted houses spattered with blood.[7]

Yet it would be wrong to regard Charles as a megalomaniac unconscious that excesses of tyranny often make bad policy. In 1245–64, when he struggled against bitter resistance to establish his authority in Provence, there seems to have been no single execution. In this their first base he and Beatrice evidently wished confidence to be the mainstay of good government and a thriving industry and commerce; but also in north and central Italy he** ruled constitu-

---

* But he was a cultured patron of the arts and literature e.g. of Adam (le Bossu) de la Halle (b. Arras, d. Naples c. 1288), regarded in France as the first writer of comedy for the theater.

** Beatrice died in 1267, before Charles's complete conquest of south Italy and Naples. He then married Margaret of Burgundy as part of the alliance he formed in pursuit of the crown of Arles.

tionally and with a light hand, giving the cities rest from their long factional strife; and there was prosperity throughout the peninsula, above all perhaps in the ports of the south. Sicily, from which Charles's evil reputation stems, seems to have been milked more than his other domains and dependencies, probably because it was there that he was assembling his great armada for the relief of the Latin and Frank principalities of the Balkans* now sorely threatened by the renascent Byzantine power of Michael Paleologus.

The Angevins' prospects in the twelve-eighties

But for the Sicilian Vespers, Charles of Anjou, who rather than Charles the Lame was the directing genius, would very probably have succeeded in restoring an independent Kingdom of Burgundy. His enemies' coalition had fallen apart, and the Angevins' most powerful opponent in the area, Count Philip of Savoy, would if necessary have been held in check by their ally the Emperor Rudolf Hapsburg; and he was in fact shortly to suffer defeat at Rudolf's hands. There was no reason to doubt the ability of the Angevins' army at Tarascon to put down resistance in the lower Rhône valley; how far their writ could be made to run beyond that would remain to be seen. The Pope's attitude was as important as the Emperor's since it would in most cases determine that of the powerful bishops of the Kingdom – in cities like Lyons and Geneva they were the dominant authority. Martin IV was even more helpful than Nicholas III who had arranged the cession of the Arelate to the Angevins: he was a Frenchman selected, as we have seen, by Charles, yet no mere catspaw but an able, active and determined supporter of his ambitions.

Moreover Philip III, King of France from 1270, was readier to fulfil Charles's wishes than his father Saint Louis had been; indeed Louis and Charles had often had bitter quarrels. Thus Charles had the best of both worlds. He could call on French troops to help extend his dominions, but it was not a French empire he was carving out but an Angevin one, distinct and independent of France. It did not survive long in Sicily, as we have seen, but south Italy passed to the Aragonese only in 1435, and Provence remained Angevin until the death of 'Good King René' in 1480 exposed it to seizure by Louis XI of France.

---

* Charles's ambitions and qualified success in the Balkans, Levant, etc. lie outside the scope of this book.

King Robert of Naples and the Angevins' last chance

For the two centuries during which the Angevins ruled in Provence their headquarters were generally in Naples. Charles of Anjou himself was much more concerned with Italy and Sicily than with Provence once he had been offered the Sicilian crown, but his son, who as Prince of Salerno came so close to winning the crown of Arles, spent more time in Provence as King Charles II of Naples than any of the Angevin monarchs until their expulsion from south Italy in the fifteenth century.

Moreover Charles II maintained the claim to the Arelate, and in 1309 the scheme of Pope Nicholas III was revived when his son Robert succeeded to Naples and Provence. As in 1280, there would be a readjustment of power between the Emperor and the King of Naples in Italy, and once more an Angevin prince (Robert's son) would be married to the Emperor's daughter and placed on the throne of Arles. The Prince of Orange was again obliged to recognize the Angevins' rights to the crown, and it was only Robert's greed which scared off the other parties to the negotiations.

In the end the only significant step to be agreed was the transfer of the Papacy to Avignon.

In the first half of the fourteenth century there were several such schemes to restore an independent Kingdom of Burgundy or Arles.* For some years the strongest contender, backed by the Emperor and Edward III of England, was Humbert II, Dauphin of Viennois, and it was through Humbert that his great friend Robert, who had thrown the game away in 1309, had a yet more propitious opportunity. Humbert offered to make Robert heir to his lands, titles and rights for 120,000 florins (1337), which would have given him more power in the Rhône valley than any prince had had for several centuries, and he would have been in a strong position to secure the Emperor's and Pope's agreement to his coronation as King of Arles and Vienne. Humbert's offer even included control of Vienne itself, as it fell at last into his grasp during his exchanges with Robert (1338). It is hardly comprehensible that Robert did not seize his good fortune with both hands: this addition to his territories would have made him a more obvious claimant to the Kingdom of Arles than his father or grandfather had been. The moment was specially favorable: in 1337 war had broken out between France and England, and for a long time to come the new Valois dynasty would have been in no position to obstruct the advance of the Angevins up the Rhône basin from Vienne.

* Page 116 foot.

[138]

Robert however threw this second chance away; he was too taken up with the affairs of the Kingdom of Naples and he haggled long over Humbert's price; and in the end (1343) the Dauphin concluded the deal with Philip VI of France instead. The French thus won Dauphiné, which would be highly important to any contender for a restored Kingdom of Burgundy, just in time: three years later the armed might of France was destroyed at Crécy; and, although there followed a century of disaster, civil war and national disintegration, she now had a foothold in the Kingdom of Burgundy which it would be very difficult for any power to dislodge.

Robert was succeeded in 1343 by his sixteen-year-old granddaughter, Joanna. She displayed more concern with Provence than most of her dynasty, giving encouragement to Provençal literature, and I was tempted to tell of her astonishing career: she was implicated in the murder of her first husband, held in prison by her second until his death, and murdered by the cousin she chose as her heir (1382). But like her successors she made no bid for the crown of Arles; and the only remaining Angevin to have a place in this story is René I, Duke of Bar and Lorraine, who inherited Provence and Naples in 1434 but surrendered the latter to the Aragonese in the following year; and this is only because Good King René, as he is known ('king' because of his claim to Naples), lost his four closest male heirs in as many years (1471–4).* This enabled the French king of the time, Louis XI, to exploit his control of Dauphiné and win Provence. Thus came to its end a political entity which was amongst the most ancient and civilized of Europe.

---

* See footnote to p. 178, and Genealogical table D on p. 284.

One Burgundy or Four?

Burgundian 'national consciousness'?

Had Charles of Anjou won the crown of Burgundy for his heirs, the land would have been subjected to a rule which for most of its people would have been foreign. However, in few parts of Europe was nationalism so developed in the thirteenth century that alien government was unacceptable – a grasping hand was a worse enemy than a foreign tongue; and, as in most lands, loyalties in the Arelate were civic, regional, or at most dynastic, rather than national. All the same, there was a consciousness of 'being Burgundian' just as further north there was of 'being French'. In the early eleventh century Rudolf Glaber referred to Burgundy and France as distinct and equal lands and the Franks and Burgundians as separate people; and biographers of the tenth and eleventh centuries describe their heroes as 'Burgundians', for instance Pope Nicholas II (1059–61), who was born in the Savoy mountain territory of Maurienne, and Manasses the famous Archbishop of Vienne (920–959). In his stimulating essay 'Le sentiment national bourguignon' Maurice Chaume maintains that the Burgundians' consciousness of a separate individuality survived well into the Middle Ages despite Burgundy's political fragmentation and that it 'affirmed its vitality in the face of the King of France and the sovereign of Germany'. He quotes a medieval writer as deploring the inability of Burgundy's rulers – German east of the Saône, French to the west – to speak the Burgundian tongue;* and, just as one speaks today of Aix-en-Provence, people referred to Troyes-en-Bourgogne and Sens-en-Bourgogne for centuries after it had ceased to be politically accurate to place them in Burgundy. Not only the records of princely munificence, says Chaume, but the conversations of ordinary people would have shown that Burgundy was considered as stretching, as it had under the Carolings and Rudolfians, from Champagne to the Mediterranean, notwithstanding its division in feudal allegiance, since the

---

* *'Linguam burgundionem ignorant'.*

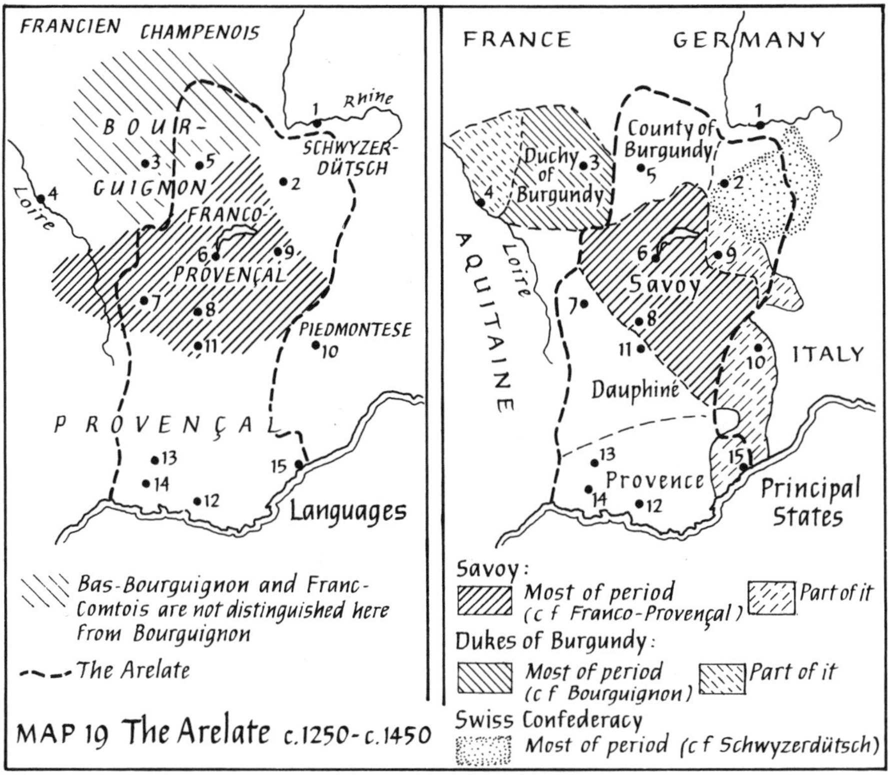
FRANCIEN
CHAMPENOIS
Rhine
BOUR-
GUIGNON
SCHWYZER-
DÜTSCH
Loire
FRANCO-
PROVENÇAL
PIEDMONTESE
PROVENÇAL
Languages
Bas-Bourguignon and Franc-Comtois are not distinguished here from Bourguignon
The Arelate
MAP 19 The Arelate c.1250-c.1450
FRANCE
GERMANY
County of Burgundy
Duchy of Burgundy
AQUITAINE
Loire
Savoy
Dauphiné
ITALY
Provence
Principal States
Savoy:
Most of period (c f Franco-Provençal)
Part of it
Dukes of Burgundy:
Most of period (c f Bourguignon)
Part of it
Swiss Confederacy
Most of period (c f Schwyzerdütsch)

Map no. 19 The Counts (later, Dukes) of Savoy rule most of the Franco-Provençal area (i.e. the Homeland), the Angevins Provence, and the Dukes of Burgundy the Bourguignon area. The Allemannic area passed from Hapsburg control to the Swiss (who spoke Schwyzerdütsch).

Towns numbered on the map:

1 *Hapsburg* The original HQ of the dynasty which in the Arelate lost out to the Swiss at Morgarten in 1315 and Sempach 1386.
2 *Bern* joined the Swiss Confederacy and led it by 1450.
3 *Dijon* capital of the Duchy of Burgundy from *c.* 1020.
4 *Nevers* Nivernais was part of or closely linked with the Duchy of Burgundy for most of the Middle Ages.
5 *Besançon* A church enclave in the County of Burgundy but later its chief city. The County was held by the Dukes of Burgundy for most of these 200 years.
6 *Geneva* Under its bishops it long defied first the Counts of Genevois and then the Counts (later Dukes) of Savoy, but the latter mostly controled it in the 15th cent.
7 *Lyons* Under its archbishops it defied all comers; was controled briefly by Savoy; held from 1312 by France.
8 *Chambéry* Usually the capital of Savoy; the home of the Holy Shroud.
9 *Sion* To Savoy for part of period with west Valais. East Valais was Swiss.
10 *Turin* To Savoy for part of period.
11 *Grenoble* Capital of Dauphiné, to France finally in 1378; but it remained in Arelate, paid homage to the Emperor.
12 *Aix* Capital of Provence.
13 *Avignon* Sold to the Pope 1348 by Joanna of Naples and Provence.
14 *Arles* Coronation city of Burgundy-Arelate. (Charles IV crowned 1365)
15 *Nice* To Savoy latter part of period.

political loss of the Duchy of Burgundy, between the French king and German Emperor.[8]

Four languages, four states

However Chaume is probably exaggerating when he claims that this was the case 'until an advanced point in the Middle Ages'. The lack of a genuine Burgundian state must by, say, the thirteenth century have diverted loyalties to the regional dynasties whose power was then becoming ever more apparent.

The consciousness of a shared identity – whatever the area in question, country, region, valley or city – depends principally on easy mutual comprehension, in a word, on language; and by this yardstick 'Burgundy' was not a single unit but rather the four which were first mentioned on page 43 above (see Maps nos 16 on p. 121 and 19 on p. 141):

Provence, where the Langue d'Oc dialects had been a literary medium for some three centuries before Charles of Anjou and where they still survive quite strongly today;

The Allemannic region, in modern terms northern and central Switzerland, where the German dialects called *Schwyzerdütsch* were and still are spoken universally (here alone in ancient Burgundy has one of the old languages remained dominant);

The Frankish region, the area of the French Duchy and of the *Bourguignon* dialects of the Langue d'Oïl, today virtually extinct; and

The Homeland, the only area at all thickly settled by the original Burgundians. Here Franco-Provençal or 'Burgundian' was the language of the people until quite recently, as is described in Appendix II.

It is not surprising that each of these four regions should have developed a sense of identity which took political form; and in all of them there were successful dynasties in power by 1300: the Angevins in Provence, the Hapsburgs in the Allemannic region, the Capetians in the Duchy* and the House of Maurienne-Savoy in the Homeland.** As the power of the King-Emperors

---

* Page 68.
** The other important Homeland dynasty, the Dauphins of Viennois (earlier known as counts of Albon), was soon to disappear, as we have seen.

declines, it becomes increasingly right to speak of four 'Burgundies' rather than one – each 'Burgundy' being a political entity with a linguistic basis; and in the next sections we shall be chiefly concerned with the attempts of those dynasties to establish their authority, at least throughout their region, if not over the whole extent of the Kingdom of Burgundy.

Provence and the lure of Italy

What, first, of Provence? We have observed how the Angevins completed the work of earlier dynasties and created a distinctive, separate state which was to remain independent until late in the fifteenth century – just two hundred years separating Charles of Anjou's attempt to create an Angevin Kingdom of Burgundy and the disappearance of its Provençal core (1281–1481). There is perhaps one reason for the Angevins' failure which should be stressed. Of the three attempts which they made on the crown of Arles, in 1281, 1309 and 1337, the first and third failed largely because of the Angevins' involvement in another land. It was because of the Sicilian Vespers that Charles of Anjou abandoned his designs on the Arelate; and his grandson Robert would presumably not have been so foolish as to bungle the purchase of Dauphiné if he too had been less involved in Italy. From this time onwards the lure of Italy plays a big part in our story.

As things were the Angevins gave little time to Provence. Had they gained the crown of Arles they might have displayed greater interest in the Rhôneland, even if it meant less involvement in their other kingdom, Naples. Provence, wealthy and efficiently run, was a good base for expansion. A king resident as often in Aix-en-Provence as in Naples would be alert to chances such as Humbert offered in Vienne and Dauphiné; and it is difficult to picture any King of Arles, even one as misguided as the greedy Robert, missing such opportunities of territorial gain. There is no point in speculating whether Angevin Kings of Arles would have won more than token homage from the Counts of Savoy or, in respect of their lands in the Kingdom, the Dukes of Burgundy, let alone the Swiss cantons of the Allemannic region; or whether successful marriages, so often more effective than the costliest wars, might have extended their dominions or influence; but it is reasonable to suggest that, other circumstances being the same, a Kingdom of Burgundy restored by the Angevins would have survived at least as long as did Angevin power in Provence, until, that is, 1481.

The emergence of the Swiss Confederation

In the thirteenth century a little-known family from a place between Basle and Zürich called Hapsburg had a meteoric rise to prominence. As we have seen, Count Rudolf was elevated to the purple and crowned Emperor in 1274. Like other emperors, for some years he saw the solution to the problem of Burgundy in the restoration of a king of its own. Charles of Anjou's son was not Rudolf's own first choice. He hoped to establish a Hapsburg dynasty in the Arelate; and, so that there could be no question of the succession to Burgundy being confused with that to Germany or the Empire, he did not pick his eldest son but his second, Hartmann; and needing the support of another European power for the scheme, which conflicted directly with the plans of Charles of Anjou and the French, he arranged for Hartmann to marry the daughter of Edward I of England. The notion of kings of Burgundy descended from Hapsburgs and Plantagenets is a fascinating one; unhappily, Hartmann was drowned in the Rhine, and Rudolf found himself swept along instead, as described above, in the grandiose schemes of Nicholas III and Charles of Anjou.

The great days of the Hapsburgs, who will figure importantly in our story, still lay a long way ahead. Between 1291, when Rudolf died, and 1438 the Hapsburgs held the imperial throne (and so the right to the crown of Burgundy) only for ten years (1298–1308); after 1438 they held it until its extinction by Napoleon in 1806. For the century and a half from 1291, therefore, we must see the Hapsburgs not as a European power but rather as a local dynasty striving – and failing – to bring even the small Allemannic region under their control. Indeed at this time, of all the four chief dynasties emerging in the 'mini-Burgundies' the Hapsburgs were the least likely to enjoy a notable future. Their ambitions were first checked by the farmers of Uri, Schwyz and Unterwalden, who in 1291 signed a treaty of mutual assistance 'to last, if God wills, for ever'. In 1308 this alliance was put to the test when the second Hapsburg emperor, Albert, tried and failed to bring the cantons to heel. Their deliverance is traditionally attributed to the heroism which gave birth to the William Tell legend; but Albert's assassination, as he rode up to Hapsburg castle, was hardly less a factor. A Swiss victory seven years later at Morgarten* was followed by new accessions to the confederacy: first Lucerne and later, more significantly, Zürich (1351) and Bern (1353) which was already a considerable military force; but the immense reputation of the Swiss as warriors dates from their victory on

* South of Zürich.

the field of Sempach in 1386, where Duke Leopold of Austria fell in company with the flower of the Hapsburg nobility. A century later, when they succeeded in smashing the most important of all attempts to restore the Kingdom of Burgundy, the independence of the Swiss was finally recognized.

The Dukes of Burgundy build up a quasi-independent state

Meanwhile, though no one could have guessed it, the state was being consolidated which was to make that attempt; it would prove a far greater threat than the Hapsburgs to Swiss independence.

It was in the Duchy of Burgundy that Chaume's judgements about *Burgundian* national consciousness probably remained most relevant. It frequently took an anti-French form, and though the dukes often supported the French kings in war and regularly rendered homage to them from about 1180, they were effectively independent sovereigns for a great deal of the time. This was increasingly the case after Duke Robert II (1272–1306) sided with the League of Mâcon against his brother-in-law Philip of France and Charles of Anjou, partly because he too nursed designs on the crown of Arles.

Under Robert's sons Hugh V and Odo (Eudes) IV the struggle between Paris and Dijon came to a head when the French crown tried to levy new taxes. In the Duchy barons, clergy and towns united in protest and extracted from King Louis X in 1315 what came to be known as the Charter of the Burgundians, which strictly and precisely circumscribed the powers and rights of royal officials in the Duchy. Then in 1328 the Capetian kings died out. The claims of Philip of Valois to the French crown were contested by Edward III of England (1327–77), and in 1346 the fortunes of France, which had ridden so high for a century and a half, were shattered on the field of Crécy. This was the beginning of a century of disaster: plague, civil war and foreign invasion brought France lower, perhaps, than at any time in her history. The dukes of Burgundy played leading roles throughout her long tragedy; in important respects they were its authors, and they were certainly, with England, its chief beneficiaries, thanks above all, perhaps, to the achievements of Duke Philip the Bold (1364–1404).

In 1361 the Burgundian branch of the Capetians also died out when Duke Philip of Rouvre succumbed, heirless, to the plague. In the struggle for power which ensued King John II of France got the better of the anti-French – one can say 'nationalist' – faction in the Duchy. After three years during which the two crowns were united in John's person, he installed as duke his son Philip

Valois who, since he was the youngest, could not expect to succeed to France as well. The separation of the two states was confirmed when John died, his eldest son Charles V becoming king and Philip Duke of Burgundy (1364).

Philip the Bold was one of the most remarkable men of his century; had his achievement – the creation of a powerful, independent* Burgundian state – endured, he would today probably be ranked almost level with Louis XI of France, Frederick the Great, Peter of Russia, Bismarck and Cavour, the men who brought into being the states of modern times. But Philip could never have created the new Burgundy without his wife, Margaret of Male. Margaret might herself seem to have been no catch for the handsome, tall and broad-shouldered Philip, as brilliant in the Council chamber as in the saddle and the field, wise, eloquent and charming, for she was described as ugly and badly dressed, vulgar in habit and taste, and fond of whistling and sitting on the grass. However she had another quality which any suitor would have found attractive: as daughter of the Count of Flanders she was by far the richest heiress in Europe.

France and England have often fought over Flanders but in none of their campaigns was there more at stake than when France pressed Duke Philip's suit against that of Edmund of Langley, son of Edward III. It was Philip who won, marrying Margaret at Ghent in 1369, and fifteen years later they inherited not only Flanders, the most highly industrialized part of Europe, but also Artois, Nivernais and Rethel; and, more importantly, the County of Burgundy** and other fiefs of the Holy Roman Empire. First peer of France Philip might be, and often its master, but it was eventually of greater significance that he was lord of large territories outside France, in the area which lent itself to the restoration of the ancient 'Middle Kingdom' of Charlemagne's grandson Lothar.

The Emperor effectively recognizes the independence of Savoy

In the end the fourth of the 'mini-Burgundies' was to be the most successful in restoring a lasting Burgundian state; this was in the Homeland, where the 'most Burgundian' of its languages was spoken. Here, as we tell in the next section, the House of Savoy built up a little state, with its own 'national' consciousness, which was very roughly similar in area to the small kingdoms of Godegisel and

* The break with France belongs rather to the reign of his son, John the Fearless.
** Duke Odo IV had gained the County in 1316. The emergence of a quasi-independent state between France and Germany may be dated from then or from 1384, when the County was reunited with the Duchy.

Rudolf I,* and which centuries later a Savoyard prince would try to expand into the wider Kingdom of Burgundy. But it was in these parts, too, that France enjoyed probably her greatest success in a century of set-backs and disasters, the acquisition of Dauphiné in 1343.

First, however, we must recall that in the fourteenth century the Emperors were still sovereign in all the territory between the Saône-Rhône stream and the Alps. In those days the crown was weak and often impotent in most parts of Europe; if England was an exception, the Arelate was not, and the Emperors' authority was slight and intermittent. Most of them were under pressure, as we have seen, to surrender the crown of Arles, for it was still a glittering prize; and only one can be said to have ruled in the Arelate as well as reigned. This was Charles IV of the House of Luxemburg who, as his relics in Prague bear witness, was one of Europe's truly great monarchs. Grandson of the Emperor Henry VII, he had fought alongside his father John King of Bohemia against the English at Crécy; his father was killed there but Charles took flight and a year later was elected to the Empire, which he proceeded to reorganize on a more stable basis than it had known for a century. Mention has been made of the Golden Bull of 1356** which *inter alia* confirmed as Imperial Electors the archchancellors of the Empire's three kingdoms – for Burgundy, the archbishop of Trier – to demonstrate that each kingdom had a rightful voice in the choice of emperors. Shortly after the second great defeat of the French, at Poitiers that same year, Charles called a Diet at Metz where he received homage from notables from all over the Kingdom of Arles and Vienne, including two introduced above: Philip of Rouvre in his capacity of Count of Burgundy, and Humbert Dauphin of Viennois, who had sold his inheritance to Philip VI of France. This success Charles followed up in 1365 with a royal progress through the Suisse Romande, Savoy and Dauphiné. The representative of the Dauphin made a great show of fêting him as sovereign, he was greeted at Avignon by the Dukes of Berry and Anjou, and the Duke of Bourbon rode in his suite to Arles. Here on 4 June he was crowned King of Arles by the archbishop. The governors of Dauphiné and Provence no less than the Count of Savoy attended, and Joanna Queen of Naples was confirmed in her title to the County of Provence.*** Charles must have been particularly gratified by the

* Pages 42 and 62.
** Page 107.
*** During this visit to the Kingdom Charles also gave his royal sanction for the establishment of a 'university of Savoy' at Geneva, the reading room of which, incidentally, saw the genesis of this book.

many proofs of French acceptance of his authority in the Saône-Rhône Basin; perhaps above all that the governor of Dauphiné, the personification of French interests and claims in the Kingdom, should accept responsibility for minting coins calling Charles Emperor and King of Bohemia and Arles.

The Valois tried repeatedly to extract either the crown of Arles or the vicariate from Charles and as regularly he refused; but in 1378 he changed his mind and appointed the Dauphin, who was only eight, as Vicar for life. This is taken by some French historians as the event which marked the union of Dauphiné with France and the break up of the Kingdom of Burgundy or Arles. However, as Fournier (our best* authority) says, in this way Charles would have his sovereignty recognized, not only throughout the Kingdom but particularly by the French: the Dauphin was to be seen as his representative, his man. Moreover, with the decline in the influence and prestige of the French crown as the century moved towards its close, the delegation of power to the Dauphin, now Charles VI of France, was forgotten and other vicars were appointed. More significantly, the Emperor Sigismund made a royal progress across his kingdom in 1415 returning through it in 1416, and even in 1435 when the cause of France had been greatly strengthened by the defection of the Duchy of Burgundy from the English camp, he rebuffed renewed demands for the vicariate to be assigned to Charles VII.

Thus well into the fifteenth century the Kingdom of Arles, however intermittent the exercise of imperial authority, was an established feature of Europe's political landscape. French-held Dauphiné, moreover, was accepted to be one of its fiefs. This was, however, no longer the case with Savoy. When in 1378 Charles IV had named the Dauphin as Vicar of the Kingdom he had carefully excluded the County of Savoy from the arrangement. From this point on, therefore, Savoy may be regarded as no longer a fief of the Kingdom of Arles but rather, in all but name, as an independent state within the Empire. Before we tell how it was consolidated into a Renaissance quasi-kingdom by Amadeus VIII – the longest lasting 'Burgundy' of all – we must retrace our steps to the beginning of its story.

---

* 'Best' because there is little competition. His judgement on this is of special interest because he regarded France's absorption of the Arelate as virtually preordained. See p. 253.

Amadeus VIII and the 'Lesser Kingdom' of Burgundy

The beginnings of Savoy

The House of Savoy emerged into history with the title of Counts of Maurienne around 1000.* They gained Savoy and other territories during the eleventh century. They prospered largely because almost alone of the Burgundian nobles Count Humbert White Hands backed the German conquerors against his own sovereign, Rudolf III; and his son Amadeus II accompanied the Emperor Henry III into Lombardy and became a good friend of his so that when they parted Henry gave him the city of Asti in memory of the many jars of foaming wine they had emptied together. This happy episode forged the link between the House of Savoy and Italy which was broken only thirty-seven years ago. Amadeus III followed the Emperor Conrad III on the Second Crusade in 1147 and adopted the white cross which the Savoyards wore on their shields thereafter and which is still the emblem of the region.

Humbert III, who reigned from 1149 to 1189, was an almost exact contemporary of Frederick Barbarossa. He was a man of irresolute spirit who was disconsolate at being born a prince and preferred the seclusion of a monastery. He only renounced his chosen state of celibacy so as to give his land an heir, but his first wife Fayfide, daughter of the Count of Toulouse, was childless. His second wife, Germaine, was from the Zähringen family that was dominant in Allemannic Burgundy. When she died having left only a daughter – who was incidentally betrothed to John, son of Henry II of England – Humbert gave up and became a Carthusian monk at Hautecombe. (The abbot as well as being Humbert's mentor later became Frederick I's Chancellor of Burgundy.) As the ancient chronicle narrates, the barons, knights and people of Savoy went to the abbot to beg him to restore their count to them, but his marriage to Beatrice, daughter of the Dauphin of Viennois, again produced only a daughter; Humbert was about to withdraw to the abbey of Aulps when he was prevailed on

* See Map no. 20, and Genealogical tables D and E, pp. 284–5.

[149]

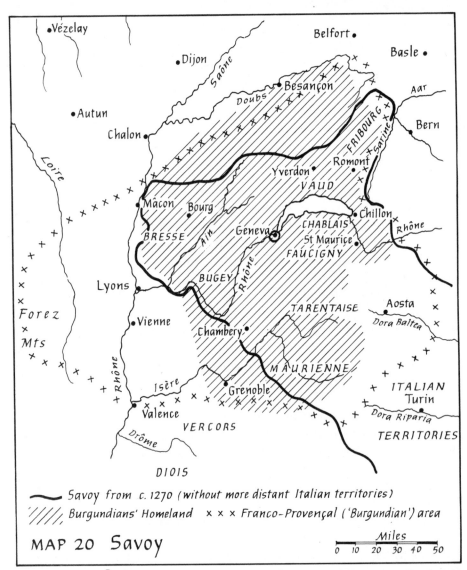

MAP 20 Savoy

Savoy from c. 1270 (without more distant Italian territories)
/// Burgundians' Homeland   × × × Franco-Provençal ('Burgundian') area

Miles
0 10 20 30 40 50

Map no. 20   Savoy-in-Gaul closely resembled the Burgundian Homeland and occupied a great part of the area in which Franco-Provençal was spoken. Franco-Provençal was the language of all Savoy, except for the latter's more distant Italian territories; French was a foreign tongue even for the upper crust until at least the fourteenth century.

to marry yet again, and his fourth wife gave him an heir who fortunately had the kingly qualities which Humbert lacked.

The expansion of Savoy

The reign of Humbert's son, Count Thomas I (1189–1233), opened a golden age for Savoy for he started the great advance north-westwards which carried his successors' sway over the Rhône into Bresse and to the Saône between Mâcon and Chalon. Even more significant was his victory over Berthold V of Zähringen which cleared the way for the conquest by his son Peter II (1263–8) of what is now the cantons of Vaud and Fribourg (Map no. 20). Thomas was also more successful than his father in reproducing his race for his bride, Margaret daughter of the Count of Genevois, raised eight sons and six daughters. According to the chronicler of Hautecombe abbey, the Westminster of Savoy, Margaret was being taken in 1196 to France by her ambitious father to become the third wife of Richard Lionheart's enemy, Philip Augustus. Thomas had fallen passionately in love with her and, ambushing her party in a narrow gorge in Bugey, defied the King of France and carried her off to the altar.* One of her two daughters, Beatrice, married Count Raymond Berenger of Provence and gave him the four dazzling girls who all married kings. The second of them, Eleanor, dominated Henry III and three of her eight uncles were given high positions in England, notably the Peter who became Count of Savoy.

From the time of Thomas I the counts were effectively rulers of a minor kingdom and there were very few states of any size in which the central power had so successfully established its authority. But it was from the time of Eleanor's uncle Peter that the greatest days of the principality may be counted. Peter II had been born at Susa in north-west Italy in 1203. Destined for the Church, he preferred secular power and military glory – the reverse of his sainted grandsire Humbert III. A chronicler tells us that when the representative of Richard of Cornwall, as King of the Romans, accepted his homage on Richard's behalf and asked him to produce title to his lands, Peter replied 'My title is my sword'. Before his succession to Savoy at the age of sixty he had been made Count of Romont by Frederick II and Earl of Richmond by Henry III.

---

* We need not be concerned with the confusion in the records about her name. Saint Genis, vol. i, p. 235.

Peter is best known in England for his building of the Palace of Savoy on the Thames between London and its suburb of Westminster. In the famous hotel which now stands on the site there is a plaque saying that Peter lodged there 'the many beautiful ladies whom he brought in 1247 from the courts of Europe before marrying them to his wards, a large number of rich young English nobles.'*

Peter dreamed of domination in Dauphiné, Lyonnais and Suisse Romande and was soon involved in a clash of interest with Charles of Anjou, since the latter's plans to reconstitute the Kingdom of Burgundy would make him sovereign from the Mediterranean to lake Geneva. In 1263 Peter took the city of Geneva under his 'protection' when the townsfolk revolted against their bishop, and soon afterwards he won the allegiance of the townsfolk of Bern. It was in this region, north and north-east of lake Geneva, that he gained his nickname of Little Charlemagne for finally bringing to heel the lords of the County of Vaud and advancing his standards to the frontiers of Allemannic Burgundy on the Sarine and Aar. Amongst these lords were the bishops of Lausanne, who have left some picturesque mementoes of their secular power in the castles of Lucens and Yverdon. To reinforce his new frontier Peter built those at Morat and Romont, but the travelers of today are more likely to be drawn to his own favorite, the palace of Chillon,** stunningly poised between the mountains and the waters of lake Geneva.

Peter's success was due in part to the friendship and support of Richard of Cornwall, whom he recognized as Emperor-elect. The pre-eminence which the Zähringen and Kyburg families had enjoyed in Switzerland was now at issue between Peter and Rudolf of Hapsburg. In his capacity as King of Burgundy Richard backed Peter and invested him with the County of Vaud and other fiefs. He also created him Duke of Chablais and, more interestingly, Duke of Aosta, for this latter title was in modern times to be held by the heirs to the Kings of Italy. Richard made Peter perpetual Imperial Vicar for Burgundy (a title often given thereafter to the Counts of Savoy), and he seems to have contemplated naming him King of Arles.

Peter considered that no one had a better claim than his own, as he sought to demonstrate by an interesting symbolic act. The crown of Burgundy and the Lance of Saint Maurice were in Germany, awaiting the next crowning of a king;

---

* Peter's palace only disappeared about 1800. My print of it shows a gaunt building less picturesque than his Swiss castles.

** Ch is pronounced Ts in Franco-Provençal. Thus it is 'Tsillon' to the oldest locals.

but what was then accepted as the saint's signet ring,* hardly less a symbol of Burgundian kingship, was in the charge of the monks of Agaune in the Swiss Valais where Peter had established his authority early in his reign. He prevailed on the monks to entrust it to him and his successors, and it figured in the installation of the dukes thenceforth until it was lost at the time of Napoleon's occupation of Savoy over five hundred years later. As we shall see, the Duchy of Savoy was to be a continuation of the Kingdom of Burgundy in more senses than the purely symbolic.

Peter was succeeded in 1268 by his brother Philip, who continued the consolidation of Peter's conquests in Vaud and Fribourg. For twelve years (1267–79) he was master also of the County of Burgundy on behalf of his young stepson Otto and when war broke out in 1281 between Charles of Anjou and Rudolf of Hapsburg, and Margaret of France's League of Mâcon, in which he was prominent, Philip was one of Europe's most powerful rulers. The Savoy which Thomas, Peter and Philip had built up west of the Alps amounted to a restoration of the lesser Burgundian kingdom of the Homeland over which Godegisel and Rudolf I had reigned long before. As we shall consider below, it also amounted to a resurgence, albeit on a limited scale, of the Burgundian Phoenix.

With only minor gains and losses the frontiers of this Savoy were to stay constant until the sixteenth century. The counts also held lands east of the Alps, and here Amadeus VIII was to make substantial additions over a century later. His reign was to see Savoy's apogee as an early Renaissance monarchy – the chrysalis from which modern states like France, Spain, Portugal and England were soon to emerge.

The Savoyards as the 'most Burgundian' of the Kingdom's dynasties

Any dynasty, native or foreign, able to restore the Kingdom of Burgundy, would have been alien in important respects to large areas in one or other part of the realm: the Angevins in the extreme south, French-born and with absorbing outside interests, no less than the northerner Zähringen who had provided the

---

* The ring was of gold and sapphire, the seal portraying the saint on horseback armed with the Lance. I am indebted for this information to Dottore Bertolotto of the Soprintendenza per i beni culturali e storici del Piemonte. (There are sketches of the ring, and a copy of it, in the Armeria Reale in Turin.)

[153]

viceroys for a long spell before Frederick Barbarossa tried his hand at more direct rule. The most 'Burgundian' of the kingdom's dynasties were, not surprisingly, to be found in the Homeland. The counts of Savoy spoke Franco-Provençal ('Burgundian') as their mother tongue – as observed above* this was the language spoken throughout the Homeland, and beyond; and it is no mere coincidence that from about 1270 their dominions corresponded fairly closely with the area where 'Burgundian' was spoken (Map no. 20), the chief omission being Lyonnais where they succeeded in establishing their rule only briefly.

From the end of the thirteenth century the counts of Savoy rose steadily in power, building on the solid base of Peter II's conquests, until their state compared favorably with Europe's smaller kingdoms: Froissart commented at the time that he would rather be Duke of Savoy than King of Scotland. Savoy was the smaller in area but surpassed Scotland in population, wealth, level of civilization, and international standing and influence.

The consolidation of Savoy by Amadeus VIII

When Amadeus VIII (1391–1434) abdicated the throne of Savoy after a long and remarkable reign, he held the counties of Maurienne, Savoy, Chablais, Faucigny, Vaud, Bugey, Bresse and Genevois. (See Maps nos 20 and 21.) All these formed part of the Homeland, as did the western half of the Valais, where he strengthened his control. In the south of the kingdom he held the County of Nice and Barcelonnette in the Alps to the north of it, and he had a good claim too to the rich counties of Diois and Valentinois. He was lord as well of the Susa valley and the Val d'Aosta, which formed pockets belonging politically to Burgundy though geographically to Italy. For a while Amadeus controled a large part of present-day Italian Switzerland, and the extinction of the cadet branch of the dynasty reunited Piedmont to Savoy. The homage of the Marquis of Saluzzo, together with the acquisition of the Pays de Gex and other territories east of the Saône, and a methodical tidying up of frontiers by purchase or force, completed the scattered jigsaw which Amadeus had inherited, and he left a compact state which stretched from the Saône north of Lyons to the Mediterranean coast east of Nice.

* Page 120. See also Appendix II.

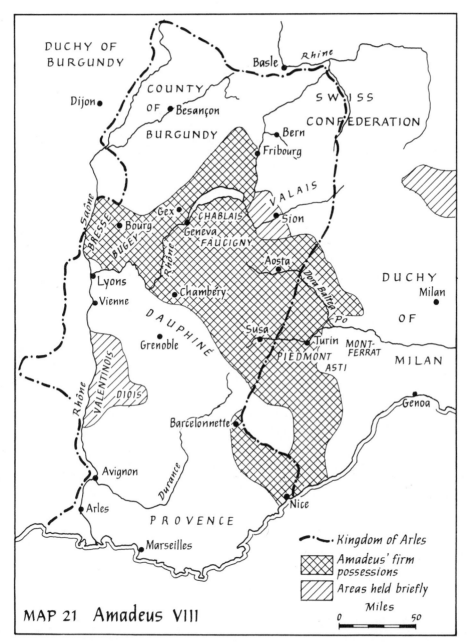

DUCHY OF
BURGUNDY

Basle

Rhine

COUNTY

Dijon

OF Besançon

BURGUNDY

SWISS

CONFEDERATION

Bern

Fribourg

VALAIS

Saône

Gex

CHABLAIS

Sion

BRESSE

Bourg

Geneva

FAUCIGNY

BUGEY

Rhône

Aosta

Dora Baltea

DUCHY

Lyons

Milan

Vienne

Chambéry

OF

DAUPHINÉ

Po

Susa

Turin

MONT-

MILAN

Grenoble

PIEDMONT

FERRAT

ASTI

VALENTINOIS

Rhône

DIOIS

Genoa

Barcelonnette

Avignon

Durance

Arles

Nice

PROVENCE

Marseilles

·—·—· Kingdom of Arles

Amadeus' firm
possessions

Areas held briefly

Miles

MAP 21 Amadeus VIII

0   50

Map no. 21   Savoy's main expansion after 1300 (cf. Map no. 20) was south-east into Italy, but at
times Amadeus VIII pursued interests also in the Arelate (Burgundy), e.g. Valentinois, Diois and
Valais.

The great achievements of Amadeus VIII 'the Peacemaker'

Amadeus was ambitious, but he was statesman rather than soldier and believed that success was the child of foresight and the careful husbanding of resources. One limited objective secured was for him worth a dozen ventured and perhaps lost. He gained the County of Genevois but accepted rebuffs from the citizens of Geneva, ever jealous of their independence. He expanded his power in the west of the Valais but he cut his losses in the east. He was too wise to humiliate his opponents, and his work as peacemaker, for instance between the warring French, Burgundians and English, won from Aeneas Sylvius Piccolomini (later Pope Pius II) the title of 'the New Solomon'.

Amadeus was the complete early Renaissance prince: patron of the arts and music (he played the lute), but above all brilliant lawgiver. The code of law, the Statuta Sabaudiae, which he gave to Savoy (1430) was as important as his work of territorial consolidation; and 'so wise were his laws', wrote Olivier de la Marche, 'that Savoy enjoyed greater wealth, security and abundance than any of its neighbors'. It was his remarkable achievement that for fifty years Savoy was sheltered from the wars and civil strife which convulsed most of Europe.

At the age of 51 this extraordinary man decided he had completed his duties as a prince and it was time to make peace with himself and with God in the solitude for which he had always had a taste. In 1409 he had founded a monastic order at Ripaille, close to the south shore of lake Geneva, which he dedicated to Saint Maurice – in no age was the patron of Savoy and of Burgundy held in greater honor. In 1434 Amadeus retired there, but after five years as its head he was called back to public life, elected by the Council of Basle to be Pope. He took the name Felix V, perhaps because he felt entitled to be happy with his life. He had however little success in healing the schisms of the Church and he abdicated in 1449, dying at Geneva in 1451.

Amadeus VIII and the Kingdom of Burgundy

Amadeus was not a man who dreamt of empire or glory, and he did not seek a crown with the consuming ambition of Charles of Anjou, Charles the Bold or Charles Emmanuel; he wanted to be sure of the possible and so his achievements were real and substantial. He built up a state with sufficient strength and coherence for it to recover from the century of disasters now to come and then survive for another three. It was a state we recognize, for here we have, in a solid and truly durable form, the 'lesser kingdom' founded by the Burgundians in the fifth century and restored by Rudolf I in the ninth.

The Emperor Sigismund had recognized that Amadeus was no ordinary prince and on his way through Savoy in 1416 had made him a duke, a title very rare indeed in Burgundian history. In 1419, when Amadeus deployed an uncharacteristic (and only partly successful) degree of force against Diois and Valentinois, which lay between Savoy and Provence, he may have contemplated the restoration of the Kingdom of Burgundy; but any such attempt would have lost him the goodwill of the Emperor and he was content for Sigismund to recognize him simply as count of those two southern territories (1426). (Map no. 21) If Amadeus aspired to dominion over the Kingdom of Arles, it was in a typically prudent manner. He was apparently satisfied to remain Imperial Vicar, the title which the Emperor Wenceslas had given him and his line in perpetuity (1398). The title helped him in the consolidation of his state,[9] and he may have looked on this as adequate springboard for any higher ambition his successors might have; but the first serious attempt on the crown of Burgundy by any Duke of Savoy was not in fact to occur for another century and a half.

Anne of Lusignan, the 'evil genius of the dynasty' of Savoy

We cannot know what future Amadeus may have contemplated for Savoy while his eldest son, also named Amadeus, was alive, but he was a young man of great gifts, energy and promise. Unfortunately disease (probably typhus) struck him down at 19 and his brother Louis was of altogether different fiber. In effect the succession passed to Louis's wife Anne, the daughter of the King of Cyprus,* who was described by contemporaries as the most wondrously lovely princess of the century, but also the most capricious and extravagant. Aeneas Sylvius said she was a wife incapable of obeying married to a man incapable of commanding. Another contemporary remarked 'Never, perhaps, did the follies of a woman lead to greater disasters'. The strife between the Savoyards and the 'plague of

---

* The Lusignans had reigned in Cyprus since Guy had been made king in 1192 by Richard Lionheart as leader of the crusade.

The Holy Shroud has been in Turin since 1578 (the Duke of Savoy transferred his capital there from Chambéry in 1563). It was Anne and her husband Louis who bought the Shroud from Margaret, Countess of Charny, for two castles in 1452. Before that the Charnys had entrusted it to the monks of Lirey in the Duchy of Burgundy. From 1452 to 1502 it was in Saint François, Chambéry (today the cathedral), from 1502 to 1578 in the Sainte Chapelle of Chambéry castle.

[157]

Greeks' whom she had brought with her from Cyprus lasted for thirty years; and the resources so carefully built up by her father-in-law Amadeus were squandered in five years of civil war in her distant country. Anne seems not to have inherited Charles of Anjou's dream of the crown of Arles but rather his eastern ambitions, and she urged Louis to make war on the Turks, who were close to the final destruction of the Byzantine empire. It is no wonder that Louis cried out 'The Cypriots have devoured my Duchy of Savoy'.

Savoy's first absorption by France

The 'reign' of Anne of Lusignan opened the least happy of Savoy's nine centuries of existence, but the disasters which followed cannot be blamed entirely on the misplaced ambition and folly of this corrupt and willful enchantress. When her husband Louis died in 1465, Savoy's ancient and happy commitment to primogeniture was abandoned and its lands were divided amongst their five sons.* The duchy's consequent weakness was compounded by the succession first of an epileptic and then a minor; and the latter's regent, his mother Yolande, became enmeshed in the attempt of Charles the Bold to restore the Kingdom of Burgundy which is described below. She so closely identified Savoy's interests with those of the Duchy of Burgundy that she rallied to Charles not only against the Swiss but also against her own brother, Louis XI of France, who once addressed her tartly as 'Madame de Bourgogne'.

The upshot for Savoy, dragged down with Burgundy, as we must see, was the ending of its claim to 'protect' Bern and Fribourg; the surrender to the Swiss of territories long-held north of lake Geneva; and, worst of all, repeated invasion by French armies bent on conquests in Italy under Charles VIII, Louis XII and Francis I. With Duke Charles III (1504–53) Savoy reached her nadir. In 1519 Geneva revolted successfully and in 1536 became an independent republic in alliance with the Swiss cantons. In the same year Francis I, who spoke contemptuously of the House of Savoy as 'the Doormen of the Alps', annexed Savoy and Piedmont, and it seemed that the duchy had disappeared for ever from the map of Europe.

In the meantime a tragedy of even greater importance was played out beyond Savoy's northern borders; and for this drama, perhaps the most poignant of all Burgundy's long history, it is now time for us to set the stage.

---

* Only two are shown on p. 285.

Charles the Bold,
The King denied a Crown

The 'New Monarchies'

In the fifteen and sixteenth centuries Europe emerged from the Middle Ages by way of the Renaissance and Reformation. A wind of change blew open the windows of the mind, bringing back the humanism of the ancients, so that old-time faith gave ground to doubt, experiment and discovery. The watershed between the old age and the new was far from clear-cut but may be placed in the closing decades of the fifteenth century. It was now that the horizons of Europe started moving towards the limits of the globe. Groping along the coast of Africa the Portuguese rounded the Cape in 1486; and, although Columbus's landfall in the West Indies in 1492 was by no means the first European contact with the New World, it led unlike its predecessors to settlement and conquest. Europe was on the march to mastery of the planet; and the mind too had new horizons. In 1470 the printing press reached Paris and within years was at work all over the continent. Whereas at the beginning of the fifteenth century there had been but a few score thousand manuscripts, by the end of it there were perhaps ten million books.

However, the development which most sharply distinguishes the modern world from the medieval is the emergence of the New Monarchy. Of medieval institutions the Empire, Papacy, parliaments, and feudalism were in retreat, and only the kingdom made ground, steadily gaining power previously shared with the three Estates, clergy, nobility and municipalities. The absolute sovereignty of the state was coming to be accepted; all executive, legislative and judicial power was increasingly focused on the center; and provincial separatism was crushed along with feudal liberty and noble license. The triumph of the New Monarchy was made possible by many factors: the power of the new artillery to destroy baronial levies and castles; the growing wealth of the cities which provided a source of revenue far richer than earlier rulers could tap; and there were others, but the most significant in the end were the new techniques of government which had been evolved in the Italian city states and which made possible the efficient administration of areas larger than at any time since the disintegration of the Roman Empire. It was not Macchiavelli but Italy itself that fashioned the Prince.

Four of the new monarchies went on to play a specially important role, notably in Europe's conquest of the world. All were successfully established in the last quarter of the fifteenth century, more precisely between 1477 and 1492. In France Louis XI and Charles VIII brought the duchies to heel between 1477 and 1488. Spain was united by Ferdinand and Isabella between 1479 and 1492, by which time despots had brought civil wars to a triumphant close in Portugal and England as well. In the former John II had recourse to the simple expedient of executing all possible opponents, some eighty noble heads rolling in six years (1481–7), whereas in England the same result had already been achieved for Henry VII, when he acceded in 1485, by the bloodletting of the Wars of the Roses.

Burgundy the best placed 'new monarchy' 1425–75

Together with the Empire and Holland these four monarchies were ascendant for most of the half millennium since then, Portugal falling back and then Spain, and France and later England moving to the front. But it was another state which pointed the way and which may fairly be called 'the first new monarchy'. Arnold Toynbee maintained that it was the remarkable dukes of Burgundy who showed how the political techniques evolved in the Italian cities could be applied in the administration of large territories.[10] In any event in the second and third quarters of the fifteenth century no princes were more successful in deploying their lands' resources and particularly the wealth created by their cities' industry and trade, and no state was so free as Burgundy of the troubles which marked those five decades. Italy and Germany were never to become new monarchies and the divisions of the fifteenth century were not to be healed for four hundred years; and at that time Portugal, Spain, France and England, which we know now were destined to rule most of the known world, were barely less afflicted by unstable government or civil war. It is hardly necessary to recall the unhappy condition of France both before and after the expulsion of the English (1454) or the internecine dynastic struggle in England between Lancastrians and Yorkists; and the kingdoms of Iberia were in no more fortunate circumstances.

The relative peace and prosperity which Burgundy, by contrast, enjoyed in

[160]

Two Cistercian abbeys: *(above)* Pontigny, 1150–70, with simple lines so different from Cluny's towered silhouette. *(Below)* Bellapais abbey, Kyrenia, twelfth century and later. The Cistercians built their monasteries all over Latin Christendom. There were few more romantically situated than this one in the Lusignans' kingdom of Cyprus. (p. 85)

Two churches of destiny: St. Trophîme, Arles *(left)*. From 417 'the primatial church of the Gauls' later the coronation church of Burgundy. The present church *c.*1100–80. Through this doorway finished *c.*1152, Frederick Barbarossa passed on his way to be crowned in 1178. *(Below)* Palermo, Church of the Holy Spirit, twelfth century, of unhappy association for Charles of Anjou. This was where the Sicilian Vespers started. The church is built in Norman–Moorish style. (pp. 108, 135)

(*Above*) The tomb of Philip the Bold, the Dukes' Palace, Dijon, 1381–1411. (*Below left*) One of the mourners around Philip's tomb. (*Below right*) Isaiah, one of the wonderful group sculpted by Claus Sluter in the now disappeared abbey of Champmol, at the gates of Dijon, 1395–1400. (p. 166)

The Christ in Sluter's group at Champmol, generally known as
d

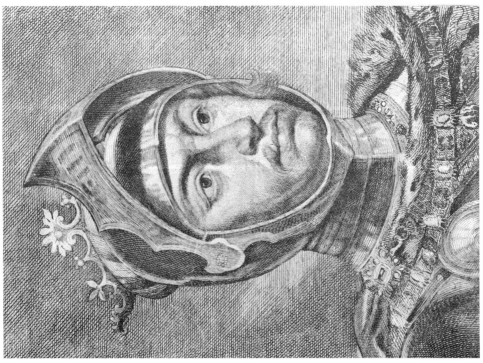

Charles the Bold, from a painting by Jan van Eyck, c.1470.

the second and third quarters of the fifteenth century were due to the immense strides she had made in the previous fifty years. In 1375 Philip the Bold, with whom we left the Duchy's fortunes on page 146, was still little more than one of the great feudatories who were struggling to control the throne of France, whereas in 1425 his grandson Philip the Good was, in all but name, monarch of a new 'Middle Kingdom' strangely reminiscent of the ephemeral creation of 843.* Indeed events between those years conspired to build up the dukes' strength outside France rather than within it: Philip the Bold's inheritance in 1384 of Flanders, the County of Burgundy and other territories in the Empire; the feud of Philip's son successor John the Fearless with the so-called Armagnac faction leading to his murder of its leader in 1407; and his alliance with Henry V of England, the soon-to-be victor of Agincourt (1415). When John the Fearless was assassinated in his turn in 1419, his son Philip the Good backed Henry's claims to the French crown and supported his reduction of northern France and occupation of Paris. What was of special importance was that, whereas the tide turned against the English after the relief of Orleans by Joan of Arc in 1429, Philip the Good of Burgundy went on from strength to strength. At the tripartite conference at Arras in 1435 he arbitrated between France and England, gained recognition of his country's independence from the former, and cavalierly abandoned his alliance with the latter. From this point on the English were gradually expelled from all of France but Calais, whereas for forty years Burgundy was to be the most mighty state of Christendom.

Thus, when Philip was succeeded by his son Charles the Bold** in 1467 he left him a state which had enjoyed a long spell of peace and economic expansion unmatched elsewhere. It is hardly too much to say that Burgundy's territories, stretching from the Jura mountains to the North Sea, formed an island of order*** and prosperity amidst the general strife and chaos of the time. Or rather two islands, as is shown on Map no. 22A: first, in the south, there were the Duchy and County of Burgundy, the original ducal territories with Dijon as their center, together with Mâconnais and Charolais, to which should be added the County of Nevers and other lands which belonged to a cadet branch of the

* Page 59. The northern part of Lothar's area on Map no. 9. The dukes are shown in Genealogical table F on p. 286.
** Charles le Hardi in his day, e.g. in Chastellain. From about 1825 he became Charles le Téméraire (the Rash) to French writers. He is Karl der Kühne (Bold, Daring) to the Germans. British historians have mostly called him 'the Bold' though 'the Rash' is more apt.
*** The last serious internal opposition was in Liège in 1468.

ducal family. Then, forming a separate block in the north, there were the territories acquired since Charles the Bold's great-grandfather, Philip the Bold, became Count of Flanders in 1384: the North Sea and Channel coastline from Friesland to the Somme; all of present-day Belgium and Luxemburg and half the Netherlands; and also the French departments of the Somme, Pas de Calais and the Nord.

When Charles the Bold acceded to this vast empire in 1467 the gap between the two blocks of territory was, at its narrowest, only some eighty miles wide. With the exception of the King of England, the territories of no important monarch of the period 1375–1475 formed a compact mass and even England was divided for many of those years between the rival houses of York and Lancaster. The provinces which readily accepted the writ of the sovereigns of Castile were few and far between; even in France the areas in which the king's power counted for more than the nobles' were scattered throughout the land. So, despite the gap, by the standards of the time the empire of the dukes of Burgundy was compact; and Charles was not slow to extend a covetous hand to the territories between. He missed a good chance of gaining indirect control of Champagne, but two years after his accession he won large areas of Alsace, and in October 1473 René II, the new Duke of Lorraine, the vital missing link, recognized Charles as his 'protector' and signed a treaty permitting Burgundian troops to pass through his lands and giving Charles a number of fortresses.

The junction of Charles's northern and southern territories created a state which was not Christendom's most populous (with seven millions as against France's fifteen and England's three) but which, given its relative centralization and administrative efficiency, was without doubt the most powerful. There had been a single currency throughout the dukes' lands for forty years (since 1433, the year incidentally of Charles's birth). Only in Italy was there as great a concentration of industrial and commercial wealth as Charles had at his disposal in his northern provinces, and neither in Italy nor anywhere else was that wealth brought into the service of the new monarchies more successfully. Consequently his exchequer was richer than the French or Venetian, far more wealthy than those of England or Austria, and in 1471 he could demonstrate the permanence of his power by establishing a standing army, that hallmark of the modern state. Thus, endowed with resources which had been unknown since the heyday of the Roman Empire over a millennium before, in the fourteen-seventies the Duchy of Burgundy was the European country most firmly set on the road to great power.

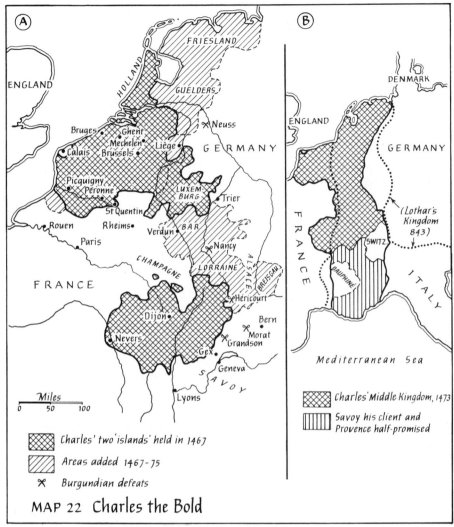

![cross-hatch]	Charles' two 'islands' held in 1467
![diagonal]	Areas added 1467-75
✕	Burgundian defeats

MAP 22 **Charles the Bold**

![cross-hatch] Charles' Middle Kingdom, 1473

![vertical-lines] Savoy his client and Provence half-promised

Map no. 22 A   In 1467 Charles already held the two 'islands' (cross-hatched)

He added Guelders etc (in the north), Breisgau and Upper Alsace (east) and, more importantly, Bar and Lorraine linking up the islands

Varying degrees of control by Charles are not shown, e.g. over Nevers (a cousin's) or over church lands such as Verdun.

Map no. 22 B   In 1473 Charles already held most of his new kingdom and Savoy was his client and Provence half-promised to him.

The 'Grand Dukes' as Renaissance monarchs

Philip the Good and his son Charles the Bold disported themselves as though they knew that they had created something greater than both the city state and the medieval kingdom, something to which the future would belong. Moreover Charles saw his Burgundy as the leading state of a renewed Holy Roman Empire, and long before their conference at Trier in 1473 he had pressed Frederick III to recognize him as his heir to the purple; and the leaders of Christendom did indeed regard the mantle of empire as having fallen on the 'Grand Dukes of the West', as Philip and Charles were called, for no other dynasty was capable of saving Christendom from the Turk, who now even threatened the Emperor's capital, Vienna. The dukes were not slow to accept that the leadership of the Christian world was theirs, and at Lille in 1454 Philip and Charles (then 20) vowed solemnly to take the cross in company with the knights of the Order of the Golden Fleece and to wreak vengeance on the Infidel for his capture of Constantinople in the previous year.

The Order of the Golden Fleece was founded on 11 January 1430 at Bruges during the celebration of Philip the Good's marriage to Isabella of Portugal, his third duchess and the mother of Charles the Bold. It became one of the most important institutions of Christendom, not only Europe's most exclusive club of which kings were proud to be members, but also the First Estate of all the Grand Dukes' realms which expected them to obtain its concurrence before they engaged in war. It even claimed the right to censure their behavior; and Charles accepted in good part complaints made by the eleventh Chapter in 1468 that he spoke to his servants with undue severity and failed to curb his all too swift temper in his dealings with princes.

The Order's most showy manifestations were the tournaments which served as a sort of early Renaissance Olympics, attracting noblemen from far and wide who on their return home would speak, as was intended, of the magnificence of the ducal court, and perhaps above all of its ostentatious banquets. They would tell how between the many courses, richly spiced and served with an elaborate ritual, an elephant might be brought into the hall; or a gigantic pastry containing twenty-eight flesh and blood musicians; or a table constructed to represent a cathedral complete with organist playing his organ. Then there was the automatic device set up at Hesdin castle which showered the guests with soot or flour, another which tipped them into a pool.

The Burgundian leaders may now seem a cross between foolish dreamers and vulgar, upstart *nouveaux riches*, but they were taken seriously in their day, as representative of an age which sought to reconcile ancient virtues with new aspirations. Their garish extravagance, which recalls the worst of Hollywood, was tempered by etiquette and ritual, and their court was to be the model, in all its magnificence and its emphasis on protocol and precedence, for the courts of Charles V and Louis XIV. Moreover the patronage of no ruling house has had a greater influence on the artistic development of western Europe.

The dukes' achievement does not lie chiefly in the field of architecture: for a dynasty which rivaled the Roman emperors and Louis XIV in the sumptuousness of their court and their patronage of the arts, the dukes were relatively modest builders. Their most important surviving building, the Palace of the Dukes at Dijon, has perhaps less significance for architecture than for cooking, for no kitchens can have contributed more to the art of the table than those which can still be seen there today. The remains of Philip the Bold's great monastery of Champmol (mostly built 1377–85), perhaps the dukes' most notable edifice, are in a mental home in the suburbs of Dijon, but even had it survived its architecture would probably have counted less with us than its sculpture and painting. It is in these two arts that Burgundy made its great contribution to Europe's renaissance, in painting one as great perhaps as Italy's.

The Burgundy of the dukes, it must be recalled, only corresponded in part with the Burgundy which created so much fine painting and especially sculpture in earlier centuries. Most of the artists gathered together by Philip the Bold and his successors, and often personally chosen by them, were from Flanders, Brabant, Holland and Limburg – in fact from modern Belgium and the Netherlands; and others came from France, Aragon and Avignon; but the schools which they founded (sculpture in Dijon, painting in Flanders) may truly be named 'Burgundian' and not only because their founding was a conscious act of Burgundian policy: it is no accident that the Dutchman Sluter, for example, should have created figures of such typical Burgundian realism since he had around him so much inspiration in the stonework of the previous three centuries. Perhaps more than any other single man Sluter was the founder of Renaissance and modern French sculpture; but he was also the heir to Burgundy's past.

When Ghiberti began work on the doors of the baptistry in Florence and helped give wings to the reborn sculpture of Italy, Sluter's doorway at Champmol had already been completed (1401). For fifteen years Sluter and his colleagues had been creating sculpture the like of which had not been seen since the finest days of the Hellenic world. Their masterpieces at Germolles, the castle of Philip the Bold's duchess (built 1382–96), have been lost; of the

Calvary (1395–1404) at Champmol only the so-called Well of Moses remains; but happily we can still visit Philip the Bold's tomb (1381–1411) in Dijon, which was finished after Sluter's death (c. 1405) by his nephew Claus de Werve. Sluter's Moses bears comparison with Michelangelo's of a century later. While there is a touch of gaudiness and arrogance about Philip's tomb in the ducal palace, the figures of the forty-one mourners which surround the base, with their variety and skill of execution no less than their evident and wholly convincing grief, are amongst Europe's greatest treasures in stone.

No court can ultimately have had a greater influence on the development of European painting than the Burgundian court at Ghent, Bruges and Brussels. The group of talented artists which Philip the Bold assembled at Dijon may be regarded as the founthead of the Flemish School. Among them were the three Limburg brothers who are perhaps best known to us for their hand in the *Très riches heures*. While Sluter was carving the figures of Philip the Bold and Duchess Margaret for the doorway of the Champmol chapel, Broederlam was working on the altarpiece (1394–9).

Philip the Good, who moved his court from Dijon to Flanders, engaged Hubert and Jan van Eyck. Jan's portrait of Giovanni Arnolfini and his wife in the National Gallery in London (1434) is a fine example of what the Netherlands excelled at – real people presented in all the detail of the homely background they had themselves created – and we can judge how far these heirs (however indirect) of the realism of old Burgundy had moved into our own world when we contrast this portrait with work done in Florence at the same period: Fra Angelico's Annunciation in the convent of San Marco, for instance, or even the remarkably alive figures painted by Masaccio (perhaps the first great Italian painter of the Renaissance?) in Santa Maria del Carmine (1426); for in some respects the Flemish painters were far in advance of their Florentine and Sienese contemporaries.

There are other arts in which the Burgundy of the Valois dukes excelled, notably stained glass, tapestry and music. Philip the Bold brought Jean de Thioys to Dijon to work the glass of the superb Burgundian-Gothic church of Notre-Dame (1385) and the Fleming Robert de Cambrai to decorate the chapel of Champmol (1389). Burgundy's tapestry-work was even more import-ant; it was one of the finest manifestations of the early Renaissance and for most of the fifteenth century virtually all of the best tapestries woven in Europe were the work of schools which flourished under the dukes.

To early Renaissance music Burgundy's contribution was as significant as it was to the other arts and once again we can credit it to ducal patronage. The best-known of the early composers who worked for the dukes are Guillaume Dufay and Gilles Binchois. Both Flemish,* they were greatly influenced by the work of the Englishman John Dunstable (d. 1453). Both were in Holy Orders too (Binchois was chaplain to Philip the Good), but it was not thought at all odd that they should write love songs in French, the tongue of the court, as well as more serious religious or commemorative works in Latin. It is doubtful whether any Burgundian of their day better expressed their countrymen's robust and earthy joy of living than these two priests, as for instance in Dufay's '*Bon jour, bon mois*' and his tribute to the product which best symbolizes the less spiritual part of Burgundy's essence: '*Adieu ces bons vins de Lannoys*'.

The support which the dukes gave to their chapel choir produced a stream of less well-known composers. In the time of Charles the Bold, Okeghem and Obrecht were outstanding, but the greatest of them all was Josquin des Prés (*c.* 1445–1521), master of the palace choir under Charles's daughter, Duchess Mary. The influence of these Burgundian composers, and perhaps particularly Dufay and Josquin, was immense, and the emergence of north Italy as the leader of European music in the sixteenth century must in part be due to Josquin's work at Florence, Milan and Ferrara, and to the influence of other Burgundians who served Italian masters, such as Willaert at Venice and Arcadelt at Florence.

The century from 1375 to 1475 was a veritable Age of Maecenas and all four dukes were men of culture. In an age when books were only just coming to be of interest to laymen, Philip the Bold founded a library and Philip the Good and Charles the Bold were avid readers. Philip the Good himself wrote poetry, an example to later Renaissance monarchs; and his patronage of literature was as notable as his grandfather's of sculpture. The court of the dukes produced no writers to compare with the giants who strode through the age of Louis XIV, but in the fifteenth century the finest literature in the French language came not from France but from Burgundy and particularly from her historians. That we know so much of the splendor of the court at Brussels, Ghent and Bruges, and of the activities especially of Philip the Good and Charles the Bold, we owe to Chastellain, La Marche, Commynes and several others.

These historians were interesting men in their own right. Georges Chastellain, whose long *History of the Noble Deeds of Christendom* is mostly lost, was official court historian and one of the few commoners to bear the Golden Fleece. Olivier de la Marche was able to leave us such a full account of Charles

* Strictly Dufay was born at Cambrai (*c.* 1400).

the Bold's wedding to Edward IV's sister, Margaret of York, because he was its master of ceremonies. Philippe de Commynes's history of the bitter struggle between Charles and Louis XI is particularly fascinating because he knew both men very well, having served Charles as a courtier-diplomat before he deserted to Louis.

Most of the 'Burgundians' mentioned in this section came from what we today call the Low Countries, and notably from Belgium. 'Burgundy' cannot claim credit for the work of Netherlanders in the way that it can for the marvels of Cluny's sculptors three to four centuries before, for the artists and composers in question were Burgundians only by virtue of Philip the Bold's fortunate marriage to Margaret, the heiress of Flanders. For us in this present study the importance of Sluter, the van Eyck brothers, Okeghem and the many others, lies elsewhere: first, their brilliant achievements were a worthy adornment of (may we say it?) the first kingdom of modern times, this Burgundy which the dukes had not only restored but placed at the head of Christendom; but also probably no single dynasty – classical, medieval or modern – had ever done so much for western art as the dukes did in creating schools which flourished long after they themselves were gone, and which exerted an immeasurable influence on the arts of other lands including Germany, France, England and even Italy.

Philip the Good and Charles the Bold: a sorry contrast

In some respects the Court of Burgundy shone with its greatest brilliance under the first of the great Valois dukes, Philip the Bold who died in 1404; but it rose to its greatest power under Philip the Good (1419–67) and Charles the Bold (1467–77). It was under these remarkable princes that the best opportunity arose that was ever offered to the Burgundian Phoenix. Philip created it, Charles cast it away.

Burgundy's tragedy is that Charles did not inherit Philip's finer qualities along with his mighty state. When Philip was 42 a Castilian visitor to his court described him as 'of most noble bearing, tall, elegant and chivalrous'. 'His appearance alone', wrote Chastellain, 'proclaimed him emperor and his natural graces made him worthy of a crown'. Indeed it is easier to see Philip as king or emperor than Charles, though titles meant less to him than to his son. The two men were similar in their love of music and history, their physical courage in battle, and their ability to deploy charm and eloquence. In reflective mood, commented Chastellain, Charles's smiling eyes recalled his father vividly.

However, they resembled each other in appearance less than one would expect of father and son – Philip slim and tall, Charles thick-set and, like his Portuguese mother, of swarthy complexion – and in character they were very different. It is commonplace that Philip had thirty known mistresses and Charles none. Philip was pleasure-loving, Charles austere. Philip was lacka-daisical, even lazy, Charles industrious and hard-working. Philip was good-natured, Charles suspicious and vindictive. Both were autocrats who chose good lieutenants, but Philip delegated well whereas Charles meddled. Philip controled his outbursts, Charles was governed by them. Whereas Philip's decisions were rooted in moderation, patience, restraint and a readiness to listen, Charles's judgements were too often unbalanced by the heat of anger, and even in his cooler moments he would act impulsively or be blinded by misplaced contempt for his enemies, arrogance or overweening ambition. Commynes wrote that above all else he desired glory such as history had accorded to princes of antiquity.

Charles seems to have become more unstable with the passage of time, perhaps through some affliction* which affected his behavior more than his physical well-being; and, as is too often forgotten, for several years he pursued his goals with commendable restraint, relying less on arms than on diplomacy.

The Emperor betrays Charles the Bold on his coronation day

At least from the reign of Robert II in the twelve-seventies the dukes, when they were not bent on controling France itself, had pursued two objectives: Burgundy's independence of the French crown and its consolidation into a powerful state. The logical conclusion of these policies was the destruction or emasculation of the French monarchy and the elevation of Burgundy to be a kingdom, and both were brought within Charles's reach by negotiations with England and with the Empire. In 1471 his help was decisive in the installation of his brother-in-law the Yorkist Edward IV on the throne of England, and in the ensuing three years plans were put in hand for Charles and Edward to renew the Hundred Years' War, divide France between them and complete the work of Charles's father, Philip the Good, and Philip's brother-in-law, the Duke of Bedford, of fifty years earlier; and before long Charles was forging a powerful coalition against France.

* e.g. venereal disease? It seems unlikely in so chaste a man and so faithful a husband.

[169]

The parallel negotiations with the Emperor Frederick III were more difficult and tedious, but they seemed to offer Charles an even more glittering prize, not only a crown – for what state deserved more than Burgundy to be a kingdom? – but perhaps also Frederick's promise of the succession to the Empire, for Frederick was his senior by nearly twenty years, and Maximilian, the Emperor's heir, was still in his teens.

A successful conclusion to the negotiations was even more important to Frederick than to Charles, since for most of his long reign (1440–93) the Empire was on the verge of total collapse, and the leaders of the west looked not to the Emperor but to Philip the Good and Charles the Bold for their salvation from the Turks, who were now frighteningly close to the imperial frontiers. There was indeed no greater contrast than between the hopes of Burgundy and the despair of Austria, and no surer means of salvation for the Hapsburgs than an alliance with Burgundy through the marriage of Maximilian to Charles's heir, his daughter Mary. However, Frederick, one of the least effectual rulers of history, was so decision-shy that it took seven years (1463–70) to persuade him to seize what his cousin Sigismund called, and rightly, 'the greatest piece of luck that had for long befallen the house of Austria'.

Three more years were to pass while Frederick's and Charles's ambassadors fenced and parried over the terms of the compact, above all over Charles's demand for a crown. At last in November 1473, as we saw in the Prologue, the Emperor formally agreed to the reconstitution of the Kingdom of Burgundy in favor of Charles and his heirs, male or female. It would comprise both the lands which he already held within the Empire and the other territories which traditionally formed part of the Kingdom; and for his part Charles promised to furnish Frederick with 'up to ten thousand troops for the succor of the Faith' (presumably against the Turks) and 'for so long as the Emperor may be at war with the King of France'.

As Charles contemplated the tapestries portraying his great hero and model Alexander the Great which decorated his headquarters in Trier, we may imagine him indulging in dreams of conquest. He saw himself indeed as 'Alexander' to his fittingly-named father: like Philip of Macedon, Philip of Burgundy had forged and tempered the weapon which his son would wield in victory. But not even Alexander, Charles may have mused, would have executed with greater skill the pincer movement which he and Edward would shortly make on Rheims and Paris. He could relish the thought of his brother-in-law's coronation in Rheims as King of France with almost as much pleasure as his own in Trier as King of Burgundy, for Edward, like his other allies, would be no more than a junior partner in his new order in Europe, and in due course, perhaps, he would do homage to him as Frederick's successor as Emperor.

Preparations continued apace. The new sovereign's crown and scepter, cloak and banner, were put on show, and Trier was in the grip of mounting excitement. But Charles was soon back to fretting and fuming since the Emperor now procrastinated over the date for the great day. Many medieval sovereigns relied on the advice of astrologers in decisions large or small, but Frederick practiced their skills himself. From his study of the stars, a contemporary wrote, the Emperor 'comprehended and predicted the most sublime things'; and, when we consider the date which Frederick chose, 25 November, we can see that astrology must have guided him at this time and that he was waiting until there was a favorable conjunction of celestial bodies – for instance, for such a prestigious event, one bringing together the Sun and Jupiter, and this occurs only once a year. In 1473 the conjunction fell in the last days of November, and it was placed in Sagittarius which was specially propitious for a holy occasion like the anointing of a king.

But we can also understand that Frederick's reading of Charles's natus, which he had undoubtedly studied before they met at Trier, would have given him pause. Here any good astrologer would find a man of boundless ambition, immense drive, enormous endurance and obstinacy, and dogged courage; a cruel, ruthless and acquisitive man without any conscience, but one who was a faithful, even passionate husband, whose wives would meet with misfortune. (Charles lost two, Catherine of France and Isabella of Bourbon, before he was 34.) Besides this the subject evidently had charm and magnetism and was a cultivated man who was fond of music and of collecting beautiful things. He was a man of moods and, while he was generally of good temper, his rages could be dangerous. He was proud and arrogant, never admitting a mistake nor learning from one. Secretive and revengeful, he would not forget or forgive an injury. He would have no difficulty in believing that his goals were noble or his policies truly for the good of his subjects. The natus showed that he would have had a rich inheritance from his father, but he would have resented his father's longevity (Philip lived to be 71), and he would have longed for the succession and the independence that it would bring.*

We may be sure that Frederick believed he already knew what sort of man

---

* All this was written by a modern astrologer who knew nothing about Charles but the time and place of his birth. Frederick doubtless approached the problem in a similar manner.

faced him when they met at Trier, but he obviously reflected long not merely where Charles's ambition and impulsiveness would lead him but above all how his fate might affect Frederick's own; and on this his astrology would have given him a clear enough sign, for given the opposition of their moons success for Charles probably spelt trouble for the Emperor. But what must have struck Frederick most of all was the dominating feature in Charles's chart: disaster, and disaster with terrifying and unexpected suddenness. This was not a star to fix one's chariot to.

We shall never know for sure what made up Frederick's mind for him, or even whether he ever intended to carry out the promises he made at Trier to restore the Kingdom of Burgundy for Charles. Historians tell of the influence brought to bear on him by his advisers and the pressure exerted by Louis of France, and how he was infuriated by the insufferable arrogance of the younger man, with whom he had almost daily contact. But in addition Frederick may have been swayed by a conviction that Charles was doomed, and also perhaps anyone closely tied to him. In any event, early in the morning of 25 November, only a few hours before Charles's coronation as King of Burgundy, Frederick slipped away under cover of darkness with a few retainers and, although he left a message for Charles suggesting time and place for the completion of their business, he never again fully committed himself to what had been agreed at Trier. As for the marriage of his son Maximilian to Mary of Burgundy, if it was predestined (he must have said to himself) it would come about without his having a hand in it.

Charles was enraged by Frederick's treachery but had little reason to doubt that he would be able to bring him to honor their deal before long: the Empire needed his support far more than he needed Frederick's; and he proceeded to issue ordinances for the organization of his kingdom, which he had drawn up before reaching agreement with Frederick at Trier, and with which he had secured the Emperor's concurrence. At least in theory the Burgundian territories were under the ultimate judicial authority of either the Imperial Court or the Parlement of Paris. These ordinances, passed soon after Charles arrived at Thionville (between Trier and Nancy) on 27 November, now set up a sovereign Burgundian court and other supreme bodies to administer his dominions.[11] Thus, with at least the acquiescence of the Emperor, Burgundy could claim once more to be a separate sovereign state.

Mechelen (Malines), north of Brussels, was Charles's first choice as seat of these federal institutions, which initially could only be concerned with the northern block of his territories. But he was already looking ahead to the union and consolidation of all his lands north of the Jura (Map no. 22B); and, as we shall see, two years later he had chosen Nancy, the chief city of Lorraine and more centrally placed, as the capital of his kingdom.

Charles and Edward IV plan the partition of France

In 1473, however, Dijon, the capital of the Duchy of Burgundy, was still Charles's chief city south of the northern block, not least on grounds of history and sentiment; but only now, late in January 1474, did he make his first ceremonial appearance there; and he took the opportunity to refer to his claims to the crown of Burgundy. He had convened the Estates of the Duchy, attending mass with them in the great abbey church of Saint Bénigne. Then, at the ducal palace, he dined them off the magnificent gold and silver which had so impressed the lords of the Empire during the conference at Trier. After the banquet he spoke to the Estates about the Kingdom of Burgundy which 'had for a long time [he said] been usurped by the French and made into a vassal and tributary duchy. This should give all his subjects cause for sorrow, but he had plans, known only to himself, which the future would reveal'.

It was clear that he was as concerned with France as with his unfinished business with the Empire; and these words amounted to a declaration of war against the Kingdom of Burgundy's old enemy and oppressor. Six months later (25 July 1474) he and his brother-in-law Edward IV signed in London a treaty which put the seal on the renewal of the Anglo-Burgundian alliance which Charles's father, Philip the Good, had abandoned in 1435. Each ally would commit at least 10,000 troops to the invasion of France the following summer (1475); the English force would thus be roughly as numerous as those which Edward III and Henry V had landed for the Crécy and Agincourt campaigns. Charles would recognize Edward as King of France as Henry VI had been before him, but in return Edward would cede to Charles large areas of France and Charles would not pay homage to the new King of France for any of his lands; and so the Burgundian State would finally become free of any taint of inferiority to France and, whether Charles won a crown of his own or not, his country would unquestionably rank with the most honored or powerful of Europe.

Thus in the summer of 1475 Charles was within reach of both great objectives: the consolidation of a Burgundian empire and the defeat of France, perhaps even her destruction, and thus the termination, at last and finally in

Burgundy's favor, of the thousand-years' conflict with the Franks. Louis XI would be made to pay, after all these long centuries, for the aggression of that earlier Louis – or Clovis as he is known to us. The grand alliance which Charles had built up against Louis XI included Aragon as well as England, thus threatening France from both north and south; the King of Naples and his son the Prince of Taranto, the latest choice for Mary of Burgundy's hand; and Yolande of Savoy, who not only continued to betray her brother, Louis XI of France, but skilfully brought Louis Sforza of Milan out of the French camp and into the Burgundian. There seemed every prospect of many great lords of France, not least the Duke of Brittany, joining Charles against Louis XI, just as several of them had rallied to him ten years before in the League of the Common Weal. This confrontation reached its climax with the landing of the English army at Calais on 4 July. 'Never' wrote Commynes, the Burgundian historian of the times, 'had a King of England since King Arthur brought so many men at once across the sea'. Indeed the force was more numerous than that which Edward had promised to Charles in the Treaty of London a year before, and it was excellently set up with the most modern arms and equipment. Charles, when he shortly joined Edward at Calais, declared happily that the English were strong enough 'to conquer France and Italy even as far as Rome'.

Charles recovers Lorraine but misses his chance in France

At the conference in London in July 1474 Charles had promised to wear down the French forces from the beginning of the campaigning season of 1475, and that when Edward landed he would find ample supplies and a large Burgundian force. They expected the two armies to have little difficulty in advancing together on Rheims.

Edward was a short while behind schedule but in every other respect he had fulfilled his part of the bargain. This, however, was not the case with Charles, who had suffered a number of reverses since the conference in London. Alsace was in revolt and the Swiss had beaten a Burgundian force at Héricourt near Belfort in November 1474, the first defeat ever suffered by Charles. Next, the duke had foolishly become involved in a quarrel on behalf of a kinsman over the archbishopric of Cologne and he let his army be tied down in the siege of the neighboring town of Neuss. The Emperor, provoked by Charles's designs on German territory, formed an alliance with Louis XI and between them they persuaded René II of Lorraine, who had been a satellite of Charles since the previous November, to defect from the Burgundian cause and to declare war on the duke (May 1475). Thus Charles, who had hoped to be able to concentrate on his great objective in the west, the destruction of France, found himself unexpectedly involved in the east; and, when he raised the siege of Neuss on 13 June, it was not for the invasion of France but for the reconquest of Lorraine, so vital to the unity of his empire. Edward was justifiably angry that on landing at Calais he should find no Burgundians or supplies, only the news that the Burgundian army was still in the east. Indeed when Charles reached Calais ten days later (14 July) it was with only a few men.

Charles explained to Edward the difficult choice he faced: he could join him at once in battle against the French but without his army; or he could join him in only a few weeks after the completion of his campaign in Lorraine with the capture of Nancy. Charles's choice was in fact between the dukes' two objectives: the consolidation of their territories and the destruction of France. Which should Charles go for first: Nancy or Paris? He must have been fated to choose Nancy; it was his city of destiny. However, in seeking his brother-in-law's acceptance, he promised that there would be no question of abandoning the campaign against France, only of a few weeks' delay, during which the English forces could attain the first objective, Rheims, which as Charles pointed out they were quite strong enough to do on their own. As soon as it had settled matters in Lorraine, the main Burgundian army would join the English at Rheims so as to be present for Edward's coronation there as King of France. Meanwhile Charles and the small force with him would keep Edward company.

Edward had no choice but to fall in with this new scheme (see Map no. 22A on p. 163), and it was only two or three days after Charles had joined him that they advanced southwards by way of Doullens to Saint Quentin, a key stronghold which was held by the Count of Saint Pol. Saint Pol had been one of Charles's army commanders in his first war against Louis XI in 1465 and in the first days of August he wrote to Charles promising to serve both him and Edward against any of their foes. The English accordingly approached Saint Quentin, as they would have any friendly town, without taking precautions. To their great surprise Saint Pol's men sallied out of the fortress to attack them and the English, caught off-balance, withdrew to their camp in blinding rain, bitter and furious not only with Saint Pol but also with Charles.

This was to prove the turning point. If Charles had stayed in the battle area, even more if he had brought over some of the troops from Luxemburg which had been assembled for the final attack on Lorraine, the English would almost certainly have been willing to continue the campaign and advance on Rheims

[175]

and Paris. As it was, Charles had just ridden eastwards to join his army and settle his account with René of Lorraine, and a day or two later an envoy from Louis XI arrived at the English camp near Péronne to discover if Edward might conceivably be ready to treat. The timing was singularly fortunate for Louis. Edward was tired of his costly and so far fruitless campaigning and longed for the pleasures of his court in London; he felt he no longer owed any loyalty to Charles, who had pressed him so hard and long to invade France, only to let him down; and he saw an opportunity of driving an excellent bargain with Louis. The King of France indeed was only too anxious to bring hostilities to an end. As he saw matters, once Charles had brought Lorraine to heel, he and Edward could be expected to unite their forces, and they would probably be joined by the Duke of Brittany and many others who were waiting for an Anglo-Burgundian success before declaring themselves. Consequently when Edward's ambassadors met Louis's on 14 August and demanded an immediate payment to cover the costs of Edward's campaign and a pension of fifty thousand crowns a year for life, Louis's acceptance was granted within a day.

If Louis could hardly believe his miraculously good fortune, Charles was astounded that Edward should abandon him so swiftly without any consultation when success was within their grasp. The duke, traveling with all haste, reached his brother-in-law's camp on 19 August and tried to talk him into renewing hostilities. The two princes exchanged angry charges of treachery. 'The duke [Commynes wrote], speaking in English, recalled some of the great deeds which English kings had performed who had crossed to France and the sufferings they had undergone in order to win honor there. He complained strongly of the truce ... but the King of England took his words very ill'. He upbraided Charles for breaking the agreement made in London and refused to forgo his rich pension and embark again on the rigors of war.

So with this bitter argument France finally emerged the victor in the Hundred Years' War* and Burgundy lost her last chance of defeating her great foe. Even at that time it must have seemed a golden opportunity thrown away, for Charles went on to conquer Lorraine only ten weeks later, restoring his lines of communication between his northern and southern territories and demon-

---

* Our name for it. The English kings did not regard their claims to the French crown as terminated in 1454: 1475 was effectively their last attempt on it.

strating to Edward and Louis that, had the former only been patient, the latter would have been crushed.

Nancy, Charles's chosen city of destiny

The supporters of a tennis champion who is two sets ahead do not despair when he casts away the first of three match points. No more did Charles's adherents lose faith in his ultimate triumph when he missed that chance to defeat France. In the months following his bitter row with Edward near Péronne Charles's star was again in the ascendant. Once more it was on Nancy that his dreams focused, and as soon as the city was in his hands (11 January 1476) he informed the Estates of Lorraine of his plans to create an empire in terms more explicit than those expressed to the notables of Dijon in January 1474. No city, he asserted, pleased him as greatly as Nancy. Besides it was at the center of his lands (better placed than Mechelen), and he would accordingly make it his capital and the seat of Burgundy's sovereign court of justice; and from here he would dictate his laws to the Germans and the French. He would enlarge the city and make it more beautiful and better fortified. Indeed it was his intention, he declared, to end his days there.[12]

We can only guess what the members of the Lorraine Estates thought of the prospect of Nancy becoming the center of Charles's empire. Some of them may have assumed that he had in mind no more than a greater kingdom of Lotharingia, the name which now only meant Lorraine, but which in olden time embraced all that lay between the Kingdom of Burgundy and the North Sea. Since he was Lord from Somme to Sarine,* and from Friesland to Lake Geneva, he already held more than 'Lotharingia' and a wiser prince would have settled for that, or at least have consolidated it before renewing the advance. But others knew Charles better and realized that his remarks to the Lorrainers referred to the Middle Kingdom of Lothar, Charlemagne's grandson, which had stretched to the Mediterranean and beyond; for the most part, after all, this was what the Emperor had granted him at Trier just a year before (Map no. 22B), and it only remained for him to secure the rest of the Kingdom of Burgundy. 'Frankish Burgundy' formed the old core of Charles's dominions; the Burgundians' original Homeland, now the Duchy of Savoy, was his satellite; and the third part of the ancient kingdom, Provence, had been

* The river west of Bern.

promised to him by 'Good King René'.* Within days of subduing Lorraine he was preparing to invade the fourth region, the Allemannic, where Frederick III's dynasty had been ousted by the Swiss.

As we have seen, the reports of Charles's coronation at Trier in November 1473 alarmed the Swiss, and early in 1474 they sent ambassadors to the duke who addressed him from their knees as though they were his subjects. But before the end of the year the cantons had decided to declare war on him, through a combination of sympathy for the Alsatians in revolt, increasing friction with Charles's supporters in present-day western Switzerland, and the liberal use of gold by the 'Universal Spider', Louis XI, always anxious to avoid direct confrontation with his enemy if he could destroy him by other means.[13] Charles seems to have been more concerned to avoid war with the Swiss than he is usually represented,[14] but when his army was freed before the end of 1475 by its conquest of Lorraine, he could no longer overlook the cantons' many provocations: their support for the Alsatian rebels and for René II, their surprise attack at Héricourt, and their repeated incursions against his dependents, leading notably to the cold-blooded massacre of perhaps 1500 citizens at Estavayer. This charming little town on the southern shore of Lake Neuchâtel retains as much of the atmosphere of the period as any in Switzerland, and its battlements are largely those on which the victims fought the Bernese assailants in 1475.

It was in vain that his more cautious advisers spoke of the difficulty of campaigning in the mountains in winter and, when early in January 1476 Swiss ambassadors came to Charles to urge arbitration of their differences, he gave them a harsh welcome, recalling how they had ravaged the County of Burgundy, attacked Savoy and seized the lands of his friend, the Count of Romont. The lords of Romont and Chatel-Guyon, whose fortress of Grandson the Bernese had also seized, urged Charles on to war. We may be sure that they, and the Savoyard nobles at his court, kept reminding him that the areas owned, occupied or threatened by the Swiss had once

* René I's promise was probably vaguer than is suggested by the sources who tell us of the deaths of his eldest son John I in 1474 and of John's sons in 1471 and 1473, but seem to discount the position of René's nephew Charles IV let alone his grandson René II. René I, who died in 1480, had delegated his title to Provence to Charles III (his brother and Charles IV's father), but he had died in 1472; it was Charles IV who, having taken over Charles III's claim, eventually made over Provence to Louis XI. René II, who appears in these pages as Duke of Lorraine, defied this as a betrayal; his troops resisted Louis XI in Provence, but in vain (1481). Whatever the strength of René I's promise to Charles the Bold, for *him* it would have been pretext enough to intervene in Provence in due course. See Genealogical table D, p. 284.

formed part of the Burgundian kingdom which he was in process of restoring.

To the Estates of Lorraine Charles declared on 11 January 1476, 'The French and Germans fear me. They know I am powerful and can protect you. I will maintain the peace, excepting only against the Swiss since they have persecuted my cousin the Count of Romont. And with them I shall deal next month'. That evening he left to begin the war which a year later, all but six days, was to prove so decisive.

The remaining match points lost at Grandson and Morat

Today, perched on a mountainside commanding the west end of lake Neuchâtel, Grandson's thirteenth-century castle is one of Switzerland's most interesting tourist attractions. In the Middle Ages it was the headquarters of a Savoyard family with English links hardly less important than those of the counts. The poetry of Othon de Grandson is said to have influenced Chaucer; it was Bishop John Grandisson (as he is known in England) who gave Exeter cathedral its magnificent nave and the longest stretch of Gothic vaulting in the world (1327–69); while legend has adorned the leg of his sister, Catherine Countess of Salisbury, with the garter which gave the name to an order of chivalry no less renowned than the Golden Fleece.*

When Charles's army appeared beneath the walls of the castle on 19 February it had already recovered all the territory occupied by the Swiss as far as the town of Morat. It was bitterly cold and snowing hard. Nine days later the little Bernese garrison of four hundred surrendered and were hanged as a reprisal for Estavayer. With his next objective Neuchâtel, Charles sent his advance guard into a narrow pass where they were surprised by the Swiss. One foolish move compounded another, and his troops were soon in disarray and rout; and, although he suffered relatively few casualties, he lost no fewer than five hundred guns. Europe was astounded: the mighty duke was not invincible after all. However, Charles was determined to restore his fortunes at once. While his enemies gained heart and many of his friends wavered or deserted him, he struck the Swiss again, in June, laying siege to Morat, a Savoyard

---

* For four generations of Grandson family involvement with the English court see Béat de Fischer, *2000 ans de présence suisse en Angleterre*, p. 21. For recent doubts about Catherine's claims see especially M. Packe, *King Edward III* (1983), pp. 113, 170.

frontier-fortress which the Bernese had seized from the Count of Romont, and this time Charles's army was massacred. A large part of it was caught with its back to a lake and no way of escape, when it was set upon by superior numbers led by René II of Lorraine. The Burgundians left no fewer than 8000 on the field.

The fruits of decades of skilful diplomacy were thrown away by these two disasters. This time Charles's coalition fell to pieces and outside Burgundy the last important supporter left to him was Yolande of Savoy, more faithful to him than he deserved – or believed. Having taken refuge with her after Morat, at Gex north of Geneva, he quite unjustly suspected her of treachery and had her kidnapped and incarcerated at Rouvre south of Dijon. Here she was seized by a French task force and henceforth had no choice but to throw in her lot with her brother Louis.

Return to Nancy

Meanwhile René II followed up the victory in which he had been so prominent by investing his old capital, Nancy, so that once again the lines of communication between Charles's northern and southern territories were in grave danger. Charles promptly called together the Estates of the County of Burgundy, and then of the Duchy and of Flanders, to vote funds for a new army. He would raise, he said, forty thousand men (in those days a vast force), even if it meant taxing all his subjects one quarter of their goods; and he spoke yet again of the Kingdom of Burgundy he would establish. The assemblies were shocked that he could still make such demands of them, each of them showing less compliance than the last. Burgundy, they replied, was powerful enough already and required no further conquest; the war was unnecessary and the people should not be called on to contribute to a quarrel so little justified.

Meanwhile Charles's counselors urged him to be patient while he restored his fortunes, raised loans, rallied his allies and built up an army again. Let Nancy fall – within a year or so he would be able to recover it and set his strategy in motion again, first if he wished against the Swiss, later against the French. It was sound advice; a more temperate man would have taken it since it obviously held out such excellent prospects of success. After all, at forty-two he had the time for the highest enterprises even if he were not blessed with his father's three score years and ten.*

* More precisely 71.

Charles, however, was possessed by a demon: he was determined to save Nancy from René at all costs, and within only two months of the disaster at Morat he was again on the march without waiting to gather more than some six thousand men. Even the discovery of the city already fallen did not give him pause; he was still set on recapturing it whatever the odds. But the battle was lost before it was joined, for his Italian troops had abandoned him for René.

This time Charles paid for his temerity with his life. His body was found two days later in a muddy pond, naked and gored by wolves. Nancy, fought on 5 January 1477, was one of the decisive battles of the western world.

The English alliance the match-winner

A great deal has been written elsewhere about the reasons for Charles's failure,* and here we shall touch on only two themes, the English alliance and Charles's personality, leaving more general comments about the failure of Burgundy for later pages. As we shall elaborate there, the fall of Burgundy was due in the final analysis to the rise of France; here we suggest that this was brought on largely by the failure of Charles the Bold and also Philip the Good to make the best use of the English alliance.

At no time did Burgundy achieve independence from France so securely as in the half-century between 1420 and 1475; at no time was she so close to the destruction of her great enemy as at those two high-points in her story, thanks largely to her alliance with her natural confederate, England. In 1475 one might well have asked, which was to destroy the other, Burgundy or France? Philip the Good and Charles both recognized that they could only create and preserve a Middle Kingdom of Burgundy if they could successfully withstand France. The dukes had created an independent Burgundian state in the half-century between 1380 and 1430, but it needed, say, another half century (1430–80) of consolidation before its security would be placed beyond all doubt. It was imperative that this consolidation should be achieved before the French monarchy regained its full strength after the troubles of the Hundred Years' War; and so it is exceedingly difficult to understand how in their turn both Philip and Charles allowed France to recover.

Philip made a signal error in abandoning the English in 1435 and watching passively while the French drove them from all their vast possessions on the

---

* See for example the works in Appendix IV under 'The Duchy and Dukes of Burgundy'.

Continent but Calais. Charles was no wiser to leave Edward IV's invading forces in the lurch in 1475, when he could have marched with him on Rheims and Paris rather than alone on Nancy, his city of ill omen. On this supreme folly Commynes, the courtier-historian who deserted him for Louis XI, wrote: 'God had allowed his mind and judgement to become disordered, for all his life he had striven to open a way into France for the English, and at this moment when the English were ready, he remained stubbornly determined to embark on an impossible undertaking'. Charles's early success in conquering Lorraine showed that that at least was not 'impossible', but it was certainly a prize to be ignored until Charles had secured a greater one, the destruction of France. Commynes, however, probably had in mind Charles's ambition to create an immense Middle Kingdom, on which he without doubt overreached himself. However, it must not be taken as inevitable that Charles would bring disaster on his country, despite Frederick III's reading of the stars. Commynes, it is true, said of Charles: 'After over one hundred and twenty years of peace under three illustrious princes* . . . it pleased God to send this duke Charles who involved them [the Burgundians] in bloody wars, in winter as well as in summer, to their great affliction and expense'. But La Marche and other excellent contemporary sources wrote more highly of Charles. Thomas Basin, for instance, summed up his reign with these words:

> If only he could have tempered his greatness of spirit with moderation and prudence! But, as it happens often with princes, he prided himself on his own judgement and listened only to his own wisdom, rejecting good advice most of the time or listening to it little, and making up his mind according to his view of what he wanted done.

But Basin drew a distinction between his earlier and his later years, remarking that 'at the beginning of his reign, after the death of his father, he showed himself moderate and good at governing'.

In sum, had Charles conducted himself in the last two years of his reign as he had in the first seven, he might well have triumphed, with all that would have meant for subsequent generations.

---

* Philip the Bold, John the Fearless and Philip the Good.

Infelix Burgundia, Felix Austria

The Duchy of Burgundy is absorbed by France

Louis XI's occupation of the Duchy of Burgundy in 1477 might be thought to mark the end of our story; after all, Provence fell to him four years later and Savoy was overrun not long after that, so that of all the 'Burgundies' only the Allemannic, the Swiss cantons, was left riding high. But in fact, thanks largely to the courage of Charles the Bold's daughter – in 1477 she was only 19 – the Duchy's fate was not to be decided for another sixty-seven years, the County of Burgundy only passed to France after two centuries, and the larger part of Charles's territories escaped its clutches altogether, except for a few years under Napoleon.

Louis had bid for it all by putting pressure on Mary to marry the Dauphin. However, having first considered renewing the alliance with England,* she decided to fulfil the abortive Treaty of Trier as far as possible by marrying Maximilian of Austria, son of the Emperor Frederick III. On 26 March 1477, only ten weeks after her father's death, she wrote secretly to Maximilian and they were married on 19 August at Ghent. Thus the Low Countries, which had greeted the Hapsburg prince with cries of 'Long live Burgundy', were saved at least temporarily from absorption by France.

Meanwhile, rather than become French, it seems that no less than a fifth of the population of Dijon abandoned their homes and families, mostly migrating to the County of Burgundy. A revolt against the French occupying Dijon failed, but after bitter fighting Burgundian patriots recovered all the rest of the Duchy. Louis won it back but Francis I surrendered it again to Mary's grandson Charles V from 1526 to 1544. At the end of the century Mayenne, the powerful governor of Burgundy, defied Henry IV and aspired to make it his own; and the Hapsburgs encouraged his successor Biron to set about creating a separate

---

* Her stepmother Margaret of York wanted her to marry Edward IV's brother (and hers), the Duke of Clarence whom legend drowned in Malmsey wine.

state of Burgundy to which, they said, they would contribute the County and which would become hereditary in his family. Hoping to extend his power also over the center of ancient Burgundy, Biron sought the hand of a princess of Savoy. But the Burgundians considered him a stooge of the Spanish and he was eventually seized by Henry IV's men and beheaded in the Bastille (1602). The Duchy's last separatist fling occurred in 1630 when a dispute over taxation between Paris and the Burgundian authorities led to a riot in Dijon in which a portrait of Louis XIII was burnt, the Emperor was hailed as sovereign because of his descent from Charles the Bold, and many of the city's buildings were sacked.

The Franche Comté holds on longer to its freedom

The County of Burgundy was even more reluctant than the Duchy to accept French rule. Louis XI had occupied it from 1479 to 1493, when it was restored to Philip the Fair, son to Mary of Burgundy and father of Charles V. The French went over to the attack again in 1635. Once again they met bitter resistance, particularly at Dole and in the hills of the Jura; but so widespread was the terror and devastation that when peace came and the County was restored to the Hapsburgs, it had to be repopulated from Bresse, Savoy and elsewhere.

Twice more Louis XIV renewed the assault, but the end only came in 1674. Small towns like Gray, Luxeuil, Arbois and Poligny held out for several days and the conquest of the County was not complete for five months, but on this occasion the French retained the province and it has been theirs ever since, by the Treaty of Nijmegen of 1678. For the rest of Louis's reign it was treated officially as a foreign occupied territory and it enjoyed increased taxes, ruin and misery.

The Duchy was absorbed into France in the seventeenth century, and the County in the eighteenth, but it was not until late in the nineteenth that their dialects were abandoned for French by the mass of the population. (See Appendix II.)

Northern Burgundy becomes Belgium and the Netherlands

In the first act of *King Lear*, when the King of France and the Duke of Burgundy have come to seek Cordelia's hand, Lear speaks of 'the wine of France and *milk*

[184]

of Burgundy' and the French king refers to his rival as the duke of 'waterish Burgundy'. For Shakespeare and his contemporaries 'Burgundy' was not the land of vines but the Low Countries, comprising seventeen provinces which the Hapsburgs administered separately from the rest of their empire, sometimes jointly with the Franche Comté, sometimes not. Charles V, a monarch who was more Burgundian and Flemish than Spanish or Austrian, had been declared of age in the great hall of the castle at Brussels and it was here, surrounded by the knights of the Burgundian Order of the Golden Fleece and leaning on the shoulder of William Prince of Orange,* that he abdicated his rulership of the Low Countries on 25 October 1555. The pomp and solemnity of the occasion, contrasted with Charles's quiet renunciation of Castile, Aragon, Sicily and the Indies, demonstrated his regard for 'Burgundy' as the hub of his huge empire.

William, known to us as 'the Silent', struggled to create a free and united state out of the seventeen provinces, which as Huizinga said[15] rose in 'a new and special sense of nationalism' against the Spaniards. In the north he succeeded and here there emerged the Kingdom of the Netherlands, inheriting two of the main planks of Burgundian policy, resistance to French expansion and alliance with England. The provinces which William had to abandon to Alva became the Austrian Netherlands and later Belgium. But in 1784, when the Emperor Joseph II planned to turn these still Hapsburg provinces into a kingdom for the Elector of Bavaria, Belgium was not the name chosen: they were to become the Kingdom of Burgundy. The Kingdom of Belgium dates from 1830, like Holland an heir of Burgundy.

The Hapsburgs reap Burgundy's harvest

France and the Hapsburgs divided Charles the Bold's empire between them. In the end the lion's share went to France, and the Hapsburgs and their successor states, Austria and Germany, were left with not a single village; but initially by far the larger part was not France's but the Hapsburgs', thanks to Maximilian's marriage to Mary of Burgundy. Thus were the Hapsburgs heirs not only of the east Frank kingdom but of the Middle Kingdom too; and it was this Burgundian inheritance which carried them in a meteoric ascent from their nadir under Frederick III to their peak under Charles V.

* The principality near the Rhône's mouth. William even inherited claims to the crown of Arles and Vienne.

[185]

Frederick the astrologer-emperor may have seen this miracle pictured in his charts. He may have seen that an alliance with Burgundy, apparently ill-starred in 1473, might shower blessings on Austria a few years later; but whatever the stars told him about his dynasty's immediate prospects, he seems to have had a sublime faith in its destiny, apparently being convinced that the future lay not with Burgundy but with Austria, which one day would rise from the depths to the overlordship of the world. On Frederick's plates and books were inscribed the anagram AEIOU; only after his death was the solution discovered on a paper written in his own hand:

$$A_{lles}^{ustriae} \quad E_{rdreich}^{st} \quad I_{st}^{mperare} \quad O_{esterreich}^{rbi} \quad U_{nterthan}^{niverso}$$

'To Austria belongs the empire of the whole world'
'The whole earthly realm is subject to Austria'

The Hapsburgs came as close to mastery of the world as any dynasty ever did – only seventy years ago, when they had lost their vast overseas territories, they still held together an empire stretching from Switzerland to the Ukraine – and it is a commonplace that they married their way to the top:

Bella gerant fortes. Tu, felix Austria, nube.
Nam quae Mars aliis, dat tibi regna Venus.

(Let the strong wage war. You, lucky Austria, do you marry. The kingdoms which Mars gives others, you gain from Venus.)

Marriage was soon to give the Hapsburgs Spain, Naples, Bohemia and Hungary. But their most important dowry was Burgundy: if gold and silver from the Spanish Main later made the Hapsburgs the most mighty of dynasties, it was the industry and commerce of the Netherlands which first set them on the way to recovery and power. At Trier Frederick III had hesitated over the Burgundian marriage since it could only be secured on Charles's terms; after Charles's death Mary herself made the running and the marriage was secured on terms very favorable to the Hapsburgs. Indeed the marriage, which Charles hoped would give him his kingdom and Burgundy perhaps the mastery of Europe, instead gave the Hapsburgs Burgundy and the world; and so in a sense Austria was the risen phoenix of Burgundy.

Just five centuries now separate us from Frederick and Charles, and the Hapsburgs' and French dominance of the first half of this period is so

[186]

overwhelming that it is hard for us to believe that the story of Europe could ever have taken a different course. But who in Charles the Bold's time would have wagered on the Hapsburgs rising from the depths they had plumbed by 1473–6 to be masters not only of Germany and most of the Middle Kingdom and Italy but also of Spain and the Americas; and all this achieved in half a century? Far shorter odds would have been given on Burgundy achieving the far less ambitious goal which the dukes had pursued resolutely for over a century and now had in their grasp: the independence and consolidation of their state. The Burgundian dukes had fewer handicaps than the Hapsburgs: less scattered territories, less ill-defined frontiers and fewer races to reconcile. They had developed an embryonic federal system which with good fortune might in time have ensured unity in diversity even in territories with such different languages as Flemish and French, Alsatian and Bourguignon; the case of Switzerland demonstrates that plurilingual states can survive and prosper; and so does that of Belgium, where Charles the Bold's Burgundy has survived in microcosm.

It is easy to fall into the error of assuming that because something happened it was inevitable, when it may not even have been the most likely outcome. This is a theme to which we must return in the last chapter, but we have not yet completed the long story of the attempts to raise the Burgundian phoenix from the ashes. It was to suffer one final frustration.

The last Kingdom of Burgundy

Savoyards help to check the expansion of France

In 843 Charlemagne's empire was divided between his three grandsons. The new Emperor, Lothar, gained the two non-Frankish kingdoms, Italy and Burgundy, as well as the central section of the Franks' own lands. His portion not only came to be called Lotharingia (a name later confined to the central Frankish section) but has also been known as the Middle Kingdom, lying as it did between the future Germany and France, the kingdoms of Lothar's brothers (see Map no. 9).

Two centuries later the east Franks, having gained Lotharingia and added the Italian and Burgundian crowns to the German, were masters of the Middle Kingdom. To a considerable extent the subsequent history of Charlemagne's empire has turned on the endeavors of France to wrest the Middle Kingdom from Germany. For the first half-millennium, however, the Capetians and Valois were chiefly engaged with extending royal authority up to the limits of the Kingdom of France, a process we can regard as completed in 1491 with Charles VIII's acquisition of Brittany. Coincidentally rather than as a matter of long-range strategy (Charles VIII is not one of France's major figures), three years later there started the expansion beyond those limits* which had its climax when Napoleon brought all of Charlemagne's empire under French rule, direct or indirect. Italy was the first target of the French (1494–1525), their troops trampling across Savoy *en route*; but over the next three centuries it was to the north-east of their frontiers, and beyond the territories which they had seized from the Burgundians, that their pressure was the most persistent. British readers know how great a part their compatriots played in checking successive advances of the French; and in one important war their great general, Marlborough, shared the honors with the most brilliant soldier ever to lead the Hapsburg armies, Prince Eugene of Savoy.

---

* Dauphiné, gained a century before, still remained part of the Kingdom of Arles.

But there was another Savoyard captain who got the best of the French on their north-eastern frontier. Charles III may have brought Savoy to her nadir* but he also gave her her finest son.** Emmanuel Philibert was born in 1528 at Chambéry, the capital of Savoy. An exile from the age of eight, he was brought up at the court of his uncle, the Emperor Charles V. At 17 he offered Charles his sword to help defeat their common enemy, France; at 25 he was captain-general of the Spanish army of the Netherlands; and at 28, when Charles abdicated, he became governor-general there (1556). Duke of Savoy in name since his father's death in 1553, Emmanuel Philibert's chief ambition was naturally to recover his throne. Under his direction an imperialist force invaded Bresse, which the French had seized with the rest of Savoy in 1536, and occupied Lyons (1557), so long the goal of Savoyard ambitions; and it was shortly after this that the young duke, at the head of the Spanish army, inflicted on the French at Saint Quentin their most terrible defeat since Agincourt.

Duke Emmanuel Philibert of Savoy rejects dreams of the Kingdom

The Treaty of Cateau Cambrésis (1559) recognized his title to Savoy and Piedmont, but he still had to win them at the point of his sword. His homeland had long been a battlefield of the great powers. He rebuilt the shattered structure of Amadeus VIII and carried through immense reforms in its institutions, its judiciary and its social and economic life. His success is without doubt due in great part to his popularity. He had been adored by his troops, and he was now beloved by the people whom he had restored to a worthy place in the Europe of Elizabeth Tudor, Philip II and the Medicis. He was not striking in appearance. He is described as small, fair, thin and nervous with a long turned-up moustache, but he was brave and shrewd and above all patient and indefatigable. He was not only one of the finest soldiers of his century but one of its outstanding statesmen and he gave little Savoy both self-respect and national identity.

When after three years' fighting Emmanuel Philibert entered Turin in triumph (1562), he declared his intention of making it his capital instead of Chambéry. This made his Savoyards fear that he would forsake them for his

* Page 158.
** Genealogical table E, p. 285.

[189]

Piedmontese lands,* and led by a prominent member of the ducal Senate at Chambéry, Joly d'Allery, they published a manifesto proposing that the duke should declare himself a Protestant and set himself at the head of a kingdom comprising Savoy, Dauphiné and Provence, effectively the ancient Kingdom of Burgundy. Geneva, once the Burgundian royal seat and now the independent bastion of Calvinism, was to be the capital. It would be strange if a man of Emmanuel Philibert's courage, intelligence and ambition did not dream of being king, at least of the Burgundian Homeland, which would only mean adding the Suisse Romande, now being converted to the reformed church by Geneva and Bern, to the lands he already held; and in fact the duke had cause to judge his prospects bright, whether or not he renounced the Catholic faith. However, the policy which Joly urged on the duke would have entailed hostility to France and probably war, and Emmanuel Philibert was realist enough to see his mission as the consolidation of the territories he had recovered rather than their extension. Accordingly his son, Charles Emmanuel (1580–1630), inherited a united country and a state strong and centralized, and the full treasury and powerful army that successful military conquest demands. Charles Emmanuel had no doubt that this was his role in history: like another Burgundian Charles of unhappy destiny he saw himself as Alexander to his father's Philip. Had not the famous Provençal astrologer Nostradamus (1503–66) observed that he was born under Sagittarius like Hannibal and Caesar and promised him the laurels of military glory?

Charles Emmanuel, misnamed 'the Great'

Charles Emmanuel was indeed a skilful leader though not of his father's caliber. He had immense personal courage and fought in the midst of his troops as one of them, often exposing himself to mortal danger. In adversity, which was frequently his lot, he displayed constancy and perseverance. Although a zealous Catholic he was less cruel to heretics than most of his contemporaries. But his dominant trait was his voracious ambition for a kingdom and a crown. Nothing was safe from it. He rode roughshod over Estates and nobles alike and, long before Louis XIV said it, he declared 'L'état c'est moi'. Even in that age of easy treachery Charles Emmanuel became renowned for his bad faith. He asserted once that he was no turncoat: his coat, he said, had no reverse side, only

* It was in this period that the Holy Shroud was moved from Chambéry to Turin.

different colors! But his duplicity, like his ugliness, was tempered in part by his winning charm and diplomatic skill.

In some ways Charles Emmanuel was as brilliant as his father, but above all he lacked his judgement and prudence. Emmanuel Philibert had carefully husbanded Savoy's resources; Charles Emmanuel was to cast them away. The father, once back on his throne, steered a middle course between France and the Hapsburgs although his leanings were towards the former; the son married the daughter of Philip II of Spain and regarded the French as his enemy. Emmanuel Philibert had sought to recover control of Geneva by diplomacy; Charles Emmanuel, as we shall see, did not shrink from using force.

His reign falls into two parts with the dividing point at 1610. In the first he was 'obsessed by the Burgundian policy of his ancestors . . . , profiting from France's difficulties to try to reconstitute for his own benefit the ancient Kingdom of Arles and to dominate the entire valley of the Rhône'. In the second period, having recognized that France formed too strong a barrier, 'he reversed his plan of action, moved his center of balance, crossed the Alps, replaced Chambéry by Turin and dreamt [instead] of dominating and organizing Italy'.[16] We are concerned here with the first part of the reign rather than the second; and it is his work in making Savoy into a significant Italian state that won him the sobriquet 'the Great', not his achievements in Savoy proper.

Charles Emmanuel's first attempt on the Kingdom of Arles

Charles's hopes were nourished by the assassination of Henry III of France in August 1589. He had a claim to the French throne but his more definite ambitions, in which he had some encouragement from his father-in-law, Philip II, were for the crown of Arles. He blockaded Geneva and succeeded in rallying strong support for his cause in Dauphiné and Provence. In Grenoble, the Parlement listened attentively to Charles's special envoy, Chabod de Jacob, when he reminded its crowded benches of Dauphiné's and Savoy's common heritage from the ancient Kingdoms of Burgundy and Arles. Believing that his own presence would tip the scales, Charles delegated the Geneva operation to a lieutenant while he made a royal progress through Dauphiné. Moving south he defeated a French army at Riez, forty miles north-east of Aix-en-Provence (see Map no. 23). At Aix in October 1590 the Parlement voted him full powers, withholding only the title of Count of Provence.

[191]

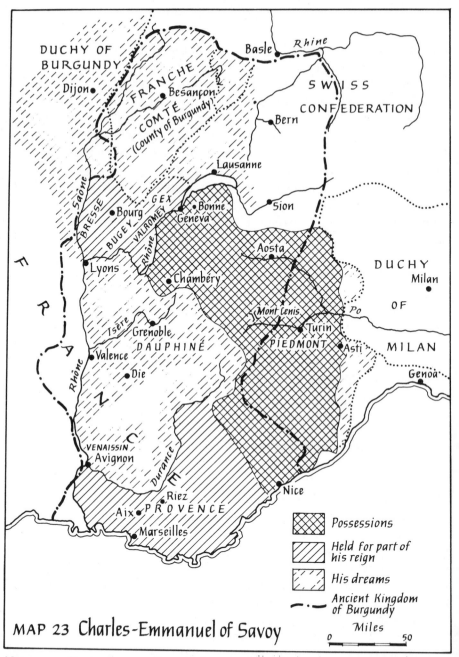

MAP 23 Charles-Emmanuel of Savoy

Legend:
- Possessions
- Held for part of his reign
- His dreams
- Ancient Kingdom of Burgundy

Miles 0 — 50

Map no. 23 Charles Emmanuel's territories were essentially the same as Amadeus VIII's, but, very importantly, he lost Bresse and Bugey and failed to recover Geneva (which had been lost since Amadeus VIII's time) let alone hold Provence.

(Far left) Charles of Anjou, a statue now in the Palazzo dei Conservatori, Rome, showing him as the elderly despot. Attributed to Arnolfo di Cambio, the Florentine architect and sculptor who was in Charles's service, and executed from life *c.*1280. *(Left)* The Angevins already held Arles. In 1282 their first major target was Vienne, the other capital of the Kingdom. Charles probably aimed to be crowned King of Burgundy in this fine Cluniac-style nave. (pp. 108, 135)

Tarascon, where the Angevin forces massed in 1281–2. (pp. 134, ill'n XXII)

Fenis, Val d'Aosta, the finest castle in Savoyard Italy, fourteenth century. (p. 204)

(*Above*) Traditional costumes of the *patoisants* of the Val d'Aosta, with (inset) a car sticker 'Let us maintain our traditions with passion' in Franco-Provençal (1983 festival at Arnad). (*Below*) Beaune: the Hôtel-Dieu founded in 1443 by Nicolas Rolin, Chancellor to Duke Philip the Good – a hospital in use until recent years.

Philip the Good and Charles the Bold shown in the 'Hercules' tapestry *c.*1460
with Philip as Hercules. In the Burrell Collection, Glasgow. (p. 166)

For over a year Charles's enterprise was in the balance. Frustrated, he at length withdrew to his ancient ducal territory of Nice (March 1592), and Henry of Navarre was recognized as King of France by the Parlement of Provence. From then on the scales tipped against Charles. The French were victorious in the valleys of the Durance and Isère, and in Piedmont, and carried the war into the heart of Savoy. Charles's subjects suffered cruelly and welcomed the peace of 1598 which put an end to Charles's claims to the French crown and to his first attempt on that of Arles. This year also brought death to Charles's father-in-law, Philip II, and another bitter disappointment to Charles himself. Obviously the bulk of the Spanish dominions would be left to Philip's son Philip III, but part, he anticipated, would be divided between one daughter, Isabella, and the children of the other, Charles Emmanuel's dead wife Catherine; and the duke had special hopes of gaining the County of Burgundy in this manner. This would give reality to his western ambitions, for his territories would then surround Geneva and the Suisse Romande, and so the greater part of the Kingdom of Arles would be within his grasp. But Philip left the County of Burgundy as well as the Low Countries to Isabella, and Charles and Catherine's children received only a crucifix and a representation of Our Lady of Pilar.

Charles Emmanuel prepares his second bid for the Kingdom of Arles

There was worse to come. By the Treaty of Lyons in 1601, Charles had to cede to France Bresse, Bugey, Valromey and Gex. Not only had Charles Emmanuel failed to extend the duchy's territories in Gaul, they were now smaller than they had been for over three centuries. Yet the duke had still not given up his hopes of restoring the Kingdom of Burgundy, and he immediately set about gaining control of the city which he intended as its capital.[17] If diplomatic pressure did not succeed he would turn to deceit, stealth, surprise and naked force. First, in talks in Turin in November 1601 he reminded delegates from Geneva of the threats posed to it by France and Bern, declared that he recognized the independence of the city and would readily defend it, and offered a treaty which recalled previous reconciliations of the city's independence ('immediacy from the Emperor' was the term often used) with the dukes' claims of over two hundred years' standing. Under this treaty Geneva would once again be under the duke's protection; and he would not station troops within the city walls but only outside it, in the castle on the island in the middle of the Rhône. Coinage would be minted with the city's arms which declared its independence being balanced on the other side by the duke's effigy and the inscription, abbreviated, 'Charles Emmanuel, Prince and Perpetual Imperial Vicar'. This was less offensive to the citizens than 'Duke of Savoy' or 'Count of Genevois or Geneva', but Charles also demanded the right to enter the city at will and to be 'accorded the honors of a great prince'.

It is perhaps not to be wondered at that the Genevese broke off the talks in indignation, but it is certainly surprising that they ignored repeated reports during the course of 1602 that Charles Emmanuel, his diplomacy rebuffed, was now preparing to use force. The duke naturally did his utmost to take the Genevese by surprise. He concealed his identity, posing as an ambassador, when he slipped across the Mont-Cenis pass from Turin to join his troops. He was dissuaded from personal involvement in the assault and waited hidden in a village some five miles from the city walls, while a force of four thousand was assembled at Bonne (ten miles distant) and elsewhere.

Preparations were made with intense care and foresight under the direction of the governor of Bonne, Brignolet (or Brunaulieu), who was also to lead the assault party composed of three hundred hand-picked men, for the most part people of substance. This intrepid group was to gain entry over the ramparts at the dead of the longest night of the year (December 11–12 by the old calendar, December 22–23 by the new). They would cross the mud-filled moat on hurdles laid flat and then scale ladders which would have been painted black and made in sections for easy transport and assembly, with pulleys to adjust their length covered in cloth to deaden the sound. Once inside the walls the scaling party was to lurk in the darkness until the moon was bright enough for them to find their way in the streets. They would then blow the Porte Neuve from within and let in the main body of troops which would meanwhile have moved up. With daylight Charles Emmanuel would make his triumphal entry, and word was already on the way to the bishops of his territories to attend on him when two weeks later he would celebrate Christmas in Geneva's splendid twelfth-century cathedral. His plans did not halt at Geneva: he was already assembling crews to cross the water and seize Lausanne and other lakeside towns which in earlier centuries had belonged to the Dukes of Savoy and the Kings of Burgundy.

The 'Escalade'

Everything went according to plan. It was a cold, misty night, dry and without snow underfoot. As soon as darkness fell the duke's forces moved on Geneva from their camps ten and fifteen miles away; when they were within earshot they followed the Arve so that the sound of its waters covered the clank of armor. Peasants were arrested on the road to stop them giving the alarm; and around midnight most of the little army was at Plainpalais, only three hundred yards from the south gate, and undetected. The scaling party moved towards the walls, with their arms and equipment muffled, across what is now the Place Neuve, and across the moat which today forms the rue de la Corraterie. The Scottish Jesuit Alexander Hume had issued them with amulets inscribed with biblical texts as a sure guarantee against a violent end, and he stood at the foot of the ladders, murmuring in the Savoyards' own speech* '*Monta pi, braves zjin, ye lou-z-egras du paradis*'. ('Get climbing, men, they are the steps of paradise').

Around one o'clock, when there was still no moon, most of the three hundred men were up the three ladders and inside the walls, and there had still been no alert. Albigny, in overall command, said 'The town is ours', and the main force prepared to move up. Word was passed back to Charles Emmanuel, who immediately sent off couriers to the courts at Paris, Rome and Madrid to report that Geneva was in his hands; and the same news went the rounds in Savoy, Piedmont and Dauphiné.

Charles's delight was premature. Brignolet had intended to keep his men squatting or lying quietly for some three hours, but their luck did not hold; the outcome would probably have been very different if he had gone into action without waiting for the moon. In any event a sentry near by on the Tour de la Monnaie heard something; another man was sent to check; and, when he gave the alarm, the 300 Savoyards quickly left a group to guard the ladders and at last set about attacking the Porte Neuve and two other targets. They overpowered the Genevese manning the gate but failed to blow it or to stop a guard from lowering the portcullis. Hearing the din of battle Albigny's men advanced to the gate and were surprised to find it denied to them. They had no choice but to withdraw.

This was the turning point. Surprise had been lost and the Genevese were already rushing to arms, many half-dressed; and a lucky shot from a cannon knocked down the ladders, making the reinforcement of the now outnumbered Savoyards inside the walls impossible. A fortnight later someone was to write in a letter that, when the Spanish regulars in Albigny's forces were appealed to for help, they declared that their dignity would only permit them to enter the city

---

* i.e. Franco-Provençal or 'Burgundian', which was also the speech of Geneva – used in the Escalade song which immortalized the episode. See p. 243.

through the gate. Once again Charles must have felt let down by Spain despite his devoted championship (as he saw it) of the Catholic and Hapsburg cause.[18]

Meanwhile a few hundred of the citizens had joined the fray with any weapon to hand. It was now that the legendary housewife Mère Royaume, living by the Tour de la Monnaie, assailed one of the invaders with an iron tureen in which she was cooking soup for her husband.[19] Fifty-four of the Savoyards were cut down in the streets; fourteen were captured; some got away by leaping from the walls back into the Corraterie moat; others fell to their death, and one landed on Alexander Hume, hurting him gravely. All was over long before dawn, and after upbraiding Albigny with 'You've made a fine mess of it', Charles hurried back to Turin without an apparent thought for his dead and wounded troops. The Savoyard prisoners were summarily executed by the Genevese; their heads and those of the dead were put on show along the walls and the bodies cast into the Rhône.

This little midnight skirmish has come to be known as the Escalade. Its anniversary, marked by the singing of an anthem in debased Franco-Provençal, is celebrated by the townsfolk of Geneva as their independence day – processions in costume wind through the 'Vieille Ville', with women fittingly armed with soup-tureens. At first Charles would not accept the outcome, and even now Burgundy seemed to mean more to him than the prospects open in Italy: when Henry IV of France sought to oust him from Gaul by offering him Lombardy in exchange for Savoy, Charles countered by ludicrously proposing to give Henry Milan, which was not his anyway, for Bresse and the Duchy of Burgundy!

Not until 1754 did Savoy finally recognize the independence of Geneva.

The death of the dream

Charles Emmanuel was the last prince to have a chance of bringing the Burgundian phoenix back to life, and it was Burgundy's misfortune not to have a finer champion at that moment of crisis. Charles of Anjou's attempt to set up an independent Kingdom of Burgundy had to be abandoned because of the Sicilian Vespers, and Charles the Bold's collapsed with his defeat by the Swiss. But for these events both men had a good prospect of succeeding. Charles Emmanuel's prospects were always worse than theirs, even though his kingdom, through corresponding the most closely with the ancient homeland, would have been the 'most Burgundian' of them; and the importance of the

Escalade in Burgundian history is not that it frustrated a nearly successful attempt, but rather that it finally put paid to serious ambition to restore the Kingdom. The Escalade has another significance for us: it is one of history's many strange symmetries that this last endeavor should be frustrated on the battlements of the Kingdom's first capital city.

The end of the last Kingdom of Burgundy

The disasters brought on them by Charles Emmanuel's pursuit of a crown were rightly judged by some Savoyards as presaging the end of their country which would now, they foresaw, become a mere dependency of Piedmont. From now on, indeed, the Duchy of Savoy would have an Italian rather than a Burgundian destiny.

The Italianization of the Dukes of Savoy from Charles Emmanuel onwards did not prevent their becoming satellites of France. In 1685 Louis XIV instructed Duke Victor-Amadeus to wipe out the Valdensian heretics whose persecution in the previous generation had been immortalized by Milton's famous sonnet (see page 93). The duke prevaricated and complied only with reluctance, and the Valdensians put up such heroic resistance that he conceded their request to be allowed to migrate to Protestant Switzerland, but three years later they decided to return, preferring persecution at home to safety in a foreign land.

The strain which this disagreeable episode placed on their relations was a factor in inducing Victor-Amadeus to break with Louis XIV and support Austria and England in the War of the Spanish Succession. His exploits and those of Prince Eugene of Savoy, the leader of the Hapsburg armies and together with Marlborough the architect of Louis XIV's defeat, were instrumental in the elevation of Savoy, at long last, to a kingdom. By the Treaty of Utrecht (1713) the duke acquired Sicily with the title of king, in a union of territories which was not very dissimilar to those of Charles of Anjou some 450 years before. However, a few years later the new king was obliged by the other European powers to exchange Sicily for Sardinia, and so it was as the Kingdom of Sardinia that 'Burgundy' regained a crown! It was a true Kingdom of Burgundy in that it comprised a large part of the Homeland of the original Burgundian settlers: the lesser kingdom of Godegisel and of Rudolf I, that is, not the greater kingdom of Gundobad, Rudolf II or Barbarossa. This was the ancient patrimony of the Savoyards, the lands between lake Geneva, Dauphiné and the Alps, but it was no longer the hub of their territories, and the capital of their kingdom lay elsewhere, at Turin. Moreover the Savoyard kings were now little concerned with Burgundy; Victor-Amadeus dreamed rather of winning Naples and Milan, and of chasing the Austrians and French from Italy, thus achieving both his dynasty's and the peninsula's destiny in a united Kingdom of Italy.

Under Napoleon Savoy-Piedmont was absorbed in France for a second time. When it gained its freedom once more in 1815 few can still have dreamt of Savoy as the nucleus of a great kingdom in south-east Gaul. Those days had passed with Charles Emmanuel, the cession of Bresse and the Escalade of Geneva. Loyalty to the restored House of Savoy had become fragile and it was only a matter of time before the fate of the western territories of their kingdom was again in question. The outcome is well-known: Cavour and Victor-Emmanuel agreed in 1858 to surrender the area to Napoleon III in return for his support in their Italian ambitions, and in the referendum of April 1860 Savoy-in-Gaul inevitably chose France rather than Italy – independence was not an option offered. With this third and doubtless final annexation Burgundy's aspirations ended, as they began, in Savoy: Sapaudia was both Burgundy's cradle and its grave.

REMNANTS AND REFLECTIONS

A Language without a Country

The passing of a forgotten land

Where should the story of Burgundy be brought to an end? Not as early as 1477, even though the prospects of a great Middle Kingdom died on the field of Nancy, nor in 1544 when Charles the Bold's great-grandson the Emperor Charles V renounced the Duchy? Perhaps in 1602 when Savoy's hopes of restoring the Kingdom were stifled on the battlements of Geneva, and so it was virtually inevitable that Savoy would become an Italian state rather than survive as a mini-Burgundy, a small kingdom embracing the old Homeland? Or in 1678 when, after two generations of heroic resistance, the County of Burgundy at last fell to France? But two later dates can arguably be taken as the final curtain-drop of all: 1806, when the French snuffed out any remaining pretension to the Kingdom of Burgundy or the Arelate by dissolving the Holy Roman Empire, and so its constituent kingdoms; or 1860, when Savoy-in-Gaul, given the choice of Italy or France, chose union with the latter.

In any event the ancient Kingdom of Burgundy is now divided between its neighbors, and forgotten. The bulk of it has been absorbed in France: the Duchy and County of Burgundy, Forez, Lyonnais, Savoy, Dauphiné and Provence. The Val d'Aosta is a region of Italy. The rest – the country between Geneva and Basle together with the Valais – has joined the Swiss Confederation. Strangely, not one single village of Burgundy lies in Germany, the chief successor state of the Holy Roman Empire, even though Burgundy formed part of the Empire for so long.

Burgundy can now only be said to live on in its offspring, the Netherlands, Belgium, Luxemburg and Italy; and as part of France and of Switzerland, perhaps above all in Geneva and the Suisse Romande, not only because their inhabitants descend from the first Burgundian settlers, but because they are the areas of Burgundy least under the influence of alien cultures and so perhaps closest to what may today be left of the Burgundian ethos.

For most people 'Burgundy' spells wine; for some the rolling countryside of the Côte d'Or and the open Saône valley south of Dijon which once formed the Duchy of Burgundy; and for those very few who have heard of the *Kingdom* of Burgundy it is no more than one of those historical oddities which light up the past for a while and then fade into oblivion. What evidence can one produce today that the Kingdom ever existed? Its old administrative boundaries have disappeared, excepting only its south-eastern border in so far as it ran along the Alpine watershed which now divides France and Italy. It is true that the four regions of Burgundy have largely survived: the 'Allemannic' as the bulk of German Switzerland, the other three as administrative regions of present-day France: old Provence as Provence-Côte d'Azur, the Burgundian Homeland* as Rhône-Alpes, and the ancient Duchy as Bourgogne. But the *Kingdom* of Burgundy, the Greater Burgundy, has wholly disappeared. When the name Bourgogne became confined to the modern region just referred to – the departments of Saône-et-Loire, Côte d'Or, Yonne and Nièvre – this was no more than political recognition of what the French naturally regard as the reality: Bourgogne, for most of them, is and was the area of the ancient Duchy, hardly more, hardly less; and it is that Burgundy and not the lost Kingdom which the schoolchildren of Saône-et-Loire are taught to cherish when they sing that they are proud to be Burgundians.

For modern 'Burgundian' writers who remain conscious of their 'country's' spirit of unity and individuality despite the all-absorbing power of Paris, Burgundy stretches beyond the Duchy, but still only as far as Bresse and Bugey, Lyons like Troyes being excluded from it. Only an author who is as steeped in Burgundy's origins and history as was Chaume regards Lyons, Vienne, Feurs, Geneva and Saint Maurice d'Agaune as Burgundian.

If today there is no trace of the Kingdom of Burgundy in administration, so also there is none in law. Gundobad's Lex Gambetta no more survives in Chambéry and Geneva than in Dijon or Marseilles. Nor is there point in looking for traces of a greater Burgundy in custom or folklore, and the costumes still preserved today derive from a period when Burgundy had already become France, Switzerland or Italy. The only visible evidence of the one-time unity of a Burgundy much larger than the Duchy will be found in architecture. There is an obvious affinity between the older churches of Savoy, western Switzerland, Lyonnais, and the Duchy and County of Burgundy; and the traveler may also be

---

* Lyonnais, which spoke 'Burgundian', was thus part of 'Burgundian' Burgundy; but it was not part of the Homeland, and it is now very roughly preserved in another region, Rhône-Loire. The County of Burgundy forms the Franche-Comté region. See endpaper map.

conscious of an affinity in the ancient streets of the cities of those regions. Even though there is little domestic architecture left today from before the seventeenth century, the centers of Lyons, Geneva and Dijon, for instance, seem to have something in common which distinguishes them from northern French, Provençal, German-Swiss or Italian towns. The traveler may also sense that he is crossing a frontier as he drives from Mâconnais northwards into the Duchy; or off La Montagne into Champagne or the Ile de France; or leaving the Reuss and the Allemannic region behind and entering Swiss cantons which were never part of the Kingdom. Yet we must concede that it is usually more difficult to recognize the external boundaries of ancient Burgundy than to tell when we are crossing an internal one, passing for instance from Burgundy proper into the Allemannic region: as one leaves behind Romont and Avenches in the Suisse Romande and comes into Bern or Luzern the border is clear, unlike for example the old boundary between Burgundy and France in Forez. In the first case the language frontier has survived, in the second it has disappeared, and with it one of the last remnants of 'Burgundy'.

To what extent the language has survived at all is a matter for the pages which follow.

Savoy and Franco-Provençal: remnants barely vanished

If this book had been written a hundred years or so earlier, say before 1860,* it would doubtless have remarked that all three of the ancient kingdoms of the Holy Roman Empire had long been prevented from recovering their identity by the intrusion of the chief continental powers, Germany and Italy being frustrated by Austria and Burgundy by France; that, unlike their situation four or even three centuries before, Germany and Italy** now had far more of their past identities – national sentiment, literature and so forth – to build on than Burgundy had; and that there was only one substantial remnant left to Burgundy, not indeed a foundation for any future recovery but only evidence of a receding past: this was the little homeland state of Savoy, at that time almost concealed in the heterogeneous Kingdom of Sardinia. A book written in those days would have made no mention of the other important remnant, the

---

* The project was conceived, and research started, in the nineteen-sixties.
** It would have been good to have had space to contrast the fate of Burgundy with that of Germany and Italy more than is done on pp. 226–7.

Franco-Provençal language which was to prevail throughout Savoy and beyond for two or three generations after that, because it was only identified by Ascoli in the eighteen-eighties. Each of these remnants deserves a few paragraphs.

Savoy: the Phoenix risen?

It is not in Savoy, generally speaking, that the traveler should expect to find the finest examples of Burgundian civilization. There is little to compare with the many relics of the magnificent Grand Dukes of the West, in Bruges, Ghent and elsewhere, or with Romanesque treasures like Saint Trophîme of Arles and Saint Sauveur of Aix-en-Provence, which recall to us such brilliant figures as Frederick Barbarossa and Charles of Anjou. The extreme north and extreme south of this long and elusive Middle Kingdom are admittedly not central to our story, and we are concerned rather with the regions where the early Burgundians settled, however lightly. However, Savoy also cannot compare with Lyonnais and the Duchy of Burgundy for relics of the remarkable renaissance of the tenth, eleventh and twelfth centuries: the cross-vaulting of Tournus, a reminder of the Second Kingdom's repulse of the Magyar 'ogres'; the enchanting sculpture of Charlieu and Anzy-le-Duc, and the magnificent churches of Paray-le-Monial, Vézelay, Autun and Pontigny. Nor has Savoy any architecture to match the churches which demonstrate the Burgundians' civilizing role all over Latin Christendom, such as Castle Acre in Norfolk and Fountains and Rievaulx in Yorkshire; nor to compare with Saint Martin of Clamecy and Notre Dame of Dijon, examples of the remarkable early Gothic style which was not to mature in Burgundy itself but rather in England, for instance at Lincoln and York.

However, in the early churches at Geneva, Saint Maurice d'Agaune and Aime, Savoy in the wider sense can boast of some of the most important evidence of the civilization of the First Kingdom; and few countries can show the traveler a finer collection of medieval castles than Chillon, Grandson, Morat, Lucens, Romont and (over in Franco-Provençal Italy) Fenis and Verres. Probably no Savoyard church deserves a detour more than Brou, in the outskirts of Bourg-en-Bresse. The edifice is not remarkable or specially 'Burgundian'. Inside, however, stand the splendidly wrought tombs of Duke Philibert (1497–1504) and his more illustrious consort Margaret of Austria, granddaughter of Charles the Bold and Regent of Burgundy (i.e. the Hapsburg-owned Low Countries). But of even greater interest is the carving of the oak stalls, which is in the highest tradition of Burgundian art and recalls the realism of the Cluniac sculptors of the early twelfth century.

Bourg has a better Savoyard pedigree than its location so far to the north-west might suggest. A hundred years before the building of Brou the town was a favorite residence of the remarkable Amadeus VIII, the principal constructor of the state of Savoy; and, had he not inherited a great part of Piedmont and had instead maintained his interest in Bresse, the Duchy's center of gravity might never have shifted to Italy, in which case our story would probably have ended very differently.

As it is, the qualified success story of Savoy allows us to suggest that Burgundy's failure was not total: in a limited sense the Phoenix did rise again. The greater Burgundy of the Kingdom fought gamely for life but in vain; but the lesser Burgundy of the Homeland, the little state of Godegisel and Rudolf, seized it firmly, being restored by the counts of Savoy and built into a Renaissance and then a modern mini-kingdom by Amadeus VIII and Emmanuel Philibert whose ambitions, unlike those of the three Charleses, were ruled by prudence and moderation. It is no mean achievement that the small country which has been absorbed by France in these past hundred years should, like the phoenix, have endured before that for six centuries.*

When the Kingdom of Savoy-Sardinia disappeared, divided between France and the new Kingdom of Italy, a majority of its people spoke Piedmontese or other Italian dialects. Up to Amadeus VIII's inheritance of Piedmont early in the fifteenth century Savoy was a far more homogeneous country, speaking from top** to bottom a single language, Franco-Provençal or Burgundian as it is fair to call it. Savoy failed to survive as a remnant of old Burgundy; but the language of what is now French Savoy managed to survive and may well continue to do so. Architecture and successor states apart, this is the main remnant left to us of all that once was Burgundy.***

The 'annihilation of the rags and tatters of Feudalism and Slavery'

For the past hundred years Franco-Provençal has been ranked by philologists along with the Langue d'Oc, the Langue d'Oïl, Italian, Iberian and

---

* Or five if one excludes the disastrous mid-fifteenth to mid-sixteenth.
** The counts of the thirteenth century and earlier almost certainly had Franco-Provençal as their first language. Those of the fourteenth century may have been brought up on French.
*** Map no. 20 shows the Franco-Provençal area and Savoy's territories in the Kingdom of Burgundy at their greatest extent.

Romanian*, as one of the dozen or so languages or dialectical groups which developed from the everyday Latin encountered by the races which settled in the disintegrating Roman Empire.

The extent of the Langue d'Oc, Langue d'Oïl and Franco-Provençal is shown on Map no. 24. From the ninth to the twelfth centuries there were only insignificant changes in these frontiers, although it must be stressed that some borders were more blurred than others, notably that in Mâconnais and Franche Comté (the County of Burgundy). The most important movement began in the twelfth or thirteenth century with the barely perceptible advance of the dialect of Paris and the Ile de France ('Francien' which became 'French'), which had the great advantage of being the language of the French court and, in so far as Latin was not used, of the administration. In the thirteenth to fifteenth centuries French was increasingly used for the written word in the other Langue d'Oïl areas, but as medium of speech it hardly displaced the local vernacular, Picard, Champenois, Bourguignon and so forth. In the Langue d'Oc and Franco-Provençal areas which came under French rule, the French language made even less headway. Not only did the regional vernaculars continue to be spoken, but here they were still written as well, indeed increasingly, for the crown accepted that they should be normal usage in public documents and in law courts, and there were several ordinances prescribing the use of the vernacular issued in the fifteenth century and later, one example being that issued by the Parlement of Dauphiné in 1531.

In 1539 there was a reversal of policy throughout France. The story goes that a provincial nobleman who had come to Paris for a lawsuit used his execrable French to tell the king, Francis I, of the court's judgement and committed a schoolboy howler which at first caused the king much mirth but later made him reflect. He decided that French must thenceforth be used for all official purposes everywhere, and in the ordinance of Villers-Cotterets of 1539 he decreed that deeds and contracts were valid only if they were written in French. We need not look far for the reasons of state behind Francis's decision: so long as the provincial languages persisted so also could separatism. The edict had the desired effect only very slowly; the dialects were progressively less used for the written word, but in many parts dialectal literatures still flourished and the vernacular was spoken as universally as before, except where as in the larger

---

* Philologists group the dialects somewhat differently, but there is general agreement on the distinctiveness of Franco-Provençal hardly less than of Langue d'Oc and Langue d'Oïl. See Appendix II.

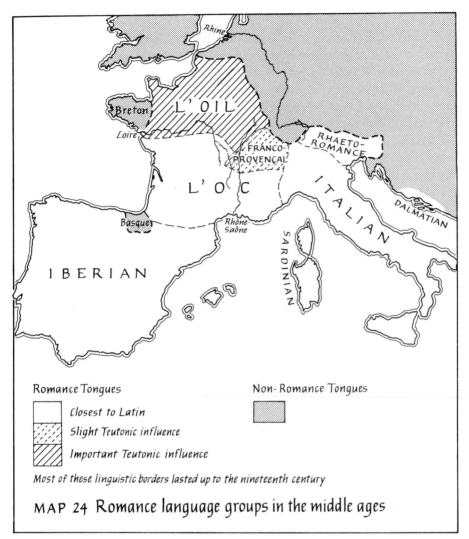

Romance Tongues

☐ Closest to Latin

▨ Slight Teutonic influence

▨ Important Teutonic influence

Non-Romance Tongues

▨

Most of these linguistic borders lasted up to the nineteenth century

MAP 24 Romance language groups in the middle ages

Map no. 24 In the Middle Ages Sardinian may have been the 'most Latin' of all the languages/dialects shown. The others unshaded (Iberian to Rhaeto-Romance) had moved away from Latin in different respects without being 'Teutonised'. The hatched areas were under Teutonic influence, 'L'Oïl' considerably, Franco-Provençal less so. The shaded areas were Teutonic (German, etc), Breton, Basque or Slavonic. Arabic areas (considerable in Spain, Portugal and Sicily) are not shown.

towns French became the language of the educated; and an official enquiry* conducted shortly after the Revolution sharpened the concern of the Convention that the dialects should have survived so tenaciously, and it called for their 'annihilation'. The result was the interdiction 'from all regions of France of the jargons which are the rags and tatters of feudalism and slavery', and the establishment of a State school, where only French could be used, in every commune.** Yet seventy years after this the census of 1863 revealed that at least one quarter of the population still had little or no French.

In 1867 the French philosopher and social reformer Pierre Joseph Proudhon wrote of the 'French nation one and indivisible' as comprising in fact 'twenty nations', and he listed them as 'Flemings, Germans, Ligurians, Corsicans, Basques, Celts, Norsemen, Lorrainers, Burgundians, Provençalers' and so on. '*Le français est un être de convention, il n'existe pas . . .*' Then, in a less easily sustainable passage, he asserted: '*Une nation si grande ne tient qu'à l'aide de la force. L'armée permanente sert surtout à cela. Otez cet appui à l'administration et à la police centrale, la France tombe en fédéralisme. Les attractions locales l'emportent*'.*** Proudhon proved to be right for the wrong reason: the French army did indeed prove to be the greatest force for national unity, for it was the great leveler of military service in the holocaust of 1914–18 which fashioned Frenchmen out of patois-speaking peasants. Even after the war there were probably fewer Frenchmen with French than with a dialect or another language as their mother tongue.

The survival of 'Burgundian'

The language group which philologists call Franco-Provençal, and which should more properly be called 'Burgundian', survived longer than most of the Romance dialects of Gaul. From the eighth to the eighteenth century, a period of one thousand years,**** it was dominant from Forez, deep in France, to beyond Neuchâtel, Sion, Aosta and Grenoble, an area larger than Denmark,

* By Abbé Gregoire. It said 'At least six million French, above all in the countryside, are ignorant of the national language; an equal number are more or less incapable of carrying on a conversation [in French]; in effect [*en dernier resultat*] the number of those who speak it purely does not exceed three millions and, probably, the number of those who write it correctly is still less'. The population of France was about 24 million.
** Law of 21 October 1793.
*** *France et Rhin*, 1867.
**** English, as a comparably formed and stable language, is not more than 600 years old.

Switzerland or Belgium. We can calculate from the census in 1863 (see Appendix II) that 2½ million French citizens still had 'Burgundian' rather than French as mother tongue. When account is taken of the peasants and townsfolk of the Suisse Romande and of north-west Italy, the total in the whole of 'old Burgundy' still speaking the ancient language comfortably exceeded three million, roughly the population at that time of Denmark or Switzerland, and greater than that of three countries which were later to become states, Finland, Norway and Ireland. Thanks to education most of those three-million-plus became bilingual in the decades on either side of 1900, but French had not displaced 'Burgundian' as the mother tongue of the majority until fifty years or so ago in the lands west of the Alps and Jura; and the process has been even slower in the more mountainous parts of the Suisse Romande.

The resurgence of 'Burgundian' in north-west Italy

Thus only two or three generations ago 'Burgundian' was a living language still in general use over most of Lyonnais and the ancient Homeland; and, as Map no. 25 and Appendix II demonstrate, it is still spoken even today in parts of the old area where it reigned for ten centuries. There are still several thousands in Switzerland and France who use the 'Burgundian' patois for everyday speech. But it is rather to north-west Italy that we must turn to find a definable compact region where 'Burgundian' is not only deeply implanted but is the prevailing language. The Val d'Aosta amounts very roughly to a thousand square miles, comparable in extent therefore to counties like Hereford and the former Westmorland in England and Dumfries in Scotland, although somewhat less populous. In the census of 1971, out of the Aosta valley's population of 109,252 about 70,000 gave French or 'its dialects' (i.e. Franco-Provençal) as mother tongue. In 1979 it was reliably estimated that the total population was some 115,000, that in fact only two or three thousand families spoke French, and that well over 50,000 people in the valley – perhaps 70,000 – spoke Franco-Provençal.

Thanks to the autonomy granted to the valley in 1948 local organizations can promote the use of the dialect and help preserve it from further encroachment by Italian, and there are signs that it may one day achieve a status as secure and respectable as, for instance, Romansch has in south-east Switzerland. Today the dialect, unlike French, is no longer in retreat and in the mountains and even in parts of the plain it is indeed regaining lost ground. It is spoken by the young

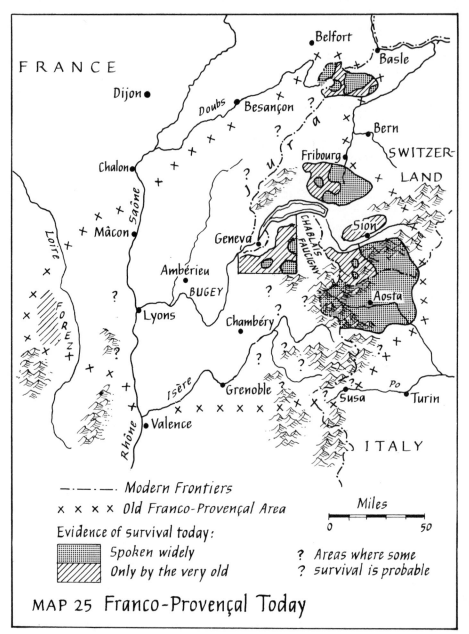

Belfort

FRANCE

Dijon

Doubs Besançon

Basle

Bern

SWITZER-

Fribourg   LAND

Chalon

Saône

Mâcon

Loire

CHABLAIS
FAUCIGNY

Sion

Geneva

Ambérieu

BUGEY

Aosta

?

Lyons

Chambéry

?

FOREZ

?

?

?

Isère

Grenoble

Po

Susa   Turin

Rhône

Valence

ITALY

—·—·— Modern Frontiers

× × × × Old Franco-Provençal Area

Evidence of survival today:

Miles

0   50

Spoken widely

Only by the very old

? Areas where some
? survival is probable

MAP 25 Franco-Provençal Today

Map no. 25 Evidence of the survival of Franco-Provençal in Switzerland and Italy is reliable, whereas in France it is patchy or not very up to date. In an area south of Ambérieu well known to the author in the early nineteen-seventies, it was then still spoken by a few old folk who will mostly have died in the meantime. It must be stressed that in the area in question the patois could be expected to perish relatively quickly, since it is open country close to modern civilization and major traffic routes. In parts more remote than this the patois may well be surviving more strongly. For instance, south and east of Geneva (see the box), and in Chablais and Faucigny, there is firm evidence of its survival.

more than it used to be and, except for immigrants from the south, parents rarely speak French or Italian to their children but rather Franco-Provençal. It is increasingly used by drama groups and song-writers, and by priests in their sermons. In some communes no speech but the dialect will ever be heard, except in post offices and other official buildings.

In earlier times the old language was not used in north-west Italy for writing, as it was in France and Switzerland until only three or four generations or so ago, but in the nineteen-sixties and seventies a modern spelling has been developed and used for present-day songs and old carols, for plays, for notices and posters, and in the schools where research into the origins of the dialect has been going on since 1962. While one magazine does not make a literature, the *Valdostani* can boast of having a periodical in their language, '*Lo Flambo*'.

Franco-Provençal is holding on with less tenacity further south, in the Susa, Orco and Soana valleys, for instance near Locana which after all is only some twenty miles north-west of Turin, but here the patois-speakers do not enjoy the protection afforded to the *Valdostani* by the autonomy statute.

100,000 speakers of 'Burgundian' today

Counting the Franco-Provençal regions of France and Switzerland as well as those of Italy, the grand total of 'Burgundian speakers' today is very probably close to 100,000. Few of them are aware of their Burgundian origins, but most of them have a sense of shared identity to which some 'nationalists' in the Val d'Aosta give the name 'Harpitan'; dreamers among them would like to create a new separate state of 'Harpitania' out of the Franco-Provençal valleys of Italy, Switzerland and France. *Valdostani* who are less militant still believe they share a wider loyalty with 'compatriots' from whom they are unhappily separated by a frontier only a century old, and they regard themselves as part of the 'Savoyard nation'; and *Valdostani* and *Valaisans*, from across the border in Switzerland, come together regularly to struggle for the survival of their language and culture.

Thus in France, where the overwhelming mass of 'Burgundian' speakers have been found for over a thousand years, 'Burgundian' is past regeneration like all other Romance dialects except for Occitan, as Provençal is usually called today; in Switzerland it similarly dies a lingering death; but in north-west Italy it lives on; and one may perhaps wonder if it might still have been spoken today in a region the size of a small European country, but for the insistence of

Switzerland, Italy (until recently) and particularly France on the use of their official languages. In 1860 a great many of the speakers of 'Burgundian' were citizens of an independent country, the Kingdom of Sardinia. However, with the vote of Savoy-in-Gaul for union with France, 'Burgundian' became a language without a country.*

The question of language must detain us a little longer.

* For the evidence on which this section is based see Appendix II, especially p. 240. Since this was set the author has obtained the most reliable figures possible of the numbers who today speak Welsh and Gaelic (Scots) as first language. No precision seems possible but it is clear that both totals are substantially less than the *c.* 100,000 who have Franco-Provençal as mother-tongue.

The Burgundian Phoenix,
the fabulous 'Might-have-been'

Language, the map-maker

The phoenix of myth was a fiction, a creature of fable and imagination. Despite neglect, misunderstanding and distortion, the Kingdom of Burgundy was by contrast not a myth but for hundreds of years historical fact. The fantasy lies rather in what might have been; what destinies the phoenix resurgent of Burgundy could well have enjoyed, given better fortune, and given above all a dynasty as successful as the Hapsburgs, Tudors, Valois and Bourbons, Romanovs or Vasa. Historians rightly eschew speculative fancy, and the justification for devoting the next few pages to it is that writers of high renown have been set to wondering about this might-have-been, probably the most fascinating of European history: Ranke, Burckhardt and Huizinga no less than Boehm, Calmette and Chaume. A slighter work may surely be granted a similar license and be allowed to ask whether Burgundy might have amounted to more than an ancient treasure-house of art, a mini-state which vanished a century ago, and a patois that survives strongly only in a region the size of a small English county.

The story of Burgundy is of enduring interest in its own right, but it is important also for the reflections it prompts on the waywardness of history and particularly, perhaps, on the manner in which we take for granted so much that has happened. There are also morals to be drawn from Burgundy's story, which a fuller study than this one could usefully consider, on the relationship between language and the concepts of people and nation, country and state. At least since the days of ancient Hellas and Judaea national consciousness has been associated with distinctiveness in language, and more recently it has been assumed that a people distinguished by its language should be entitled to independent statehood: that, at any rate in the Europe of the twentieth century, language should be chief cartographer, for is that not the usual meaning of 'self-determination'? Under this concept, states like Switzerland and Belgium may be regarded as aberrations which, but for good reasons of history, should 'logically' have been divided between their neighbors in accordance with their

[213]

languages, just as sixty years ago the great multilingual empire of the Hapsburgs was shattered into a patchwork of nation states with their borders based chiefly on language.

There was nothing pre-ordained about the frontiers of western Europe. How would the map of western Europe look today if in the age when the dozen Latin-based dialectal groups coalesced – Langue d'Oc, 'Franco-Provençal' and so forth – political frontiers had hardened along the frontiers of language? The vast area speaking Romance dialects in the Middle Ages, stretching from Celtic-speaking Brittany and Flemish Somme down to Sicily and the Algarve, would have had frontiers very different from those we know today. Gaul would have been divided into three parts, roughly Aquitaine-Provence, Burgundy, and a France confined north of the Loire.* France would stretch north-eastwards to Brussels, leaving the Flemish north of Belgium to be joined with the Netherlands. Burgundy would include western Switzerland and the north-west corner of Italy; and Catalonia might be joined with Aquitaine-Provence no more unhappily than it has been with Spain.

Language is not the only uniter and divider. The regions of the Romance world could have been grouped into nation states very different from those of modern times, had victories been defeats or had princesses been married off to other suitors. Geography, as well as dynastic marriage and war, has of course played an important part and so too have revolution and religion; but in serving to create 'nations' language has done as much as any of these features to draw the map of Europe. But one message from the story of Burgundy as of other parts of Gaul is that, while nations have often made states, states have also made nations. France, Burgundy's conqueror, is probably the most obvious European example of minorities abandoning their own language for that of the state which absorbed them, although the process of linguistic assimilation has nowhere been so successful as in the great new nation states of the western hemisphere.

'Burgundy proper' a more likely survivor than the Kingdom

Thus there was nothing predestined about the pattern of 'nation states' which have emerged in the past five centuries; and there was some 'historical bias' in

* The three Romance language groups: Langue d'Oc, Franco-Provençal and Langue d'Oïl respectively.

Burgundy's favor, because it had survived for so long and had a personality at least as clear-cut as, say, that of Italy or Germany. Not, that is, the *Kingdom* of Burgundy, which contained two areas which were hardly Burgundian: Provence and the Allemannic or Swiss region. 'Burgundy proper' comprised, as we have observed,* the regions we have termed 'Burgundian' and 'Frankish'. This is what Maurice Chaume, the historian with the strongest awareness of the Burgundian ethos, called the 'true Burgundy'. It stretched from Champagne to Dauphiné, adding Savoy, western Switzerland and Lyonnais to the Duchy and County of Burgundy. This Burgundy would have been relatively homogeneous both racially and linguistically, and probably by no coincidence this was the area of Burgundy's most distinctive feature, its medieval architecture. Indeed its racial, linguistic and artistic outlines bore a strikingly close relationship to one another – three very similar circles all with their hubs roughly at Geneva, as Map no. 17 demonstrates. In brief medieval Burgundy had an identity as clearly defined as most of Europe's 'countries', and as late as the fourteenth century it was easier to conceive of a Burgundian state than of an Italian, and 'Burgundy' was at least as much of a 'country' as Germany.

Here we may perhaps venture cautiously into the realms of speculation. The Ifs and Ans of history are beguiling playthings, and it has been difficult to resist the temptation to discuss, for instance, how significantly different the outcome would have been if Burgundy's native rulers before 1032 had not been Rudolfians but Capetians or better still Normans; or if the dynasties of Provence or Savoy had established themselves sufficiently widely to have gained recognition as sovereigns; or if the French had been defeated at Muret** in 1213 or denied Lyons or Dauphiné a century later. It seems more profitable, however, to consider the prospects of something which was hard fact: the often independent little state which dukes of Burgundy from Richard the Justiciar (880–921) onwards had built up intermittently over half a millennium and which came to what proved to be vital crossroads under Philip the Bold (1364–1404).

In his often nostalgic reflections on the fate of Burgundy, Chaume blamed the ultimate failure of the dukes on the choice of road which was forced on them by Philip's inheritance of the Low Countries through his wife Margaret in 1384. He recalled that since early in the fourteenth century the dukes had also ruled the County of Burgundy; and that their involvement in the Low

* Page 120 and Map no. 17 on p. 122.
** Near Toulouse, it was the victory which installed French power in the Midi. See p. 92.

[215]

Countries diverted the attention of Philip and his successors northwards when further expansion southwards, beyond the County towards Savoy, would have been more natural, extending their rule over the 'true Burgundy' lying between Champagne and Dauphiné.

The 'country' of Burgundy, Chaume's 'true Burgundy', was, on the basis of historical probability, more likely to be given political form by the dukes than by anyone else. In *A Study of History* Arnold Toynbee analyzed what types of contender were most likely to take over the political leadership of a society, and he noted that a state at the hub, as Savoy (with Geneva as its center) was in relation to 'Burgundy', was far less likely to succeed in unifying the society than a state on but inside the society's borders – the situation of the Duchy. The role of 'marchmen', as Toynbee called these successful champions of a culture, was played by the Romans on behalf of the Hellenic civilization, but it can also be ascribed for instance to the Prussians in Germany.* If the Duchy and County, as march provinces of Burgundy, failed to take over its leadership, then under Toynbee's analysis outsiders could be expected to do this instead.

A state composed of Chaume's true Burgundy was by no means so improbable a 'might-have-been'. Quite apart from its relative homogeneity of race, language and culture, and (assuming the success of the Valois dukes) the advantage of a strong dynasty, a kingdom of Burgundy of this scale would have had a better chance than either the Duchy alone or Savoy alone of withstanding the expansion of France. Moreover it would have enjoyed to a great extent the natural frontiers of the Rhône-Saône Basin – not that these would have been easily defensible but they would have had a measure of durability.

There is no need to conjecture at length as to how a kingdom of Burgundy of this nature might have come into existence. In happier circumstances success would probably have blessed the long, painstaking negotiations** between Charles the Bold and Yolande for some sort of union between Savoy and the Duchy of Burgundy, from which his northern, Teutonic territories might have been the most likely to break away in due course, leaving 'Burgundy proper' as a possibly more durable state; or, alternatively, marriage or inheritance might have united the Duchy and Savoy as they did the Duchy and the Low Countries, not to speak of Aragon and Castile or England and Scotland.

* Toynbee's fields of study were civilized societies like the Hellenic, Hindu, Sinic, Western, etc., not e.g. France, Germany or Italy. But this application to smaller areas he considered justifiable.

** Agreements dated 20 February 1471, 20 June and 1 July 1472, and 30 January 1475. Saint Genis, p. 467.

[216]

The dukes were not in fact successful in giving political unity to the 'Burgundian world'. They held and cemented the Duchy and County; they dominated Savoy briefly, but they never won Lyonnais or Dauphiné; and the part of Switzerland which belonged by nature to 'Burgundy proper' – the Suisse Romande – was the scene of Charles the Bold's military disasters of 1476; with the result that, when political unity came to the area (or rather to most of it), it was by the hand of an 'outsider', France.

The Valois dukes create a Middle Kingdom

Chaume's 'true Burgundy' – we may say the most 'natural' Burgundy – never came to anything, and instead history gives us a political phenomenon which is far more fascinating simply because it did happen and came close to amounting to much more.

The Duchy of Burgundy is perhaps most notable in European history as the scene of remarkable cultural achievements from the eleventh to the fifteenth centuries. But it also played two political roles: first as a political embodiment of the spirit of 'Burgundy', and secondly as the creator of the most real and most substantial 'Middle Kingdom' that ever appeared between France and Germany. The dukes were diverted from the first of these roles by their great inheritance of 1384; one can say that they failed as champions of 'Burgundy' largely because they found themselves the inheritors of Lotharingia. By contrast that inheritance was essential to their success in their second role as creators of the Middle Kingdom.

This Middle Kingdom is not the one over which Charles the Bold would have reigned had he made good the award of 1473. By pure coincidence that vast kingdom, extending from Friesland to the Mediterranean, was remarkably similar to the one allotted to Lothar at Verdun in 843,* and it proved to be no less of a will-of-the-wisp. The Middle Kingdom in question was, by contrast, very far from fantasy; it was no flash in the pan but hard and durable reality.

For three hundred years (c. 900–c. 1200) the dukes of Burgundy paid no homage to any sovereign. For the next two hundred they were feudatories of the French crown but they were quasi-independent for most of the time. By 1400 their territories extended from the North Sea to the Jura,** some in France,

* Less of course Italy. (Map no. 22B)
** They also had lands in the Arelate besides the County.

[217]

some in the Empire. Each Valois duke added and consolidated; homage to French king or to emperor became ever more nominal and rare; and the border between the dukes' lands in France and those in the Empire became ever more meaningless, until the Duchy was the great independent state we have briefly described above (page 161 onwards).

This uncrowned kingdom stretched from the North Sea to Switzerland – an area larger than England and far richer and more populous – when disaster overtook it at Nancy in January 1477. Historians not readily given to conjecture and speculation have wondered how it might have fared had Charles the Bold avoided conflict with the Swiss or had his battles with them not been so conclusive. Calmette commented on Charles's attempt to create a great, lasting and sovereign state that 'this ambition was very nearly achieved', adding that to argue that 'the failure of the venture was a foregone conclusion ... implies gratuitous acceptance of the dangerous dogma of historical determinism'. Huizinga similarly speculated as to what would have happened to Charles's empire had he won at either Grandson or Morat; or, we may add, had he assembled a larger army before moving on Nancy later that year (1476).[20] One way or another, Burgundy's survival was a more likely outcome than the actual event, since for half a century the dukes' state had been Christendom's first in power and efficiency, and to contemporary observers few can have seemed more sure of permanence on the map of Europe.

We are more conscious today of Burgundy's weaknesses than thinking people were in 1476. A state so extensive would have been gravely handicapped by its internal divisions of race, language, culture and custom – it was a true 'Middle Kingdom' between France and Germany in that it brought together the Romance and the Teutonic worlds – and it could hardly have coalesced as successfully as Spain did, let alone France; but its divisions were hardly sharper than Switzerland's or Belgium's in more recent times; and it would never have been subject to stresses from within as disruptive as those of the ramshackle Hapsburg empire which after all endured into the present century. Nor, we may suggest, need it have been broken in two by religious and political conflict as were the seventeen provinces of the Netherlands under Philip II of Spain and William the Silent, since it is hardly likely that Burgundian heirs of Charles the Bold would have adopted the deeply divisive policies of Philip and Alva; their interest would have lain in fostering the provinces' growing sense of national unity.*

* In 1531 Charles V built on the 'federal' experiments of Charles the Bold by establishing a Council of State for the co-ordination of policy throughout the seventeen provinces.

All in all there was a fair chance of Charles's empire, or the bulk of it, surviving until it was exposed to the sort of external pressures which arose from the expansionist policies of Louis XIV of France (1643–1715). (See Map no. 26) Then, with two centuries of consolidation behind it, might not Burgundy have withstood the French advance better than did the Hapsburgs in Flanders and Franche Comté? It could hardly have been as weakened as they were by the Thirty Years' War. It would very probably have had the support of England – in a sense England's support of the Low Countries' independence from the sixteenth to the twentieth century has constituted an extension of the old Anglo-Burgundian alliance* – and faced with such opposition Louis XIV might have been diverted in the direction chosen by other French kings bent on territorial expansion, towards the 'natural frontier' of the Alps and above all the wealth and glamor of Italy. In any event one is left wondering how much more substantial, solid,** powerful and durable a Burgundy modern history would have known if Charles the Bold's folly had not thrown the game away.

Most historians weighing up such imponderables would probably conclude that, although about half of the Valois dukes' Burgundy has survived in three independent states until today, the political edifice they put together before 1476 was never likely to endure throughout the half millennium since then. They would probably be right. For a while at least the advantages Burgundy had in the fifteenth century – it was rich, well governed, relatively compact and populous – might well have confirmed the winning lead which Burgundy had secured over the other new monarchies in the two preceding generations (pp. 160–2). But just as Portugal and Spain were to fall back and be overtaken by France and England; indeed just as Holland itself lost ground after its herculean efforts against Louis XIV's aggression, so this hypothetical Burgundy – in effect a much larger Holland – might in any case have gone into decline in, say, the early eighteenth century.

If this large conjectural Burgundy had disappeared from the map of Europe, say in the seventeenth or eighteenth century, it would have been a significant exception to the pattern of European history. All the states lying north or west of

---

* One must be careful not to carry this sort of speculation too far. In the circumstances visualized here the Netherlands might have been strong enough for England to fear more than she did fear them at the time of Cromwell and Charles II (might Holland in these circumstances have been able to hold on to colonies she actually lost? Might New York now still be New Amsterdam?!) But in the final analysis England would generally have backed the 'Burgundians' (Dutch, etc.) against an expansionist France.

** Even as things are we must recognize that the three North Burgundy countries have in the last generation partially 'solidified' in the union called Benelux.

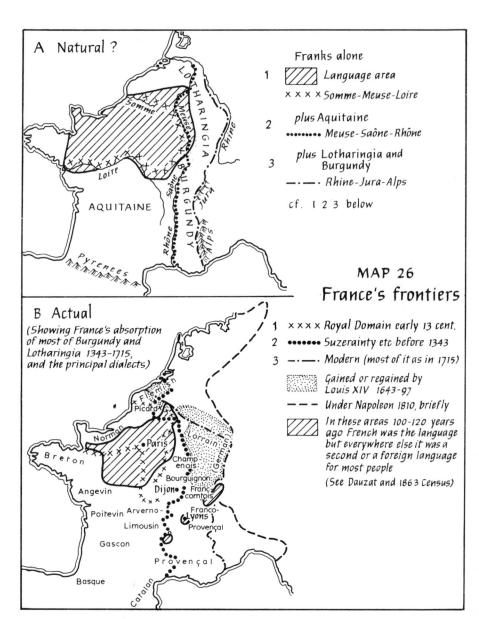

A Natural ?

Franks alone

1 ////// Language area
  x x x x Somme-Meuse-Loire

2 *plus* Aquitaine
  •••••••• Meuse-Saône-Rhône

3 *plus* Lotharingia and
    Burgundy
  —·—· Rhine-Jura-Alps

cf. 1 2 3 below

LOTHARINGIA
Somme
Meuse
Rhine
Loire
BURGUNDY
Saône
Jura
Rhône
Alps
AQUITAINE
Pyrenees

MAP 26
France's frontiers

B Actual

(Showing France's absorption
of most of Burgundy and
Lotharingia 1343-1715,
and the principal dialects)

1 x x x x Royal Domain early 13 cent.
2 ••••••• Suzerainty etc before 1343
3 —·—· Modern (most of it as in 1715)

::::::: Gained or regained by
        Louis XIV 1643-97

— — — Under Napoleon 1810, briefly

////// In these areas 100-120 years
       ago French was the language
       but everywhere else it was a
       second or a foreign language
       for most people

(See Dauzat and 1863 Census)

Flemish
Picard
Norman
Paris
Lorrain
Breton
Champ-
enois
Bourguignon
Angevin
Dijon
Franc-
comtois
Poitevin
Arverno-
Limousin
Franco-
Lyons
Provençal
Gascon
Provençal
Basque
Catalan

Map no. 26 Many French have believed that France has 'natural frontiers': the sea, the Rhine-Jura-Alps to the east, and the Pyrenees to the south. Under Napoleon those frontiers were achieved for a while, with something to spare; and France has those frontiers today except for the Rhine north of Strasbourg. But less extensive frontiers would also have been 'natural'. Indeed the Meuse and Saône formed the approximate eastern frontier of France (the Kingdom of the West Franks) until the 17th C., together with the Rhône until the 14th C. 'Natural frontiers' related to language would have been the Somme, Meuse and Loire, i.e. Neustria, or west Francia without the Franks' conquests in Burgundy and Aquitaine.

Louis XIV was turned back from his high-water mark of 1697 by William III of England and Holland: he was the embodiment of the Anglo-Burgundian alliance.

the Holy Roman Empire which enjoyed independence in the sixteenth century have survived until the present day. The new monarchies established before 1600 were the nation states of 1850 – France, Spain, Portugal, England, Sweden, Denmark and Scotland,* together with Savoy, a duchy in the fifteenth century, a kingdom in the eighteenth. The outline of modern Switzerland, a state which never had its own monarchy, dates from the first half of the sixteenth century; the Netherlands and Belgium from the second half, the former in revolt from the Hapsburgs, the latter then still in subjection to them. Thus, apart by and large from France's eastern frontier, the map of 1850 was little different from that of 1600, the frontiers of today** appearing in the seventy years which followed 1850. In particular, Germany and Italy emerged as Savoy was being absorbed by France; so that the outstanding changes in the last half-millennium involved the three kingdoms of the Holy Roman Empire: Germany and Italy united, Burgundy shattered!

Charles the Bold's Middle Kingdom: vicissitudes 1643–1945

So much for the fantasy: the fact is that the richer half of Charles the Bold's empire did survive and still does. The Duchy of Burgundy was the only large territory to fall to France, the lion's share of Charles's domains going, as we have said, to his Hapsburg descendants. When Louis XIV acceded in 1643, the Hapsburg portion – this shattered Middle Kingdom – was still about as large as England, even if the Rhine is taken as its eastern border and Holland excluded, for France's limits were then on the Saône and the Meuse and barely passed the Somme. Her advance towards the 'natural frontiers' of the Rhine and Alps*** was not by any means single-minded, and there were periods when Louis listened to those, above all his great minister Colbert (1661–83),**** who

* England and Scotland formed a union in 1707, on which more below: Scotland has certainly not disappeared!

** We are obviously not concerned here with the changes made by Soviet expansionism to eastern Germany and to Poland's frontiers.

*** Map no. 26.

**** Louis XIV effectively chose expansion eastward, rather than expansion overseas, in the period of Colbert's decline. Colbert, advocate of colonial and commercial power, found France with 18 warships in 1661 and left her with 276 on his death in 1683. He gave France navy conscription; her army conscription dates only from Napoleon. See, e.g., Murat, Inès: *Colbert* (1980). Map no. 26 shows France's eastern expansion under Louis XIV up to 1697. The 'advance' from the Meuse-Saône line may be dated from 1679 with the so-called '*politique des réunions*'.

urged political and economic consolidation more or less within France's existing frontiers, and advocated expansion overseas rather than towards the Rhine. At any rate France's *Drang nach Osten* achieved only partial success: the state of Burgundy may have been destroyed but its remnants continued largely unconquered, and in the end France did not gain more than a limited stretch of the Rhine – from Strasbourg to Basle. Only under Napoleon did the French fully attain the Rhine-Alps line.* In the early years of this century the Rhine was at no point under French control; and, although in 1919 France again took over Alsace and Lorraine, the survival since 1815 of the Netherlands, Belgium and Luxemburg (as well as of Switzerland) bears witness to the ultimate failure of France to absorb more than half of Charles the Bold's Middle Kingdom.

A final word about the Middle Kingdom which, we should recall, first appeared in the ninth century, only to split into three almost at once.** In this section we have not been concerned with the central part which has survived in the form of Switzerland and, until 1860, Savoy, or with the southern portion which was revived in the following decade in the Kingdom of Italy. We have been involved with the northern part, Lotharingia, which emerged again under the Burgundian dukes in the fifteenth century – a middle kingdom which has survived in the Netherlands, Belgium and Luxemburg. It needs no fantasy or speculation to conclude that this form of the 'Middle Kingdom' might have taken several different shapes from the patchwork we assume today to be the final (and now immutable?) outcome. The possibilities were almost infinite, ranging perhaps from the Meuse-Saône line laid down at Verdun in 843, which was not far from the border which Colbert was ready to accept, to the French high-water mark under Napoleon (Map no. 26). Where the 'west Franks'' frontier has been since 843 has determined the size of the Middle Kingdom – initially Lotharingia and the ancient kingdom of Burgundy and its components (notably the Duchy and County of Burgundy and Savoy), and later Burgundy's successor states, the Netherlands, Belgium, Luxemburg and Switzerland.

---

* Napoleon III hoped to emulate him; but, far from achieving the Rhine-Alps frontier (notably by absorbing Belgium), he lost Alsace and Lorraine.

** All of the lands mentioned here formed part of the Middle Kingdom of Lothar (843). Alsace and Lorraine were part of the Empire (Germany) from the tenth century until conquered by Louis XIV in the seventeenth, and reverted to Germany in 1871 and to France in 1919. Napoleon took over all of the lands mentioned (indeed all of the Middle Kingdom) except Switzerland. Before 1815 the threat to the survival of the Netherlands, Belgium and Luxemburg was chiefly from France (Louis XIV, Napoleon); more recently from Germany (the Kaiser, Hitler).

England (or, more recently, Britain) has had a compelling interest since medieval times in the survival of some sort of Middle Kingdom, whether to block the advance of France or of Germany or to act as buffer between them. After five years in various roles in continental Europe, both west and east, in 1945 the author was appointed to the Peace-making Section of the Foreign Office and found himself sharing a monastic cubicle with Arnold Toynbee, the world historian who had been invited by the British Government to advise on the settlement most likely to establish a lasting peace in Europe. We were soon to be chiefly concerned with the relationship between the western allies and the Soviet Union, a matter of direct emotional involvement for the author, who had worked in the Polish Resistance; but there were also problems in western Europe such as the French territorial claims on areas in north-west Italy which had formed part of Savoy, and above all we were determined that tensions over the middle ground between France and Germany should not embroil Europe in war ever again.

One tends today to forget how fortunate Europe has been in the conversion of the militarist and aggressive German Reich into a stable and pacific democracy, reconciled with France in the European Community they have created together. This outcome was hardly to be foreseen in the autumn of 1945, when the Foreign Office 'peacemakers' were busy preparing the drafts of the treaties which they would negotiate with their American, Russian and French counterparts in preparation for the Peace Conference of 1946; and so they naturally gave thought to the future security of France's eastern frontier. The dismemberment of Germany was not considered seriously, nor was the demilitarization of the German Rhineland which had proved so futile after the previous world war; but, the British 'peacemakers' asked themselves, should Germany's provinces on both banks of the Rhine be taken from her and made the kernel of a buffer state? Should Alsace and Lorraine be added to it? Switzerland, ever ready to defend her neutrality, would anchor the southern end of the area separating France and Germany which the peace treaty would thus create; could new guarantees to the Netherlands, Belgium and Luxemburg similarly secure the northern end? And should Italy also be brought into the scheme in any way?

The author was bidden to assist Professor Toynbee in his paper weighing up these ideas, which, as Toynbee remarked with a smile, concerned the possible relevance of the ancient Middle Kingdom in the world of today. It was with some nostalgic regret that they came to the conclusion that in 1945 the Middle Kingdom had greater historical fascination than actuality. For instance, how

[223]

could France be asked to surrender Alsace and Lorraine, as though she were on the losing side as she had been in 1871? And without those shuttlecock provinces would the buffer system have sufficient depth? They consoled themselves, both as historians and 'peacemakers', with the reflection that at least part of the Middle Kingdom still survived to serve as a glacis if one were needed again, the Netherlands, Belgium and Luxemburg: a significant part of Charles the Bold's, if only a fraction of Lothar's.

So Arnold Toynbee's Middle Kingdom was not written into our negotiating briefs and it remains one of the more improbable 'might-have-beens', almost certainly not thought of again in all the subsequent long exchanges about a settlement of the intractable problem of Germany. Thus, in recommending to his Foreign Office superiors in December 1945 that any idea of reviving the 'Middle Kingdom' should be dropped, did the author help to give the final quietus to an eleven-century* fantasy which only under the dukes of Burgundy gained any substance at all?

Savoy as a possible survivor

A survey of the 'Burgundian might-have-beens' cannot overlook the several attempts to restore the ancient Kingdom of Burgundy which for many centuries was itself no 'might-have-been' but concrete reality. It was to be 'restored and set up' for Charles the Bold, to use the words of the Trier agreement of 1473, and it was this once-real kingdom which Charles Emmanuel tried to restore a century and more later (though he would not have sought recognition as King of Burgundy but very probably as King of Savoy). Such an achievement, however, was probably never in the reach of a prince of his limited abilities. The plan to restore the Kingdom in its ancient form which possibly engages the fancy of an English reader most strongly was that made in favor of Richard Lionheart. This however proved ephemeral, and the attempt that perhaps most deserved to succeed was Charles of Anjou's, which was frustrated by the Sicilian Vespers in 1282.

It seemed reasonable to suggest on an earlier page that an Angevin Kingdom of Arles would have survived at least as long as the Angevin County of Provence did in actual fact, that is to say until 1481 (p. 143). It may be carrying speculation too far to wonder whether history would have followed a very

* 843–1945

(*Above*) Estavayer, on Lake Neuchâtel, a Franco-Provençal-speaking town whose 1500 citizens were massacred in 1475 by the Swiss – apparently only eleven escaping – because it was a dependency of Charles the Bold. (*Below*) Grandson, a view from the battlefield of 1476. (pp. 178–9)

(*Above*) Auxerre cathedral, sculpture, second half of the fourteenth century:
the Jews stoning Saint Stephen. (*Below*) Brou abbey, Bourg-en-Bresse. Two of
the famous misericords carved under the direction of Pierre Berchod
1530–32: 'Drunkenness' and 'The Chastisement'. (p. 205)

Amadeus VIII, as Pope Felix V *c.*1450, a contemporary woodcut in Chambéry museum.

Emmanuel Philibert, a miniature in the Musée Chavoisien, Chambéry.

(Left) Charles Emmanuel I at his accession in 1580 aged 18, a few years before he first aimed at the Kingdom of Arles. A painting by Jean Carrachyo, in Chambéry museum. *(Above)* The mature Charles Emmanuel turned from failure in Burgundy to success in Italy. A water color by Thierry Bellange in Chambéry museum.

The Escalade, Charles Emmanuel's defeat at Geneva, is celebrated by the Genevese every December 11 and 12: the procession and (*right*) a modern *Mère Royaume* with her *marmite*. (*Below left*) The Geneva arms worn by the horseman declare its recognition (theoretically even today!) of only two authorities: its bishop (the Key) and the Holy Roman Emperor (the Eagle) (pp. 195, 226n). (*Below right*) A Geneva house which witnessed the Escalade (fourteenth-century, façade *c.*1600)

different course if in the next four centuries the most powerful state facing France in the south-east had been not Savoy or Switzerland but a substantial Rhôneland kingdom; nor should one assume that such a kingdom would necessarily have had as good prospects of survival as Savoy or Switzerland; but it is impossible not to make the point that little Savoy disappeared only in 1860, and Switzerland, the supreme improbability, is one of Europe's most durable features!

Savoy is last but not least to be paraded before us. It has made no great mark on history, but it was the most Burgundian state of all. Sapaudia was Burgundy's first principality as well as her last. The valleys which saw Nibelung warriors descend on the plains of the Saône and Rhône were witness, fourteen centuries later, to the Savoyard Bersaglieri's surrender of Burgundy's last fortresses to the heirs of Clovis and Charles Martel (1860). Savoy was a small but real Kingdom of Burgundy, admittedly without a crown for most of its existence but, having endured for six centuries and more, it might well have survived like Switzerland, let alone Belgium and Luxemburg. Like the Swiss the Savoyards were tough fighters, their Burgundian Homeland almost as mountainous as the cantons'; but unlike them they lay in the path of advancing French armies. Moreover, when Savoy had emerged from the most bitter of its wars with France, its rulers were already Italian princes, increasingly uninterested in their ancient patrimony in Gaul. Had the dukes remained primarily Burgundian rulers, with their power based not at Turin but at Bourg, Geneva or Chambéry, they would doubtless have sought to rule a Kingdom of Savoy, rather than a Kingdom of Sardinia and then Italy; and their country would have enjoyed the immense advantage in modern times of a single universal popular language, 'Burgundian' being used alongside French rather as Schwyzerdütsch is the everyday speech of eastern and central Switzerland alongside German, the language of literature, press and officialdom.

It is easy to feel a sentimental nostalgia for this little state which survived so long and disappeared so recently. There are 'other Burgundies' today, Belgium, the Netherlands and Switzerland, but little Savoy was the heart and the hub. So this tailpiece will not be out of place.

In 1972 a movement was launched, admittedly so far without success, with thousands of copies of a manifesto addressed to '*Savoyards de naissance*' and '*Savoyards d'élection et de coeur*'. It called for an autonomous region of Savoy, formed of the most ancient provinces of the old duchy, Maurienne, Savoie, Chablais, Tarentaise, Faucigny and Genevois. It is natural that this movement should urge that Geneva should in some manner become the economic center

[225]

of this region; and it is fitting that, although Burgundy has lost its identity, Geneva, its first capital, can arguably still be held to be an independent sovereign state.*

Burgundy, Italy and Germany

In April 1860 Savoyards voted by a large majority for union with France. Ten months later the Duke of Savoy, who was also King of Sardinia, was proclaimed King of Italy. Ten years after that William I of Prussia was proclaimed Emperor of Germany. Thus in only eleven years Italy, Germany and Burgundy underwent the great changes mentioned above: two of them united and strong, the heart and homeland of the third now little more than a memory.

It is worth while briefly to compare the fortunes of the four kingdoms, France and Germany (to give their modern names), Italy and Burgundy, which made up Charlemagne's empire. During the millennium which followed, France was Europe's supreme success story, Dark Age kingdom becoming, despite setbacks, Christendom's foremost nation state. By contrast, for the thousand years after Charlemagne Germany and Italy were in splinters, the latter being taken over by foreign dynasties (Hapsburg, Bourbon) to a greater extent than Burgundy, of which at least the central region was governed by a native house (Savoy). For most of the millennium Burgundy seemed nearer to consolidation as country or state than either Italy or Germany. That Italy and Germany emerged united and Burgundy perished is in all three cases due very largely to the ultimate failure of Austria and with it the ultimate success of France.

For a great part of our period 'the Kingdom' (*il Regno*) in Italian history meant not Italy but Naples; Italian history is not concerned with one state or country any more than is Burgundian history, but with at least five: Naples, the Papacy, Florence, Milan and Venice. Burgundy is no less a field of historical study than Italy or Germany for most of the last 1500 years. Germany too comprised several states, a few of which became kingdoms in the eighteenth century.

In the fifteenth century, when several of the countries and states of today were being formed, Burgundy was a much stronger candidate for modern statehood than either Germany or Italy. From the mid-sixteenth century until

---

* It remained independent, subject only to the Holy Roman Emperor as King of Burgundy/Arles, when it became allied with the Swiss Confederation in the sixteenth century. After 1806 (when the Holy Roman Empire was dissolved) it had no authority superior to it, and some (even many?) Genevese would maintain a right to repudiate their accession to the Confederation in 1815.

[226]

the mid-nineteenth the 'Kingdom of Burgundy' in the guise of Savoy-Sardinia was more real than the Kingdom of Italy or the Kingdom of Germany.

Burgundy and Ireland

There are, however, just as intriguing comparisons to be made nearer home. Late in the sixteenth century Edmund Spenser recognized that the root of Irish national sentiment was language: 'the speech being Irish, the heart must needs be Irish'; and in the generations which have seen the decline of polyglot empires Spenser's equation has acquired almost universal acceptance: the frontiers of *states*, in other words, should correspond generally with the frontiers of *language*.

It will be of interest to apply the Elizabethan poet's maxim to Burgundy as well as to Ireland, since there were close similarities in the histories of Burgundy and of Ireland. The Anglo-Normans first invaded Ireland in 1169, and France made her first territorial acquisition in the Kingdom of Burgundy at very nearly the same time (Forez, 1166). For the next four hundred years the English language, like French in Burgundy, made little progress in Ireland, until in the sixteenth century both conquerors started imposing their tongues. In both cases the old language had been supplanted by the end of the eighteenth as the speech of the well-to-do of the towns. Thereafter parallel becomes contrast. By the eighteen-eighties Irish was spoken by far less than one-fifth of the population, whereas the great majority of the people of the Burgundian territories taken over by France still spoke the old dialects.

So much for 'language', what about 'states'? In Burgundy by that time the Estates of Savoy as well as of Provence, the Duchy and 'Free' County, had been obliterated together with all other marks of political identity. As for Ireland, by contrast, in the conquering nation no less than in the conquered there were strong pressures in the eighteen-eighties to grant Home Rule.

The end of the story can be told in a few words. Ireland's identity was restored to her, Burgundy lost hers. Ireland lost her speech yet gained freedom – a case of a country without a language; Burgundy kept her speech until almost the present day yet lost her freedom – and so was a language without a country.

This is no place to debate to what extent the Burgundians were of weaker fiber than the Irish or subjected to more draconian repression; or whether the alien culture was more acceptable, whether on its own merit or by contrast with what threatened on the other side – the Irish had no German or Hapsburg menace on their western frontier. French, Irish and English will take different

[227]

views of the events summarized above. But perhaps it is relevant that there can today be no 'Burgundian' viewpoint to balance the French as the Irish balances the English, and there is only a wraith-like, nostalgic one from Savoy or Provence; and perhaps, when we hear the facile adage that the torch of liberty is unquenchable, we should not assume that all fighters for freedom have been as successful or as fortunate as the Irish. Peoples like the Franc-Comtois have been brought to heel by violence and terror, their language and identity extinguished by the deliberate policy of Paris.

Burgundy and Scotland

If there is an Irish analogy, there is a hardly less interesting Scottish one.

In December 1361, the Estates of the Duchy of Burgundy issued what amounted to a Declaration of Independence. Basing themselves on 'the Charter of the Burgundians' of just one hundred years later than England's Magna Carta, they maintained that France and Burgundy were separate countries and their union acceptable only if the Duchy were allowed to remain distinct. They insisted that there could be no question of its becoming a French province or part of the royal domain, and so there could be no administrative changes. The union of Burgundy with France would thus be a personal one only, King John of France being ruler of two separate states. The terms which the Burgundian leaders obliged John to accept remind us of the relationship of Scotland and England between 1603 and 1707.

In the event the union of 1603 has been honored to the extent that Scotland is part of Britain and of the United Kingdom, but not part of England. Our analogy would make Burgundy part of Gaul but not of France, and it might entail finding a name for their system as ugly as 'the United Kingdom of Great Britain and Northern Ireland'; imagine, instead of 'France', 'the United Republic of Great Gaul and Northern Basqueland'! There is no need for a formula for Gaul, as there is for Britain, which denotes the union of two entities (let alone the addition of a province across the water); nor need a distinction be made between France and Burgundy today such as the English and Scots agree there should be between their two countries. For there is no pressure in Burgundy for the sort of distinctive personality which Scotland enjoys: its own separate church, legal system, government departments, bank notes, professional and other institutions, and other marks of separate identity such as it has in some international sports. Burgundy by contrast is content to be part of France.

[228]

Conclusion

The reasons for Burgundy's failure

It is time to sum up. Why was the Burgundian Phoenix frustrated? Or at any rate why was its resurgence limited to the Homeland of Savoy? Why is there today no Burgundy to correspond to France, Germany and Italy, its partners as kingdoms in Charlemagne's empire? Why, apart from the successor states – Switzerland, Belgium and the Netherlands – are we left only with the remnant of the 'Burgundian' language to be found solely in old Savoy's alpine valleys?

The chief and prime cause of all this was the expansion of France. It was the East Franks who supplanted the last of Burgundy's native kings (1038) and the Allemans of Switzerland who defeated the last Burgundian duke (1476–7); but the West Franks proved to be Burgundy's most dangerous enemies. Frenchmen may or may not be right in believing that history intended France to extend from the Pyrenees to the Rhine and Alps. It seems at any rate that geography never intended Burgundy to frustrate her expansion south-eastwards for very long. It is true that the outlines of the First Kingdom of Burgundy followed very roughly the watershed enclosing the Rhône-Saône Basin,* but only the Alps and the Mediterranean coast could be called 'natural frontiers'. The four 'mini-Burgundies' featured great rivers or mountains or both, but only Swiss Burgundy was endowed with natural defences against invasion from the north-west, and ultimately it alone preserved its independence. Thus geography did little to assist the consolidation of either the four Burgundies or the one. From the first Frank invasion under Clovis about 500 the plateau between France and Burgundy, 'La Montagne' where the Seine and Saône are parted, hardly impeded a determined conqueror, just as the Saône proved to be less hindrance than highway.

There were other causes of Burgundy's failure. Second place may be given,

* See Map no. 2.

at least so far as the houses of Anjou and Savoy were concerned, to the lure of Italy. It may also be said that the failure of Burgundy illustrates what can happen to a country which is not prepared to fight valiantly for survival, or which is not blessed with leaders of outstanding ability and dedication. Both contentions deserve more space than can be afforded them here. However, it would not be enough simply to assert that Burgundy lacked 'the will to national survival'; or that, whereas patriotism burnt strongly at times for the Duchy of Burgundy, the Franche Comté or Savoy, there was little for any wider entity. For how often indeed in the many centuries covered in this book did men die for 'Germany' or for 'Italy' until relatively very recent times? Even in France there was little *national* feeling in the centuries when dynasties like the Valois and Bourbon, Tudor or Vasa were creating nation states. In those days men would fight for land, blood-ties or honor less often in defence of 'country' than of '*contré*'. Indeed, since for a great part of this period nations were split in two by religion, as many went to battle for *foi* as for *foyer*.

In most countries nationalism is a modern growth. How strong was loyalty to 'Belgium' or to 'Switzerland' as recently as 150 years ago? And not long before that, before the *levée en masse* of revolutionary France, men took up arms more often for loot or personal glory than for any nobler cause; and when their motivation was some higher loyalty, it was often accorded less to Country than to King – perhaps to a leader of exceptional charisma, a Henry V or a Gustavus Adolphus.

Burgundy was unquestionably poor in such leaders. There were no Emmanuel Philiberts available when they were needed for the making of Burgundy between 1100 and 1500, the centuries during which England, France, Portugal and Spain emerged. The Holy Roman Emperors were hardly more alien to Burgundy than the Normans and Plantagenets were initially to England, but their involvement in Germany and Italy prevented them from becoming, as did the later Plantagenets, truly national sovereigns, identifying their subjects' interests with those of their dynasty, adopting their subjects' language and patronizing the country's vernacular literature. As for Burgundy's native dynasties, all of them failed to wrest the crown from the Emperors until Charles the Bold prevailed on Frederick III to restore the Kingdom of Burgundy for him in 1473. Never was the old dream of the Greater Burgundy – the Saône-Rhône Basin from Champagne to the Mediterranean – closer to regaining substance than in the three years from November 1473 to January 1477. When Charles the Bold proclaimed his kingdom at Nancy the reunification of Burgundy was far more probable than the reunification of Germany or

Italy. Burgundy never stood nearer to its apotheosis than when, very shortly afterwards, Charles engaged the Swiss at Grandson.

Some closing reflections

The Kingdom of Burgundy, which Charles threw away, finally disappeared only in the last century, yet its story is little known, and so far there has been only one attempt at a comprehensive history, Boehm's *Geheimnisvolles Burgund*, written during the German occupation of France in the second world war, one suspects with the intention of demonstrating that Burgundy belonged to Germany as much as to France.

The reader may not have found it difficult to believe in the lost *kingdom* introduced in these pages, since from the fifth to the fifteenth century, a period of a thousand years, its existence was universally accepted, and as recently as the early seventeenth century its crown was worth fighting for. But has he accepted that there is also a lost *country* with which history should concern itself? Until she and good fortune fell out, Burgundy had gone far in developing an identity as individual as her sister kingdoms', notably in her arts and her language. In the central regions of the Kingdom the distinctive Romance language, which the early Burgundians created out of the rustic Latin of the area they settled, was used almost universally from the eighth to the early twentieth century, some twelve hundred years; and only two or three generations ago over three million people still had it as their mother tongue.

The lost 'country' was smaller than the kingdom but was still comparable in either extent or population with Belgium, Denmark, Norway, Switzerland or Ireland. The vitality of the Burgundian patois until recently in valleys as distant as Forez, Dauphiné, Jura and Val d'Aosta, reminds us that here in 'Burgundian Burgundy' there was a chrysalis out of which a modern country larger than little Savoy might have grown, a Burgundy equivalent to Italy and Germany, the emergence of which was no less in doubt five centuries ago, or to those older creations, England, France and Spain.

The dynasties which tried to bring the Burgundian phoenix back to life may have failed, but there is nevertheless a coherent story to be told and one of which the peoples of what was once Burgundy would be proud if it were better known to them. The 'Burgundian' case has hitherto almost entirely gone by default. Even the most objective of French historians seem to have assumed that Burgundy had less right to survive than France to absorb her, but perhaps

[231]

the Frenchman who turns these pages will be generous enough to recognize that, were the Burgundians still a separate people today as are, for instance, the Irish, there would probably now be a Burgundian literature as critical of his nation's role as Irish writers are of England's. He may now recognize too that the author's attempt to see things from a 'Burgundian' viewpoint is not fired by prejudice against France, for since infancy it has been his *deuxième patrie*. His prejudice is rather against those in any land who have sought to impose their way of life and language on others for patriotism or national glory.

Patriotism, nationalism: these are phenomena with which any student of the history of a 'lost' country like Burgundy must be concerned. He is bound to wonder what arouses the feelings which we term 'national consciousness'; why groups even with different racial origins join together in a sense of shared identity which distinguishes them from other groups; and what is the relationship of 'people', 'nation', 'country' and 'state'. So too it is natural for him to ask why some nationalisms survive and others perish; whether the world would be richer if small countries had preserved their identity rather than been submerged in the wider loyalty of the Nation State; and whether Europe is today doing enough to reverse the centuries-old trend to centralism and to move back towards regional devolution. Should the withering away of national boundaries within the European Community entail regionalism as much as supra- or internationalism? Progress from nationalism to internationalism may not be enough. Happily there is little risk of the dull sameness which was coming to mark vast areas of the Roman Empire, for it would be a tragic betrayal of our history if the growth of European unity meant also a stifling uniformity. But may not regional variety within continental unity be a noble goal in itself? Some readers, perhaps thinking of Scotland or Catalonia, may say that this entails the rebirth or rejuvenation of countries and regions which have been absorbed in Europe's nation states. For others it will mean (say) Burgundy, Brittany, Provence and Languedoc, Wales, Sicily and Bavaria, each making a richer and more distinctive contribution to our western civilization.

These issues have only been touched on briefly in what is an abridgement of a more comprehensive study of Burgundy's identity and story, and we may hope that the writer who embarks one day on a definitive history will treat them fully. It may not matter that the Kingdom of Burgundy was blotted out, but the world must surely be poorer if our regions lose their identities, as Burgundy has so largely lost hers, through the trend to ever greater political units. No goal is higher than the remaking of Europe; but in reaching out for the future, we must not cast away the rich variety of our past.

Burgundy's place in history

But apart from that – and it is important – what is Burgundy's significance in history?

For most of the millennium between the fifth century and the fifteenth Burgundy stood in the forefront of European culture. In the five centuries from the fall of the Roman Empire to that of the Carolingian (*c.* 400–900), Burgundy (which usually included Provence) probably contributed as much as any other part of Europe to the preservation of classical culture without which western civilization could not have been born; but it was from the tenth century, the century of Europe's rebirth, that Burgundy's role was specially notable, and above all in the period between 1050 and 1250 when Europe began to determine the shape of its political organization, its law, and its languages, literature and arts. This was the foundation on which Renaissance and modern western culture was raised, and no country had a greater part in laying this foundation than Burgundy. Burgundy was not only one of the four kingdoms of Europe's heartland throughout the millennium between the Roman Empire and the Renaissance;* it lay at the very hub, between Italy and France, Iberia and Germany. This did not only mean that in the early days the Rhône-Saône Basin was a highway for influences from Lombardy, Provence and Moslem Iberia to penetrate northern and central Europe; it also meant that Burgundy became the nursery for a great deal that was vital to the growth of European civilization.

Burgundy's contribution to our culture was not uniformly valuable. Her decline in the thirteenth century cut short the creation of a robust national vernacular literature such as emerged in France, England, Germany, Italy and Iberia. Before that, however, in Europe's two formative centuries 1050–1250 Burgundy's contribution was relatively significant; even if important works like *Gérard de Roussillon* and *Roland* may not be counted among her creations, at that period her literature was surpassed in the Romance lands only by that of the Anglo-Normans, Walloons and Picards; and few countries have woven strands into the tapestry of Europe's legend and literature as universal as the immortal themes of Tristan and the Disaster of the Nibelungs.

No more need be said here about Burgundy's leadership in architecture and sculpture in the age of Romanesque; her development of the early forms of Gothic; and her part in spreading the new styles all over western Christendom.

* See Maps nos 3 and 14.

The monuments of her engineers and artists may still be found from Portugal and Ireland to Hungary, and from Sweden to Lebanon. Nor has there been enough space in these pages to do justice to Burgundy's contribution to medieval thought and science. Cluny set up hundreds of schools and workshops alongside its priories which spread knowledge throughout Europe; the Cistercians' role was even more important in developing and disseminating the techniques of Europe's first industrial and agricultural revolution.

Burgundy's first claim on the gratitude of Europe accordingly stems from the fact that she was the chief founthead of Christian monasticism which contributed so richly to the thought, art, science, technology, organization, manners and crusading spirit of the Middle Ages; and Burgundy's leadership in the European renaissance of 1050–1250, when her peoples were amongst the most virile and creative of Christendom, was typified by the genius which created Cluny and Cîteaux and made them the greatest forces of their time, bringing about the expansion both of the European map and of the Christian mind. The Burgundian genius, which through Bernard sought to purify the Church, also through Valdez challenged old beliefs and championed new ones; indeed the Valdensians were to survive as the only organized movement for reform until the advent of Wyclif, Huss and Luther. May it not be said that, thanks to the Valdensians, Burgundy had a pre-eminent role in Europe's first, albeit stifled, Reformation as well as in its first Renaissance?

Burgundy lay at the center of the ancient Middle Kingdom, the heartland of western civilization; so long as she preserved her intellectual energy and inventiveness she was bound to have great influence on the way in which that civilization developed. Indeed she was the mainspring of so much activity, spiritual and worldly, that lit up the medieval world that its fate and hers might seem to be inextricably linked; and it is difficult not to suspect a connection between the break-up of an order with which Burgundy was so closely associated – monasticism, the Romanesque, the idealism and internationalism of the Crusades – and the decline of Burgundy herself. From the middle of the thirteenth century Burgundy was eclipsed by the other founder-kingdoms of Christendom, France, Italy and Germany. Burgundy's mantle passed in particular to France: Gothic replaced Romanesque and the university the monastic cloister; and when around 1400 'Burgundy' recovered her place among the leaders of Europe, and her cities vied with those of Italy and Germany, it was not the old Burgundy of the Rhône-Saône Basin but the new one of Flanders and Holland.

The fifteenth-century duchy's place in history is universally recognized but not yet that of the earlier Burgundy, to which European culture owes even more, for what Italy was to the Renaissance and France to Gothic, Burgundy was to Romanesque and all it stood for. In sum, no country contributed more to the magnificent age of Europe's growth and first expansion, and one may ask whether Burgundy has still to receive from history the homage that is her due.

This book began as a voyage of discovery and it will have justified itself if it has engendered a wish in the reader to know Burgundy better and to tap her essence. It may be that 'Burgundy' evokes for most of us not an ancient dream kingdom or a dazzling medieval or Renaissance culture, but rather the pleasures of the palate. But is it entirely unfitting that 'Burgundy' should mean for us the good things of life no less than the world of the spirit – the world of Bernard and Anselm? As Gilbert and countless other artists showed, the message of Burgundy is not only to be found in the awesome severity of Fontenay, the pure lines of Pontigny, or the many uplifting Christs-in-Majesty. When Burgundians looked for beauty, they may have had their eyes on the heavens but their feet were planted firmly on their good earth. The best of their art, in the carved stone of Saulieu and Anzy and the oak at Brou, is concerned not with saints and angels but with man and his daily activity, perhaps in the belief that our Creator means us to make the most of our human existence and to help Him build a heaven on earth. Whether or not that was the intention, the lover of Burgundy is entitled to wonder how often God and man have come closer to it than in the land of the lost kingdom.

Burgundy and the epic of Northern Europe

Burgundy made a disappointingly small contribution to western literature, but this is not surprising since its culture was in decline at the time when the vernacular was blossoming in Europe. However, what is perhaps the most important theme of the epic of northern Europe derives largely from an episode in Burgundian history, the annihilation of the Burgundy army under King Gunther by the Huns in 436 which legend has called the Disaster of the Nibelungs. The heroic tale of the *Burgundian* or 'Nibelung' Gunther (Gunnar, Gunthiar) and Attila (Atli) the Hun became fused with the *Frankish* myth of Siegfried, Brunnhilde and the Ring, and passed into Teutonic languages spoken as far apart as Greenland and the Black Sea. The tale was drawn on, for instance, by the creators of Beowulf and the even earlier (sixth-century) Anglo-Saxon poem, *The wanderer*. It has been preserved for us in many versions but none so well known as the Icelandic Saga of the Volsungs (*c.* 1300) and the Nibelungenlied of Bavaria (*c.* 1200) which inspired not only Wagner's opera cycle *The Ring of the Nibelung* but also William Morris's epic poem *Sigurd* and Ibsen's play *The Vikings at Helgeland*.

Gunther and Attila, who incidentally was not present at his forces' victory in 436, were not the only characters in the Saga and the Nibelungenlied who were real figures of history. For instance Gunther's brother Gislahar appears in the sagas as Hogni, and Dietrich in the Nibelungenlied ('The Lay of the Nibelungs') is the great Ostrogothic king of Italy, Theodoric, who lived not long after the battle (454–526). De Boor suggests that Siegfried (Sigurd in the sagas) was a Frankish prince who took refuge in Burgundy and married a Nibelung princess but becoming too powerful was, like the legendary Siegfried, assassinated; while others believe that he was the Frankish king Sigebert of Austrasia who was also murdered (in 575). The most likely prototype for Brunnhilde (Brynhild in the sagas), who married Gunther and so became queen of Burgundy in the *legend*, was Sigebert's consort, Brunnhilde (Brunhild, Brunehaut), a woman of history truly larger than life who dominated the age that straddles the year 600 and who long ruled both Franks and

[236]

Burgundians. There is a likely counterpart too for the bitter rivalry of Brynhild and Gunnar's sister Gudrun, which was so largely responsible for the tragedy in the *legend*, in the struggle between Queen Brunhild and her enemy Fredegund in *history*. Gudrun probably also represents the historical figure of Ildico, Attila's wife and his murderer in real life just as Gudrun is in the legend.

As observed above, the heroic tale which is so significant in the epic of northern Europe is made up of two distinct elements, the Frankish myth of Siegfried's exploits and the Burgundian legend of Gunther. The oldest extant work of several from which the Volsungasaga is drawn is the Atlakvida, the Lay of Atli (from Iceland around 900); it narrates only the strictly *Burgundian* part of the story, omitting not only Sigurd (Siegfried) but also Brynhild, the *Frank* figures, and beginning with Atli's treacherous invitation to Gunnar which led to the Huns' massacre of the Burgundians. Odet Perrin maintains that the Lay of Atli is 'purely Burgundian' and has 'preserved all the characteristics of an original poem going back to the sixth and even the fifth century'.* The fact that so many of the characters were historical Burgundian figures (the Lay refers to Gunnar as 'lord of the Burgundians') would not in itself suffice to prove that the material from which the Lay was drawn was Burgundian, but this is strongly borne out by the way in which in Atlakvida and other early versions of the legend the narrators' sympathies lie with the Burgundians.

We may conclude therefore that the tale of Gunnar, Gudrun and Atli is of Burgundian origin; and that ultimately Wagner's *Twilight of the Gods* is the *Burgundians'* account of their own apocalypse, probably put together first by 'troubadours' at Gundioc's court at Geneva. The *Frankish* myth of Siegfried was probably added to the troubadours' tales in the seventh century when Merovingian Franks ruled over Burgundy.

Such is the Burgundian bias in the early sagas that one wonders whether the Nibelung legend reached Scandinavia, the home of the sagas, before the Burgundians were overwhelmed by the Franks (534), in other words in roughly the same period as the tale reached England – around 500. Furthermore this might perhaps explain why the region of all Europe in which the tale of the Burgundians' massacre took root most strongly, i.e. the lands of the sagas, southern Norway and Sweden, was the region in which the Burgundians originated. It is hard to believe that this is pure coincidence. It may not be stretching credulity too far to suggest that in the fifth and sixth centuries the

* Les Burgondes (À la Baconnière, Neuchâtel, 1968).

[237]

Vikings' ancestors were vaguely conscious of their kinship with the Burgundians who settled first on the Rhine and then around Lake Geneva, and so they were ready to adopt the story of the massacre of 436 as their own.

Appendix II

'Burgundian' – the language

Introduction

1. It is widely believed in France, Switzerland and Italy that the patois spoken by village folk in Savoy, the Suisse Romande and the extreme north-west of Italy, are local, debased forms of French, barbarous and coarse like the crudest English of backward African ex-colonies. The truth is very different.* The failure of the language of which the patois are remnants, in contrast with the triumphant success of French, does not mean that even in their present form they are intrinsically inferior to it. They are as rich, except in modern words, and richer, e.g. in words descriptive of mountains and mountain life; and their grammar and structure generally follow rules which recall other languages derived from Latin.

2. How does one measure the importance of a language? By the number of people now speaking it? (By that measure how should we rate Latin or ancient Greek?) Only some 100,000 people speak these patois today, and (in contrast with Latin and Greek) few of their words have come into universal usage, e.g. vogue, avalanche, glacier and moraine. The importance of this language must obviously be sought elsewhere, in fact in the following: for six hundred years or more (say, AD 700 to 1300 or 1400) it was spoken far more widely than French;** in its heyday in the tenth to thirteenth centuries it had a more respectable literature (though that is not saying much); and three or even two generations ago, which is not long, it had over three million speakers, very roughly as many as Danish, Norwegian, Finnish, Swiss (Schwyzerdütsch) and Slovak, and very many more than Irish, Gaelic, Breton, Icelandic, Albanian or Afrikaans.

---

* See Appendix IV for the chief authorities drawn on.
** I.e. more widely than Francien (the medieval French of the Paris region); not more widely than the Langue d'Oïl, the very different dialects of which extended from the frontier of Brittany to the approaches of Switzerland.

3. The estimate of three million may be arrived at as follows:

Three French departments (Ain, Savoie, Haute Savoie) had this language as the mother tongue of the very great mass of the people, according to the census of 1863. Their population then was 912,000, and of that total it was spoken by perhaps	800,000?
In five departments (Doubs, Isère, Jura, Loire, Rhône) it was spoken by a considerable majority. Of a total of 2,370,000 count	well over 1,600,000?
In Saône-et-Loire there were strong local concentrations. Of a population of 582,000 count	100,000

Total for France well over 2,500,000?

In five Swiss cantons (Fribourg, Geneva, Neuchâtel, Valais, Vaud) with population of 660,000 in 1880 the language was mother tongue for the very great mass of the people. This was so also for part of Bern canton. Count	*Switzerland*	600,000?
70,000 still speak it in NW Italy. It was spoken in 1860–80 also to the south and east of the present area. Count	*Italy*	nearly 100,000

Total well over 3 million

It must be stressed that most of the 3 million plus were bilingual and also spoke French (and some Italian). Increases with the growth of population were offset by losses to French (and Italian).

4. Finally, the area of this language (at least 18,000 sq. miles, perhaps 20,000) may have been much less than half the extent of England, but it may be compared with the area of small countries like Denmark and Switzerland.* It is indeed much wider than the three regions mentioned above – Savoy, western Switzerland and the extreme north-west of Italy – being bounded by the Forez

---

* England 51,000 sq. m., Denmark 16,600, Switzerland 15,900. Belgium has only 11,800 and the Netherlands 12,600.

mountains, Roanne, Mâcon, Pontarlier (near Besançon), Fribourg, Sierre, Pont Saint Martin (beyond Aosta), Susa, Mure (beyond Grenoble), Valence, and Saint Etienne. (See Map no. 13)

The speakers disappear but the area stays constant

5. In the last 50–60 years the number speaking the language, after flourishing for some six centuries and standing up to French for another three, has fallen from three million to about 100,000. The story of the language can be summarized as follows:

(a) *5th–8th century* The rustic Latin of the area becomes the new Romance vernacular under adaptation by the Burgundians.

(b) *9th–12th cent.* The vernacular, probably stabilized in the tenth century, is universal for speech, but Latin is generally used for the written word except for poetry. French is an alien tongue.

(c) *Roughly 13th and early 14th cent.* The vernacular is adopted alongside Latin for most written purposes, even formal ones. French is still very rare.

(d) *c. 1350–c. 1450* French is introduced alongside Latin and the vernacular for documents; but very few people can speak it.

(e) *Late 15th–late 18th cent.* French steadily becomes dominant for everything written and the educated are increasingly bilingual. However, the vernacular is still the only tongue of the masses, except in centers like Lyons, and it is still used for songs and other popular 'literature'.

(f) *First half 19th cent.* Vernacular writing dies out but vernacular speech survives more or less as strongly as before.

(g) *Say 1880–1920* Most people are bilingual in the vernacular and French.

(h) *From say 1920* The dialects are fading away except in north-west Italy. What was almost certainly the majority of the population in the area as a whole was still speaking the vernacular as its mother tongue only about 60 years ago (i.e. nineteen-twenties).

6. This immense drop – three million to about 100,000 in two or three generations – has not meant a contraction in the area where the patois can be found. It has simply meant that throughout the area the patois will today only be heard in conversation between the very old and in towns probably not at all. In some mountainous regions of south-east France and western Switzerland it is also in use by under-60s and even under-40s, but it is in general use only in the

Val d' Aosta, in the extreme north-western corner of Italy. Here it is the everyday speech of some 70,000 out of the 1971 census total of 109,252, the balance consisting chiefly of town-dwellers and Italians from outside the valley. Comparison may be made between this little remnant of Burgundy, 1260 square miles in extent, and a small county of England or Scotland, e.g. Hereford (842 sq. m., pop. 140,000), old Westmorland (789 sq. m., 68,000), or Dumfries (1068 sq. m., 88,000). Map no. 25 gives a rough indication of where the patois have survived.

7. The dialects of the rest of Burgundy were Provençal (the best known of the variants of Langue d'Oc) in the south; the Langue d'Oïl group in the largely Frankish north–Bourguignon and Bas-Bourguignon in the Duchy of Burgundy and Franc-Comtois in the County; and Schwyzerdütsch (Swiss German) in the Allemannic east. (See Map no. 13) The only one of these to continue flourishing has been the only non-Romance (i.e. non-Latin-based) dialectal group, Schwyzerdütsch, which is Teutonic.* The others have been fading away in recent generations, Bourguignon and Franc-Comtois faster than the language of the Burgundian Homeland discussed in this annex, Provençal more slowly. Throughout the millennium 900–1900, both recently and in days past, the movements in the borders between these dialects (and the patois to which they have been reduced) have been relatively small. Blurred or mixed though some of them were, most frontier areas were sharply and clearly distinguished; for instance the south-western boundary of Burgundy's old language has been amongst the most stable. The Church even substituted it for the old Roman provincial frontiers when drawing the borders of the ecclesiastical provinces of Vienne and Lyons. Vuarnet, the Genevese philologist, tells a revealing anecdote. At the turn of the century he found himself at Vizille, a few miles south of Grenoble, and he spoke to his landlady in the dialect of Geneva. Although Geneva and Vizille are separated by more than one hundred miles and several mountain ranges, his dialect seemed so familiar to the landlady that she assumed that he was a local. Yet, when he went on to Mure, only six miles further south, he and the townsfolk could not understand each other. He had crossed from Burgundy proper into Provence.

* The line eventually dividing the Romance (Latin-based) dialects adopted or adapted by some 'barbarian' invaders from the Teutonic dialects retained by others, did not follow the frontier of the Roman Empire. Britain, Holland, north Belgium, Luxemburg, Lorraine, Alsace, Württemberg, central and eastern Switzerland and Austria were the main areas 'surrendered by Latin'.

The stability of the language

8. Not only have the geographical frontiers of the language been relatively stable; the language itself has also been astonishingly constant, at any rate since the fourteenth century, as Vuarnet showed, and probably much longer. Regional variations naturally developed around local hubs like Lyons, Aosta, Geneva, Mâcon, Grenoble and Feurs, and amongst the mountain folk of Savoy and the Jura. But even at the end of the nineteenth century the patois of Dauphiné, Savoy and west Switzerland were virtually identical and those of Forez, over one hundred miles away, were still very close to them; and, though the Swiss Valais and the Val d'Aosta are separated by an immense Alpine barrier, the patois spoken there even today are very similar. Given that from the Middle Ages onwards there was little to hold these scattered dialects together and much to drive them apart, it is striking that they should have retained their uniformity. How much closer, we may ask, must they have been in the eleventh and twelfth centuries when Burgundy was still a political entity? Thus Burgundy's vernacular displayed a unity in the Middle Ages which had already disappeared amongst the dialects of France, the land of the Langue d'Oïl.*

9. The modern patois, which usually sound coarse as the speech of country-men often does, are probably a poor indication of how educated people spoke in Lyons, Geneva and Grenoble four or five hundred years ago. Moreover they are deeply penetrated by French** and (in the Val d'Aosta) by Italian. Such borrowings, particularly of words for modern things or ideas, are usually recognized easily in the speech of the *patoisants*.

---

* Three language groups (Langue d'Oc, Langue d'Oïl and Burgundy's) emerged out of the rustic Latin of imperial Gaul. (See para. 11 below) This was not the end of the process of fragmentation, particularly in France (the Langue d'Oïl) and generations later in the middle of the thirteenth century the Englishman Roger Bacon wrote that the peoples who spoke Francien, Norman, Picard and Bourguignon could not understand one another. Norman, Picard and Bourguignon had already stabilized by this time and they were hardly to develop further, unlike Francien, the dialect of the Ile de France, which in due course became the French of the Academy. The process of fragmentation and stabilization was halted much earlier in the Langue d'Oc area, Aquitaine and Provence, than in the Langue d'Oïl and by the eleventh century a standard literary form had been established. Once again Burgundy resembled the south rather than the north, her dialects also stabilizing at an early stage.

** The patois (one can say 'dialects' when they are written) were least stable in areas under strong French influence. The *'Escalade'* song of *c.* 1640 is a mixture of French and the Savoyard (or Chablais) form of Franco-Provençal. (See p. 196.)

Characteristics of the language

10. There are probably more words in the unadulterated patois which resemble French than recall the southern Romance tongues (Provençal, Italian, Spanish, Portuguese, etc.) and by most linguistic tests they are further from the latter than from French. But because of their musical quality, unaccented rhythm and enunciation of the final -a, when spoken they remind one less of French than, say, a rustic Italian or Portuguese. What is not in doubt is that the early Burgundians and their descendants left the rustic Latin they found around them far less changed than did the Franks. Very many of their words were (indeed we should say 'are') the old Latin words, unchanged or hardly so; and, if they are changed, they resemble the Italian or Spanish. Often they remain closer to Latin than even the Italian or Spanish do.

Latin	*Italian (Spanish)*	*Burgundy's vernacular*	*French*
ala	ala	ala	aile
amica	amica (amiga)	amica, amiga	amie
amo	amo	amo	aime
bibere	bere	bere	boire
duo	due (dos)	dos	deux
folia	foglia	folia	feuille
hic	qui	hic	ici
homo	uomo	homo	homme
lavare	lavare	lava	laver
manus	mano	man	main
meta	meta	metya	moitié
niger	nero	neyro	noir
panis	pane	pan	pain
paucus	po	pou	peu
plovere	piovere	plove	pleuvoir
poma	pomo	poma	pomme
quator	quatro (cuatro)	catro	quatre
ripa	riva (riba)	riba	rive
tela	tela	tela	toile
tota	tutta (toda)	tota	toute

and the imperfect tense:

donnabant	donavano	donavant	ils donnèrent

What should the language be called?

11. The examples just given show that the Burgundians' Romance language was (and is) something distinct from both French and the southern Romance tongues. In agreeing on its distinctiveness philologists count it amongst the ten or twelve Latin-derived languages which are generally accepted, along with Langue d'Oïl (with French as its best-known example), Langue d'Oc (Provençal, Gascon, etc.) and those of the Italian, Balkan and Iberian groups.* They generally call it 'Franco-Provençal'** but, as Armand Decour wrote in *Le Patois de Bettant* (1966), that name suggests a mixture of bad French and Provençal, which was just what uninformed observers have taken the language to be. In fact, as he and others like Dauzat as well as Ascoli have demonstrated, we are concerned here with a distinctive language which is not French and not Provençal, nor indeed is it an intermediate stage between the two. As Decour commented, it might with less misconstruction be regarded as a step between French and Italian. If, however, it were right to call the language 'Franco-Italian', then (Decour commented) Catalan should be called 'Hispano-Provençal', and one might add that Dutch should then be 'Anglo-German'! (And Francien, lying between the initially more successful dialects of Picardy and Normandy, might in different circumstances have ended up known as 'Picardo-Norman'?!)

12. All in all it is best to retain the now accepted Franco-Provençal; but, since the language with which we have been concerned was created by the Burgundians out of Latin (as French was by the Franks), readers may think we have been justified in often calling it 'Burgundian'.

---

* There are of course different classifications but all generally distinguish Franco-Provençal, e.g. that of Tagliavani. He puts Sardinian and Rhaeto-romansch with Italian; Dalmatian either with the Italian group or with Roumanian in the Balkan; and Catalan either with Langue d'Oc, Franco-Provençal and Langue d'Oïl in his 'Gallo-Roman' group, or with Portuguese and the Spanish dialects in his 'Ibero-Roman'.

** First so called by Ascoli in 1878 (the French often write 'francoprovençal'). Decour suggested 'lugduno-romand', Lugdunum being the Latin for Lyons, and Vuarnet '(la langue) romande', as in 'la Suisse romande', the area of Switzerland which used to speak the language for which we are seeking a name. 'Romand' is the French word for what the people of the region used to describe their language, e.g. 'romancio' was used in a record written in the vernacular in Geneva in 1460; it said that an appeal made by the townsfolk to the bishop was presented both in 'romancio' and in 'galico' (French). But how should we translate 'romand' or 'romancio'? (Romansch in south-east Switzerland is a different Latin-based language.)

(1) From the Life of Saint Beatrice, virgin of Ornaciu, a nun at Poleteins near Lyons, by her prioress, Margaret (*c.* 1300); (2) From the Statutes of the Brotherhood of the Trinity of Lyons (1306).

(1)
La via seinct:
Biatrix virgina de Ornaciu

Illi eret tres humis de cuor et de cors; illi eret mout cheritousa et pidousa et sumiz denens de tota maneri de humilita que potet necessita a ses compaignes. Illi fut de mout granz jeunos et abstinences, tan quant sa feybla complexions ho poet portar. Illi eret mout enteriment obediens, et de mout grant oreison assiduaz, et de si grant devocion que pluisors veis illi cuidavet de tot perdre lo veyr, per les laygremes que illi gitavet; et se eret mout benigna de paroles, humiz et de grant exemplo. Illi eret mout curiousa et fervenz en metre tot son entendiment a fayre y a dire y a veyr y a oir totes les choses que li senblavont que puyssant tornar al edifiament de sa arma et de les autres genz.

She was humble in heart and body, very charitable, compassionate and in every way full of humility towards her companions. She fasted and abstained as much as her weak constitution let her bear. She was of complete obedience and assiduous in her prayers, and her devotion was so great that many thought she would lose her sight through the tears that she shed; and she was kind in speech, humble and of fine example. She was attentive and fervent to do, say, see and hear everything that she thought could help to edify her soul and other people.

(2)
El nom de la Seincti Trinita de Deu del Paro et del Fil et del Saint Esperit l'an deicelui Nostre Seignour M. et CCC. et vi el meis de decembro furont escrit en cest present paper li confraro de la frari de la Trinita de Lyon, li qual ant achata del lor argent la mayson de la dita frari et paia de tot, li quaus maisons est asisa a Lion en rua nova.

In the name of the Holy Trinity of God the Father and of the Son and of the Holy Spirit, in the year of Our Savior 1306 in the month of December, the fraternity of the brothers of the Trinity of Lyons were registered in this present document, who [as they] in that year bought with their money the house of the said brothers and paid in full, which house is situated at Lyons in New Street.

[246]

Appendix III

Some notes on architecture

Works dealing with Burgundy's medieval architecture are listed in Appendix IV. This appendix only contains a few notes to supplement or explain points made in pages 79 to 90.

A Romanesque architecture

Romanesque spread all over Latin Christendom, from Ireland and Portugal to Palestine, and readers will not need reminding of its chief characteristics, of which the rounded arch and window are probably the best-known. The features which art historians particularly associate with Romanesque in *Burgundy* are of course to be found elsewhere, but notable amongst them are the *cupola* surmounted by a *tower* at the crossing, prominent *transepts* and a spacious *narthex* (porch).

The visitor to Burgundy will find there relatively few 'high Gothic' churches whether or not *'Burgundian* Gothic' (see *C* below). He will find as fine a selection of 'half-Gothic' as anywhere in the world (*B* below); and wonderful examples of Romanesque in any part of Burgundy from Langres to Vienne and from Nevers to Sion (Map no. 12), of which here are a very few:

Tournus (Saint Philibert). Much of the narthex is from *c.* 875–950; the main walls *c.* 950–1000; the columns and the intersecting groined aisle vaults from *c.* 1000–1025; the nave vault (transversal) from *c.* 1075–1100.

Romainmotier, Switzerland. Nave 996–1028 (wood ceiling). Nave stone vault after 1050. *Chapaize*. Completed *c.* 1040. (Both modeled on *Cluny II,* *c.* 955–81, stone vault added *c.* 1000; Cluny II had immense influence in Burgundy and beyond; now no trace)

Payerne, Switzerland. (Also Cluniac) Largely *c.* 1000–1050. Barrel vault is of this period (imitated on grander scale in Cluny III?)

Anzy-le-Duc. 'The best example of Burgundian architecture before Cluny.'

[247]

Partly before 1050, nave after 1050. Outstanding sculpture, probably
c. 1070–80.

Nevers (Saint Etienne). Consecrated 1095, in which year the nave of Cluny III
was finished. For me Saint Etienne is the 'purest' Romanesque in Burgundy.

B The emergence of Gothic

Cluny III was perhaps the climax of Romanesque. Where should one look for
the beginning of Gothic? And what may fairly be termed 'half-Gothic'?

The development of medieval styles of architecture was a constant process
which it is wrong to compartmentalize; the people of the twelfth century did not
think in terms of 'Romanesque' turning into 'Gothic', of one style emerging
from another; and art historians are accordingly careful over their choice of
terms. It is for instance an over-simplification to say that Romanesque like the
style of classical Rome conveys the impression of solid mass and horizontality,
whereas Gothic suggests lightness and vertical movement. However, if one
accepts that there is some validity in that contrast, we may say that the
beginnings of the soaring character of Gothic should be sought in the lines of
the nave* of *Cluny III* (1088–95, most of rest by 1109), with the emergence of
the new style thereafter being a process of increasing emphasis on verticality
until the climax is reached in the completion of the choir vault of Beauvais in
1272 (157 ft 6in high). But even if this concept of the horizontal giving way to
the vertical is right, there is no single point at which we can say that 'this is
Gothic and that was not'.

Another approach is to establish roughly when and where architectural
features like the pointed arch, the pointed vault, the intersecting vault rib and
the flying buttress first appeared in western Europe. One must remember that
these features, which are generally associated with Gothic architecture, were
also used in churches which art historians regard as Romanesque. Given their
development of pointed arch, pointed vault, vault rib and flying buttress, the
monks of Cluny may perhaps have a stronger claim to have 'invented Gothic'
than Abbot Suger when he rebuilt *Saint Denis* nearly fifty years (1137 onwards)
after they had raised the nave at Cluny (1088 plus).

Cluny III (like Durham) was one of the few churches north of the Alps to be

---

* The transept which has survived gives us an impression of this. Cluny's nave, at 92 ft, topped
not only its greatest English contemporary, Durham (72), but almost all England's Gothic naves.

[248]

rib-vaulted before 1100 – the rib, which Focillon* regarded as the touchstone of Gothic, apparently originated in Lombardy but the Italians left it to others to exploit. Cluny may not have been the first church outside Italy to incorporate the rib vault, but it was certainly one of the first in which the *pointed arch* was employed. The pointed arch seems to have been introduced to Europe by Abbot Desiderius in building done at Monte Cassino north of Naples around 1066,** and it was copied by Saint Hugh (Abbot of Cluny), who visited Monte Cassino in 1083, in the construction of the choir and nave at Cluny III from 1088. The abbey church at *Paray-le-Monial* (1100–10), which is essentially a smaller-scale version of Cluny III, is probably the oldest structure extant in Christendom in which the pointed arch was used extensively, and its pointed vault may be the first ever raised since initially Cluny III had a rounded or 'barrel' vault. (The latter collapsed or cracked seriously in 1125 and was replaced by a pointed vault supported by flying buttresses, 1125–31.)

The reader who wishes to see other early examples of the pointed arch and pointed vault might visit *La Charité-sur-Loire* (1100–6), *Avallon* (1100–10), *Saulieu* (1110–20) and *Autun* cathedral (1120–46), all Cluniac churches. In their buildings from *c.* 1130 the Cistercians also generally used the pointed arch and pointed vault, e.g. *Bonmont* (1131–40), *Fontenay* (1130–47) and *Pontigny* (mostly 1150–70). None of these is quite Romanesque or quite Gothic; the finest 'half-Gothic' church is Autun. (The vault and arches of the famous nave at *Vézelay* (1120–45), which is neither Cluniac nor Cistercian, are rounded.)

The English reader wishing to see an early vault rib (the 'touchstone of Gothic') has only to visit Durham; it was used by 1093 in the aisles and was already then projected for the nave, some thirty years before its use in France.

Finally, where should we look for the genesis of 'full' Gothic (if it is right to mark this off from what developed into it)? Most authorities see its genesis in the rebuilding which Abbot Suger did at Saint Denis close to Paris from 1137. Is there a link between Saint Denis and any form of developed Romanesque? The answer is probably to be found in the Paris church of Saint Martin des Champs, since there is little doubt that Suger took it as his model. Saint Martin des Champs is today a science museum in the center of Paris displaying primitive aircraft, cars and bicycles, which stand in the same relationship to

---

* *The Art of the West*, written from a French viewpoint.

** Pointed arches were perhaps first used north of the Alps in Saint Front, Périgueux, about this time.

modern vehicles as the old building does to the magnificent High Gothic of Beauvais. At that time Saint Martin was a Cluniac abbey still being completed on the outskirts of the capital in Burgundian half-Gothic (1130–40). The ambulatory of Saint Martin closely resembles that of the Cluniacs' second greatest church, La Charité-sur-Loire. There is more than one possible explanation of the development of Gothic, but in so far as it is worth while to seek a single line of development from Romanesque to Gothic, a convincing case may be advanced that it ran from Cluny III by way of La Charité and Saint Martin to Saint Denis.

C Burgundian Gothic

Most readers will be familiar with the differences between the Gothic of England and that of France (i.e. particularly the Ile de France and Champagne). The differences between Burgundian and French Gothic, before the churchmen and citizens of Burgundy began to foresake their own style for the 'opus francigenum' (the French style) around 1300, were almost as marked.

Burgundian church architecture of the thirteenth century was the product of three centuries of steady development of features which were not unique to Burgundy but which were specially typical of it. They were features which are associated in particular with the Cluniacs and which were mentioned above; the cruciform design with its pronounced transepts and the cupola above the crossing surmounted by a tower. In the thirteenth century, when the flying buttress was being increasingly used in France (once again in the limited geographical sense), the same purpose in Burgundy was often served by the concealed internal buttress.* Churches typical of Burgundy had a larger triforium than those of France, usually with an interior passage, and the narthex retained the importance which it had had in Burgundian Romanesque.

R. Branner (Studies in Architecture, vol. III, *Burgundian Gothic Architecture*, Zwemmer, London 1960) writes of 'a homogeneous style ... Burgundian Gothic' appearing abruptly in Notre Dame de Dijon, Auxerre cathedral and Saint Martin's at Clamecy, and having a 'wide success in the region' (p. 37), the region being roughly that of Burgundian Romanesque (see below). 'Abruptly'

* Also used at Durham c. 1120.

refers to the beginning of the thirteenth century, or more precisely 1207 at both Clamecy and Auxerre.

The main stream of Burgundian development may be regarded as Cluny II, Anzy-le-Duc, Cluny III (Paray etc.), Autun, Notre Dame de Dijon (1230–51), and Saint Bénigne de Dijon (1281 plus). Because the Cistercians eschewed bells and often therefore towers, the cruciform design, transepts, cupola and central tower which marked out the buildings just mentioned were dropped or played down in their churches, e.g. Fontenay, Bonmont.

The French, for different reasons, also made less of the transepts and often dispensed with the cupola;* so that at most there was only a light spire** where a large tower would previously have stood; this considerable reduction in weight, coupled with the proliferation of the flying buttress, helped the French towards their objective, vaults of the breath-taking heights of Beauvais and Amiens.

As already remarked, the Burgundians adopted French ideas from around 1300: these usually comprised high vault, small transept, and massive towers at the west end and not over the central crossing. The cathedral church of Saint Jean in Lyons was begun in what we may term 'early Burgundian Gothic' between 1165 and 1180 but was finished in French Gothic; and Saint Nizier de Lyon, which dates from the fourteenth and fifteenth centuries, has no 'Burgundian' in it but is a splendid example of Flamboyant which would do credit to the Ile de France or Champagne. (Vienne cathedral tells the same story.)

Most of Latin Christendom 'went French' as Burgundy did. However, England's national style of Gothic owed more to Burgundy, very largely to the Cistercians, but hardly less to the Cluniacs since the English retained the tower-capped cruciform of Paray and Autun, Jumièges and Durham; and they went on to perfect it: if the French reached for heaven with the vault of Beauvais, the English sought it with the great central towers of Canterbury and York and the spire of Salisbury.*** Is it too fanciful to regard England as not only the home of some of Burgundy's best Romanesque but as the most important site of Burgundian Gothic?!

---

* Cf. Bourges.
** Cf. Notre Dame de Paris. The present spire is nineteenth-century.
*** Spires on the Continent were rarely at the crossing, as was common in England. (Jumièges is in Normandy; consecrated 1067.)

D   The extent of Burgundian Romanesque and Gothic

French art historians (see p. 84) have defined the area of Burgundian *Romanesque* as enclosed by Auxerre, Châtillon-sur-Seine and Langres in the north; Épinal, Neuchâtel and Sion in the east; Savoy, much of Dauphiné and Vienne in the south; and the upper Loire valley in the west. This entails a precision that is unnecessary, and it is sufficient to define the area as comprising simply the four ecclesiastical provinces of Burgundy proper we have met before: Lyons, Vienne, Besançon and Tarentaise. (See Map no. 12.)

Branner saw Burgundian *Gothic* as having a similar extent, but this is more arguable, since there are far fewer examples of thirteenth-century architecture in Burgundy than of the preceding two centuries – too few, perhaps, to lead us to firm conclusions as to its extent. However we can say that the Gothic in Burgundy was distinct in that century from both English and French styles, though displaying similarities with each of them.*

---

* There are of course many features besides the basic design which could be compared, and on this Bannister-Fletcher has done a monumental work in comparing French and English Gothic in *A History of Architecture on the Comparative Method*. Unfortunately he did not compare and contrast French and Burgundian architecture, or English and Burgundian, and for this Branner is probably the best authority.

Appendix IV

Bibliography

The geographical area covered by this book is as large as England's and the historical time-scale is as long, and so the bibliography which follows is very selective indeed. It is not intended to do more than help the reader who may wish to go more deeply into one or other aspect than has been possible in a brief work on such a vast subject. Thus, at the risk of apparent discourtesy and ingratitude, it omits many hundreds of authors whose work has been of inestimable help to me these last seventeen years. I think, however, that all the writers to whom I am chiefly indebted have received mention. Since a great deal of my research was conducted while I lived in Geneva at the hub of the old Kingdom of Burgundy, many of the works drawn on cannot be found in Britain even in the British Library, but nearly all the others listed are in the always wonderfully helpful London Library.

It hardly seems necessary to list standard works on the Middle Ages or general European or French histories; and very few biographies are included. In making my choice my criterion has been less whether a work has been useful to me than whether it could be useful to readers.

As one would expect, most of the secondary sources are French. Readers will judge their historical objectivity for themselves, but it is probably not unfair to the French writers concerned to say that they have taken it not only for granted but as right and just that France should have expanded to the wide frontiers it has enjoyed since the eighteenth century. Fournier, who is probably the fullest authority on the Kingdom of Burgundy after it ceased to have native kings, wrote a passage which may be taken as the 'French' vantage point: '*C'était à la France que devait appartenir le royaume d'Arles. La géographie, qui en avait fait une partie des Gaules, l'avait en quelque façon prédestiné à devenir une partie du royaume capétien*' (*Le Royaume d'Arles et de Vienne*, Alphonse Picard, Paris 1891, p. 521).

Boehm, whose work is mentioned below, sees the story from the German point of view, or more strictly that of the Holy Roman Empire; and, in so far as there can be a Burgundian viewpoint, it is best represented by Chaume. In this book I have tried to steer a middle course.

In contrast with the considerable space given to the Duchy of Burgundy in the fifteenth century, sections on the Kingdom are rare in general European or French histories, e.g. the Cambridge Medieval History, the Methuen series, H. A. L. Fisher,

Lavisse, Guizot and Glotz. The separate chapter on the Kingdom of Arles (chiefly in the fourteenth century) in the Cambridge Medieval History by Fournier is an important exception.

Nearly all the works mentioned below or in the Notes are in the London Library, 14 St James's Square. A single asterisk means the book is not to be found there or in the British Library (and probably, therefore, not in Britain), but it will be found in large libraries in France or Geneva.

A few abbreviations are used, e.g.:

H. (in a title) = History/Histoire of/de etc.

s. = siècle.

contr. = article or chapter contributed to.

biog. = biography of.

trans. = translated (from).

ed. = edited or directed by.

General Works

So far there is only one comprehensive history of the Kingdom in any language: Boehm, M. H., *Geheimnisvolles Burgund* (Munich, 1944). It is a detailed history of the area of the First Kingdom, and it takes the story up to and in some respects beyond the French annexation of the Free County of Burgundy late in the seventeenth century. Boehm stresses Burgundy's identity as something distinct from France and claims many figures as 'Burgundian' that are normally regarded as French, e.g. Rousseau, Diderot, Proudhon, Lamartine and Bossuet.* He ignores the distinctiveness of the language, and gives little space to Burgundian culture or art; and he treats Savoy (and Provence) inadequately.

The following works are more limited in scope but still very valuable:

Chaume, M., *Les Origines du Duché de Bourgogne*, Dijon 1925; *Le Sentiment National Bourguignon*, Dijon 1922

Steyert, A., *Nouvelle H. Lyon*, Lyon 1897

Drouot, H. et Calmette, J., *H. Bourgogne*

The First Kingdom

Deanesley, M., *H. Early Medieval Europe* 476–911, London 1956**

Perrin, Odet, *Les Burgondes*, Neuchatel 1968

---

* Berlioz, who also came from the area (Grenoble), is the famous Frenchman with perhaps the most obvious Burgundian name.

** Henceforth, if no city is named, publication should generally be assumed to be in Paris or London.

Wartburg, W. von, *Les origines des peuples romans*, trans. German 1941
Salin, E., *La civilisation mérovingienne*, 1949
Pirenne, H., *Mahomet et Charlemagne*, 1939
Lot, Pfister and Ganshof, *H. Moyen Age*, vol. i
Moss, H. St L. B., *Birth of the Middle Ages*, 1935; and *Economic Consequences of the Barbarian Invasions*, 1937
Burns, C. Delisle, *The First Europe*, 1948
Coville, A., *Recherches sur l'h. de Lyon du V s. au IX s.*, 1928
Jahn, A., *Die Geschichte der Burgundionen*, Halle 1874
Coutil, L., *L'art mérovingien et carolingien*, Bordeaux 1930
Perronot, Th., *La Toponymie Burgonde*, 1942
James, E. F., *The Origins of France*, 1982

The Second Kingdom

Deanesley and James as above
Poupardin, R., *Le Royaume de Bourgogne 888–1038*, 1901
Chaume, M., *Recherches d'H. Chrétienne et Médiévale*, Dijon 1947
Glaber, R., *The Histories* (Several editions).

The Holy Roman Empire period

Bryce, Lord, *The Holy Roman Empire*, 1928
Duby, G.: *La société aux XIe et XIIe siècles dans la région mâconnaise*, 1971
*Jacob, Louis, *Le Royaume de Bourgogne sous les Empereurs Franconiens*, Grenoble 1908
Fournier, P., *Le Royaume d'Arles et de Vienne 1138–1378*, 1891
Hill, Boyd H., *Medieval monarchy in action: the German Empire, Henry I–IV*, 1972
Pacaut, M., *Frederick Barbarossa*, trans. 1970
Resmini, B., *Arelat in Kräftefeld der französischen, englischen und angiovinischen Politik nach 1250 und das Einwirken Rudolfs v. Hapsburg*, 1980
Haskins, C., *The Renaissance of the Twelfth century*, 1927

The Duchy and Dukes of Burgundy

Vaughan, R., biogs. of the 4 Valois dukes, 1962–1973
Bartier, J., *Charles le Téméraire*, 1970
Richard, J., *Les Ducs de Bourgogne et la Formation du Duché du xie au xive siècle*, Paris 1954; *H. Bourgogne*, 1965

[255]

Kendall, P. M., *Louis XI*, 1971
Barante, M. de, *H. Ducs de Bourgogne de la Maison de Valois*, 1838
Calmette, J., *The Golden Age of Burgundy*, trans. 1962
Drouot, H. (with Calmette), *H. Bourgogne*
Kleinclausz, A., *H. Bourgogne*, 1909
Cazaux, Y., *Marie de Bourgogne*, 1967
Cartellieri, O., *The Court of Burgundy*, 1929
Huizinga, J., *The Waning of the Middle Ages*, 1924
Thielemans, M. R., *Bourgogne et Angleterre 1435–67*, 1966
Jarry, E., *Provinces et Pays de France*, vol. II, 1948

Contemporary histories etc. of Charles the Bold

Commynes, P. de, *Mémoires*, éd. Coulet 1963
Chastellain, G., *Oeuvres*, éd. Kerwyn de Lettenhove, Brussels 1863–6
Basin, Thomas: éd. Ch. Samaran
Marche, Olivier de la, *Mémoires*, éd. Baune and Arbaumont 1883
Molinet, J., *Chronique*, éd. Doutrepont, Brussels 1935–7

Lyonnais

Steyert as above
Deniau, J., *H. Lyon et du Lyonnais*, 1951
Kleinclausz, A., *H. Lyon*, 1939–52
Bleton, Auguste, *Petite H. Populaire de Lyon*, Lyon 1885

Provence

Ed. Barattier, E., *H. Provence*, 1969
Busquet, *H. Provence*, 1954
Manteyer, G. de, *La Provence du premier au douzième siècle*, Paris 1908
Poupardin, R., *Le Royaume de Provence 855–933*, 1901

Savoy

Saint-Genis, V. de, *H. Savoie*, Chambéry 1868
Dufayard, Ch., *H. Savoie*, 1941

Previté-Orton, C. W., *The Early H. House of Savoy*, 1912
Marie-José, Reine, *La Maison de Savoie*, 1956
Perrin, A., *H. Savoie*, Chambéry 1868
Avezou, R., *H. Savoie*, Paris 1963
Belgiojoso, Princesse de, *La Maison de Savoie*, Paris 1878
Manteyer, G. de, *Les Origines de la Maison de Savoie en Bourgogne 910–1060*, Gap 1925
Katz, Robert, *The Fall of the House of Savoy*, London 1972
Beauregard, Costa de, *Mémoires Historiques sur la Maison Royale de Savoie*, Turin 1816

Switzerland, Geneva, the Escalade

Muller, J. de, *H. Confédération Suisse*
Bertrand, P., *Survol de l'H. Genève*
Picot, J., *H. Genève, 1811*
*Legrand, *L'Escalade de Genève*, 1952

Other Regions

Duby, G., *La Société aux XIe et XIIe siècles dans la région mâconnaise*, 1971
Zanotto, André, *H. Vallée d'Aoste*, Aosta 1980
Henri, Abbé, *H. Vallée d'Aoste*, Aosta 1929
Manteyer, G. de, *Les Origines du Dauphiné de Viennois*, Gap 1925

Saints and Religious Orders

Butler, *Lives of the Saints*
Brooke, C. N. L., *Monastic World 1000–1300*, 1974
Hunt, N., *Cluniac Monasticism in central Middle Ages*, 1971; *Cluny under Saint Hugh*, 1967
Knowles, D., *Christian Monasticism*, 1969
Also Evans and Conant, see under Art.

Art and Architecture

Evans, J., *Romanesque architecture of the Order of Cluny*, 1938 and 1972; also *Cluniac art of the Romanesque period*, 1950

Porter, A. Kingsley, *Romanesque sculpture of the Pilgrimage Roads*, 1923 and 1966
Oursel, C., *L'art de Bourgogne*, 1953
Branner, R., *Burgundian Gothic Architecture*, 1960
Conant, K. J., *Carolingian and Romanesque Architecture*, 1959
Lasteyrie, *L'Architecture Religieuse en France à l'époque romane*, 1929
Cadafalch, Puig i, *Premier Art Roman*, 1935
Valléry-Radot, J., *Les églises romanes*; also cont. *L'art roman en France*, 1961
Aubert, M., cont., *L'art roman en France*, 1961
Eygun, F., *Architecture romane*, 1931
Gimpel, J., *The Cathedral Builders*, 1980, trans. 1983
Oursel, R., *Invention de l'architecture romane*, 1970
Dunlop, I., *The Cathedrals' Crusade*, 1982
The many other authorities drawn on include Lavedan, Gromont, Benoit, Focillon, Rahleves.

Language

Dauzat, A., *Les Patois*, 1927; *La Géographie Linguistique*, 1922; and most of the rest of his work is relevant.
Ascoli, *Schizzi Franco-provenzali*, 1873
Stimm, H., *Entwicklungensgeschichte des Frankoprovenzalischen*, 1952
Elcock, W. D., *The Romance Languages*, 1959
Brun, A., *L'introduction du Français dans les provinces du Midi*, 1923
Bec, P., *La Langue Occitane*, 1967
Bourciez, E., *Elements de Linguistique Romane*, 1923
*Vuarnet: *Patois de Savoie, Dauphiné et Suisse*, Thonon 1907
*Monnoye, *L'idiome bourguignon*
*Decour, A., *Le Patois de Bettant (Ain)*, 1966
Wartburg, as above.

Literature

Aebischer, P., *La Chrestomathie Franco-Provençale*, 1950
Sampson, R. B. K., *Early Romance texts*, 1980 (pages 97–107)
Hackett, W. Mary, *Girart de Roussillon* (Contains the Bodleian text of the *chanson*)
Bartsch, K., *Altfranzoesische Chrestomathie*, Leipzig 1866
H. des Littératures, vol. III.
Holmes, V. T., *H. Old French Literature*, 1948

Legends, Sagas

Murrell, E. S., *Girart de Roussillon and the 'Tristan' Poems*, Chesterfield 1926
Ham, E. Billings, *Girart de Rossillon*, 1939
Meyer, *Girart de Roussillon*, 1884
Finch, R. G., *The Saga of the Volsungs*, 1965
Ed. Gutman, R. W., *Volsunga Saga* (trans. by W. Morris), 1962
Lettsom, W. N., *The Fall of the Nibelungers*, 1850
Needler, G. H., *The Nibelungenlied*, 1904
Armour, M., *The Fall of the Nibelungs*, 1897
Casey, R., *The Lost Kingdom of Burgundy*, 1924 (Tales from many parts of the Kingdom)

Race

Sauter, M.-R., *Le Problème des Burgondes*, Geneva 1941

Valdensians

Monastier, A., *H. l'église vaudoise*, 1847
Montet, E., *Les vaudois de Piedmont*, 1885

Appendix V

Notes

For *names* of people or places I have generally used the form which would seem most intelligible to an American or English reader. However, since most works on Burgundy are in the French language, I have tended to accept the French form rather than one which would be closer to the dialects of Burgundy. Thus it would be confusing to refer to the great Burgundian bishop of Autun, known to his contemporaries as Lethgier or Leodegar, in any but the French way, Léger. (However, the French name Eudes seems less suitable to the region than Odo.) In general I have avoided terms which may not be clear to the lay reader even at the risk of raising the eyebrows of professionals. For instance I never use 'Mesorhodanic' or Decour's 'Lugduno-romand' (Lyons-Romance) for the language most widely spoken in the Kingdom of Burgundy, and I would reject the only slightly less objectionable 'Franco-Provençal' were its use not so general among philologists; and I hope I have made out a convincing case for the use of the simple word 'Burgundian' instead.

Prologue

1. See H. Stein, '*Un diplomate bourguignon au XVe siècle, Antoine Haneron*', Bibliothèque de l'École des Chartes, vol. xcviii, Paris 1937. The agreement was in Latin and some 300 words in length, excluding the list of the Imperial and Burgundian delegates. Haneron was one of the latter.

Phoenix on the wing

1. See for instance Kenneth Clark, *Civilisation*, p. 8. (Based on a popular and excellent television series)
2. E.g. Peter Salway, *Roman Britain*, p. 479; A. H. M. Jones, *Later Roman Empire*, p. 248; J. N. L. Myres, *The English Settlements* (1986), p. 208f, for the contrast.
3. The earliest references to the Burgundians are by Pliny the Elder *c.* 59 (reign of Nero) and Ptolemy before 170 (Marcus Aurelius), the former placing them near the Baltic, the latter between the Oder and Vistula. The most interesting are those in Ammianus Marcellinus (Bk xxviii) which bring out differences in culture and

social organization between the Franks, Allemans and Burgundians, which are very greatly to the advantage of the Burgundians. Writing shortly after the event he also tells how Emperor Valentinian appealed *c.* 370 to the Burgundians for help against the Allemans because the former had 'regarded themselves as Romans' since their settlement in the Rhine-Danube triangle by Emperor Probus in 278 (Bk xxviii, Ch. 5).

4. Perrin, O., *Les Burgondes*, p. 96. This may be the best work to consult for the Burgundians' beginnings.

5. Like Aetius 'the last of the Romans' before him, Gundioc was made *Magister Militum Galliarum*, strictly 'Commander-in-Chief of the Gauls', but effectively governor-general or viceroy of the several provinces of 'Gaul'. Perrin, op. cit. p. 342, gives good grounds for the contention that the Burgundians' viceroyalty embraced the six provinces listed below. What seems conclusive is that the areas involved (e.g. see lists of cities in Perrin p. 197 *et seq.*) continued to form the Kingdom of Burgundy for many centuries; and that the Church's ecclesiastical provinces, i.e. archbishoprics (as indicated here in the parentheses), thenceforth corresponded to these Burgundo-Roman provinces, the main difference being that Viennensium was broken into the separate archbishoprics of Vienne and Arles virtually from the start.

Lugdunensis Prima (ecclesiastical province of Lyons, including Autun, Langres, Chalon and Mâcon)

Maxima Sequanorum (eccl. prov. Besançon, incl. Basle etc.)

Alpium Graiarum et Penninarum (eccl. prov. Tarentaise)

Viennensium (eccl. provs. Vienne incl. Geneva etc. and Arles incl. Avignon, Marseilles etc.)

Narbonensis Secunda (eccl. prov. Aix-en-Provence)

Alpium Maritimarum (eccl. prov. Embrun)

6. Perronot, Th., *La Toponymie Burgonde*. But see also Perrin, p. 349, and works in the bibliography by Wartburg, Sauter and Dauzat.

Places of Burgundian origin end in -*ans*, -*an*, -*ens*, -*ins*, -*inges*, -*enges*, -*anges*, -*z*. Even if only names in -*ans* are taken (as in Perronot's analysis on p. 269), about half the names in Suisse Romande and Franche Comté will be seen to be Burgundian, the balance being Celtic or Latin. High proportions are to be found also in other departments east of the Saône – Ain, Haute-Savoie and Savoie (the river between Chalon and Vienne was almost certainly the western limit of the *main* Burgundian settlements); but only small proportions west of the river: one-eighth in the department of Côte d'Or, one-fifteenth in Saône-et-Loire, and smaller still in Rhône and Loire, as also in the fringe area all around–Isère, the Valais, the frontier land shared with the Allemans between Aar and Reuss, Nièvre and Yonne (the two western departments of the modern French region of Burgundy), and the Val d'Aosta annexed in 576.

[261]

Thus (1) in the areas east of Chalon-Vienne which today correspond with the lands donated to the Burgundians, Burgundian names represent about half of Perronot's considerable sample. The Burgundians may not have formed as much as half the population there but they were anyway a very important part of it, probably because many areas had become depopulated. (2) West and north-west of Chalon-Vienne there was lighter Burgundian settlement. (3) Almost all of the Kingdom, excepting only Provence, can be said to have had some Burgundian settlement. (See Map no. 6.)

The other evidence (cemeteries, the dispersion of the Burgundians' Romance language and of their cattle, and traces of their civil and criminal codes) tends broadly to bear out these conclusions about the *dispersion* of the Burgundians. All this, however, tells us little about their *numbers*.

7. Perrin, op. cit., p. 90.
8. For the close links between Burgundy and Constantinople see Wellesley, Egon, *Eastern Elements in Western Chant*, p. 201; and Granakoplos, D. J., *Byzantine East and Latin West*, p. 42. Also see *Liturgia* ed. Abbé Aigrain (Paris 1935).
9. Bede II, ch. XV.
10. For the persistence of Roman civilization: Deanesley, M., *H. Early Medieval Europe*, p. 117 f.; Pirenne, H., *Mahomet et Charlemagne, passim*; James, E. F., *The Origins of France*, pp. 46–8; Palangue, J. R., in *H. Provence* (ed. Baratier), p. 98; Glotz, *H. Moyen Age* vol. I, p. 174.
11. Esp. by Charles Bonnet. See his articles in *Archéologie Suisse* 4, 1980, pp. 174–91, and *Vallesia* XXXIII, 1978, pp. 75–7; and his book *Les premiers édifices chrétiens de la Madeleine à Genève* (Geneva 1977).
12. Deanesley, M., *H. Early Medieval Europe*, p. 222.
13. Steyert, A., *H. Lyon*, p. 66. Roman roads were long called *chaussées de Brunehaut*.
14. Pirenne, H., *H. Europe*, p. 37.
15. Baratier, E.: *H. Provence*, p. 113.
16. There were long gaps in almost every diocese in Burgundy (and Aquitaine), e.g. also Aix 596–794 and Autun 696–762: Duchesne, Mgr.,*Fastes episcopaux de l'ancienne Gaule*, vol. I pp. 229, 261, II p. 181.
17. 'Christian civilization of the sixth and seventh centuries is above all a civilization of Burgundian origin', an overstatement by Chaume, *Le sentiment national bourguignon*, p. 204. However, for south Gaul as the most Romanized part of the western Empire see Deanesley, p. 54; and for Italy's decline being faster and deeper than Burgundy's see Pirenne, *Mahomet et Charlemagne*, p. 69. Spain was obviously the most affected by the Moors' invasions. For a fascinating discussion as to whether the main break at least in economic continuity came less with the Teutonic invasions than with the Moors 3–400 years later, see Pirenne, *Mahomet et Charlemagne*; Lopez, R. S., *Mohammed and Charlemagne* (1943) and *East and West in the Early Middle Ages* (1955); Baynes, N. H., *M. Pirenne and the Unity of the*

Mediterranean World (1955); and Dennett, D. C., *Pirenne and Mohammed*. Pirenne is supported by, *inter alios*, Deanesley and Trevor-Roper.

18. Toynbee, Paget, *Specimens of Old French* (Oxford, 1892), p. 10.
19. Wartburg, W. von, *Les origines des peuples romans*, p. 138.
20. Murrell, E. S., *Gérart de Rossillon and the 'Tristan' Poems* (Chesterfield 1926).

The Paragon of Excellence and Beauty

1. G. N. Wright, 'Order from a Wilderness' in *Country Life* of 28 December 1972.
2. Oursel, C., *L'Art de Bourgogne*, p. 75.
3. Conant, K. J., *Carolingian and Romanesque Architecture*. Many passages stress the importance of Burgundian architecture and its wide-spread influence.
4. For the view that France's contribution to medieval architecture has been seriously overvalued, see Kingsley Porter, A., *Romanesque Sculpture of the Pilgrimage Roads*, e.g. pp. 6, 10, 12 *et seq.*
5. Evans, J., *The Romanesque architecture of the Order of Cluny*. See e.g. figs 114, 115.
6. Brun, A., *L'introduction du français dans les provinces du Midi*.
7. Elcock, W. D., *The Romance languages* (Faber), p. 397.

'Ashes'

1. Gaul as we know it was often described as 'Galliae', the Gauls, as in Magister Militum Galliarum. 'Gallia' in the singular was often reserved for Burgundy as distinct from 'Francia', especially by German historians. So too 'Gallican' could mean Burgundian.
2. Roger of Hoveden, *Chronica*, in Rolls Series, ed. W. Stubbs, vol. iii (1195) p. 301. Hoveden's comment on Henry VI's objective appears in connection with the situation in 1195, when it was probably attainable only if he and Richard I were at one – not always the case. Both died prematurely, Henry in 1197, Richard in 1199. Philip Augustus lived till 1223 and, in the absence of strong rulers in Aquitaine-Normandy or Germany, made France the power she remained for most of the centuries to come.

   Hoveden (Howden), who is drawn on throughout this section, is probably the most trustworthy of our sources for the period.
3. Hoveden, op. cit., iii 202, 203.
4. For Savaric see Church, C. M., *Chapters in the Early History of the Church of Wells* (London 1894); pp. 89, 93, 99, 101–2; or his *Four Somerset Bishops* (London 1909), p. 52, etc.
5. *Cambridge Medieval History*, vol. V, p. 469.

6. Hoveden iii 225: 'After this [i.e. autumn 1193] the Emperor gave to the King of England, establishing it by his charter (*et carta sua confirmavit*), the following territories: Provence, Vienne, Viennois [the later Dauphiné], Marseilles, Narbonne [never in Burgundy], Arles, Lyons, ['the lands' omitted?] above the Rhône as far as the Alps [imprecise but this anyway excluded Aosta and Susa?], and all that the Emperor has in Burgundy (*quicquid habet imperator in Burgundia*) [possibly the scattered Hohenstaufen domains in the Kingdom, more probably a reference to the County of Burgundy, inherited by Henry from his mother]; and the homage of the King of Aragon [probably for his lands and rights in the Midi], and the homage of the Count of Diois [between Provence and Dauphiné] and the homage of the Count of Saint Gilles [i.e. the Count of Toulouse].' These lands, Hoveden says, comprised five archbishoprics (no doubt Lyons, Vienne, Arles, Aix; and possibly Besançon is meant rather than Narbonne, Tarentaise or Embrun), as well as 33 bishoprics.

7. Hoveden iii 227.
8. Hoveden iii 226.
9. Ralph of Diceto, *Opera Historica*, Rolls Series, ed. W. Stubbs, vol. ii, p. 113; Hoveden iii 202, though its place in the Rolls Series is early 1193 and the event was early 1194; Norgate, K., *Richard the Lionheart*, p. 336; Bryce, J. V., *The Holy Roman Empire*, p. 184.
10. Hoveden iii 236, footnote.
11. Hoveden iii 300.
12. Bryce, op. cit. p. 184.
13. E.g., J. Gillingham (1973), p. 213; P. Henderson (1958), p. 238.
14. Steyert, A., *H. Lyon*, p. 366.

Phoenix Resurgent

1. Fournier, P., *Le Royaume d'Arles et de Vienne* (1891) is the fullest source, but see also E. Barattier, *H. Provence* (Toulouse 1969), p. 175.
2. For Provence's population growth: Fevrier, P-A., *Le développement urbain en Provence de l'époque romaine à la fin du XIVe siècle*, p. 138.
3. Fournier, op. cit., p. 235.
4. Simonde de Sismondi, *H. des Republiques Italiennes* (1840), vol. II, p. 467.
5. Sismondi, op. cit., p. 518.
6. Villani, Giovanni (*c.* 1275–1348), *Chronica*, Book VII, chap. 1.
7. Sismondi, op. cit., p. 441.
8. Chaume, M., *'Le sentiment national bourguignon'*, p. 215.
9. Marie-José, *La Maison de Savoie*, vol. 2i, p. 286, gives examples of Amadeus VIII's use of this authority outside territory which was strictly his.

10. Toynbee, Arnold, *A Study of History*, iv p. 198 and (for Burgundy) iii p. 349.
11. Cazaux, Yves, *Marie de Bourgogne* (Paris 1967), p. 148.
12. From the so-called Chronicle of Lorraine.
13. So named by the Burgundian historian, Jean Molinet.
14. Cazaux, op. cit., p. 170. While partisan for Charles, Cazaux bases his case on excellent authorities.
15. Huizinga, J., *Burgund, eine Krise des romanisch-germanischen Verhältnisses* (Wissenschaftliche Buchgesellschaft, Darmstadt, 1967), p. 53. See Note 20 below.
16. Dufayard, Ch., *H. Savoie*, (Boivin et Cie., 3 Rue Palatine, Paris VIe, 1922) p. 170.
17. The several accounts of Charles Emmanuel's stealthy assault on Geneva in 1602 do not always tally. I have mostly followed that in Picot, J., *Histoire de Genève*, vol. ii, p. 297 *et seq.* (Geneva, 1811); but Muller, J. de, *Histoire de la Confédération Suisse*, vol. xii, p. 360 *et seq.* (Paris and Geneva 1841) is valuable; and of the histories of Savoy, Saint Genis, V. de, vol. ii, p. 234 *et seq.* (Chambéry, 1869) is the fullest. Armstrong, E., in the *Cambridge Modern History* (Ed. 1904) vol. iii, pp. 415–21, is excellent for the general picture, the duke's ambitions and the story of the Escalade.
18. E.g. *C.M.H.* vol. iii, p. 420.
19. Dufour, L., *La mère Royaume et sa marmite* (Geneva 1880).
20. Calmette, J., *The Golden Age of Burgundy* (Weidenfeld 1962), p. 287; and the Huizinga lecture of 1932 mentioned in Note 15 above. The latter (a booklet) seems not to be readily available in Britain (or the USA?), unhappily, since it is a remarkable analysis of the situation in the area of the Middle Kingdom in the fifteenth and sixteenth centuries; of several 'might-have-been' possibilities; and of the hard and too often forgotten *reality* of Burgundy in the sixteenth century, i.e. after the disaster of Nancy in 1477. Huizinga's speculation, which is more far-reaching than mine, is based largely on the books and letters of the nineteenth-century historian Jacob Burckhardt.

Dates

Dates in *italics* are not specially to do with the history of Burgundy or its component states.

Some early dates are approximate (or are disputed).

Dates of kings, etc., will not normally appear here as well as in Appendix VII.

Abbreviations will be normal ones or easily understood, e.g. d. = died, acc. = acceded. Burgundian(s) may be Burg'n(s), etc.

Beginnings: Making of Burgundy

Probably before 100	Burgundians from S. Norway/Sweden to Poland via Bornholm (Burgundarholm).
At least from 150	Contacts with Roman civilization.
278	Settled by Emperor Probus in Rhine-Danube triangle (Württemberg). Some also in Britain where help put down revolt.
287	In war with Allemans driven east into Bavaria.
Probably from *c.* 300	Christianized (Arians).
370	'Because they are Romans' Burg'ns fight for Emperor against Allemans.
405–6	Huns' pressure forces Burg'ns into Rhine valley.
410	*Alaric (Visigoth) sacks Rome.*
413	Burg'ns ceded lands on Rhine, center Worms. Gunther ?410–37 recognized as king by imperial authorities. 'First Kingdom' can be dated from now or from 443.
418–22	*Visigoths settle Aquitaine.*
436	Burg'ns massacred by Huns.
443	Settled in Sapaudia (Savoy, W. Vaud, N. Dauphiné).
c. 450	*Traditional, Anglo-Saxon invasion of Britain.*
451	Burg'ns help imperial forces under Aetius defeat Huns.
457–8	Sequania (County of Burgundy, Franche Comté) awarded to Burg'ns.

457–70	King Gundioc makes Geneva capital.
460–80	Burg'n settlement outside 'Homeland'.
461	Ricimer Patrician (chief minister) in Rome makes Gundioc Magister Militum (imperial governor-general) of Gauls.
470	King Chilperic makes Lyons capital.
472	Burg'ns repulse Allemans (settled middle and upper Rhine and E. Switzerland).
472–4	Gundobad (Gundioc's son) Patrician in Rome.
474	Kingship shared between brothers Gundobad, Godegisel (in Geneva) and Chilperic II, but Gundobad (474–516) increasingly master from Champagne to Mediterranean.
476	*Last Roman emperor in West.*

First wars with Franks/French. Burgundy stays separate under Merovings

487–93	*Theodoric, Ostrogoth, conquers Italy, d. 526*
c. 493	Chilperic's daughter Clotilda marries and converts Clovis, Frank king (481–511, now master most of N.E. Gaul).
?490–510	*British defeat Saxons Mount Badon.*
507	*Clovis conquers Aquitaine.*
c. 510	Sigismund, heir to Gundobad, becomes catholic. Built in these years were Geneva's 'double cathedral', palace on Roman praetorium, St Germain and Madeleine, and (in Valais) Abbey of St Maurice d'Agaune.
523	Sigismund (acc. 516) captured and murdered by Franks.
534	Franks (Merovings) control Burgundy.
537	*Army of Justinian (emperor in east 527–65) takes Rome. Byzantines gain and keep footholds in western Mediterranean for several centuries.*
575	*Brunhild rules in Austrasia. Lombard invaders reach Benevento, S. Italy.*
575–6	Aosta and Susa to Burgundy.
590–604	*Pope Gregory the Great. Sends Augustine to England 596.*
593–613	Brunhild rules in Burgundy.
616	Burg'ns secure charter from Clothar II. Effectively separate again until 735 except 629–39 Dagobert restores Frank authority.
657–81	Ebroin rules as mayor of the palace, murders St Léger c. 677.

Saracens. Carolingian oppression

711 plus	*Saracens (Moors) overrun Spain.*
720	Saracens take Narbonne; 721 sack Luxeuil, N. Burgundy; 725 Carcassonne, Nîmes, Autun, etc.
732	Sarcens defeated by Charles Martel at Poitiers. But continue as threat to West for 2–3 centuries.
737	Charles Martel finally master of Burgundy, dies 741.
741–68	His son Pepin III rules; king of Franks from 751, founding Carolingian dynasty.
771–814	Charlemagne sole king. (800 crowned Emperor)

Burgundian struggle for independence. Threats from Saracens and Norsemen

835–53	Guerin count of Mâcon starts struggle against Franks.
841	Lothar I (grandson of Charlemagne) defeated by brothers Louis and Charles at Fontenay (nr. Auxerre). Leads to partition of Verdun 843 (Charles's border eventually becomes frontier of France).
842	Saracens sack Arles. (846 desecrate St Peter's Rome)
855	Lothar I leaves Burgundy and Provence to youngest son Charles. Gerard of Roussillon in control.
859	Norsemen devastate Provence, defeated by Gerard. He founds Vézelay abbey.
861	First serious threat of Norsemen to Frankish Burgundy.
863	Charles of Provence dies. Gerard divides kingdom between C's sons Lothar II (Lyons, Vienne) and Louis (Provence).
870	Gerard defeated. Boso count of Lyons and Vienne; later of Provence, Chalon and Autun.
877	Death of Gerard.

Re-emergence of Burgundy (Second Kingdom)

879	Boso crowned at Mantaille nr. Vienne.
880 plus	His brother Richard the Justiciar called Duke of Burgundy.
883	*Saracens sack Monte Cassino. Roman Campagna made a desert.*
886	Charles the Fat buys Norsemen off Paris by 'offering' Burgundy.
887	Boso dies. Son Louis infant, recognized King of Lower Burgundy (Provence), from Chalon and Autun to Mediterranean.

887	*Charles the Fat deposed. Arnulf King of East Franks and Emperor. Odo Count of Paris made King of West Franks.*
888	Rudolf Guelph Count of Vaud becomes King of Transjuran (Upper) Burgundy as Rudolf I.
891 plus	Saracens established at La Garde-Frainet (Les Maures) in Provence.
c. 900	Lay of Atli (Iceland): first written version of Gunther legend. (300 years later, by a coincidence, Volsungasaga and Nibelungenlied – in respectively Scandinavia and Bavaria – appear almost simultaneously, both combining Gunther and Brunnhilde-Siegfried legends)
900 plus	*Duchy of Lorraine (Lotharingia) merged in Kingdom of East Franks (Germany).*
905	Louis of Provence blinded. Hugh of Arles Count of Provence dominant.
910	Cluny abbey founded.
911	*Richard the Justiciar allied with Robert Marquis of Neustria (future Duchy of France) defeats Rollo, Norse leader, at Chartres. Rollo founds Duchy of Normandy.*
919	*Henry I (the Fowler) founds Saxon dynasty of east Franks.*
919, from	Magyars regularly invading Burgundy.
921	Richard the Justiciar dies. Son Raoul Duke of Burgundy (923 King of West Franks).
933	Rudolf II (of Transjuran kingdom) reunites Kingdom of Burgundy, gaining Provence from Hugh of Arles, who becomes King of Italy.
c. 930–948	Hugh (nephew of Hugh of Arles) apparently first Count of Maurienne (i.e. Savoy). Grandfather of Humbert of the White Hands.

Emergence of Germany and France

935	Death of Raoul, followed 936 by separation of Duchy of Burgundy (Mâcon, Chalon, Autun, Dijon) and Duchy of France (Langres, Troyes, Sens, Auxerre, as well as Paris).
936	*Otto I King of Germany.*
937	Rudolf II succeeded by Conrad the Peaceful, a minor. Magyars sack Tournus, ravage Lyonnais.
951	Adelaide sister of Conrad marries Otto I, beginning of German influence.

955	*Otto crushes Magyars at Lechfeld. A turning point for revival of civilization.*
961	*Otto King of Italy, 962 Emperor – effective creation of Holy Roman Empire.*
973	Saracens expelled from La Garde-Frainet (Provence), largely through Abbot Majolus of Cluny.
987	*Hugh Capet King of West Franks i.e. France.*
994	Rudolf III of Burgundy presides at installation of Odilo as Abbot of Cluny, i.e. it is in Burgundy not France.
c. 1000–48	Humbert White Hands Count of Savoy and Maurienne.
1002–26	Otto William Count of Burgundy and Mâcon.
1006	Emperor Henry II seizes Basle from Burgundy.
1015	Robert Capet of France defeats Otto William for Duchy of Burgundy.

Emperors gain Burgundy

1016	Rudolf III recognizes Emperor Henry II as heir, leading to revolt led by Otto William 1016–26.
1024–39	*Conrad II Emperor.*
1031	Robert Duke of Burgundy (Duchy now hereditary in junior branch of Capetians).
1032	Rudolf III dies. Odo of Blois chief rival to Conrad for Kingdom of Burgundy until death 1037.
1034	Emperor Conrad crowned King of Burgundy at Payerne and Geneva.
1038	Conrad's control effective, though Burg'ns long rebellious. He makes his son Henry King of Burgundy i.e. of a separate kingdom. He succeeds in 1039 as Henry III of Germany and I of Burgundy.
c. 1045/50	Burg'n chronicler Rudolf Glaber dies.
1056–61	Rudolf Rheinfelden viceroy of Burgundy.
1061–87	William Count of Burgundy viceroy of Burgundy.
1066 plus	*Normans conquer England.*
1073	Investiture quarrel starts over bishop for Die, i.e. in Burgundy.
1076	Archbishop of Lyons builds bridge only replaced 1846.
1077	*Henry IV kneels to Pope at Canossa.*

Crusades, Monastic Orders

1078	Hugh I Duke of Burgundy leads crusade in Spain.
1078–1111	Bethold II Duke of Zähringen viceroy of Burgundy.
1084	Carthusian order founded.
1085	Burgundian troops active in capture of Toledo from Moors.
1095	Pope Urban calls for freeing of Holy Land. Dedication of Cluny III.
1098	Cistercian order founded.
By 1100	'Alexander of Macedon' written in a Burgundian dialect.
1110	Bosonids die out. Provence goes mostly to Berenger of Barcelona.
1119	*Guy Archbishop of Vienne becomes pope Calixtus II, concludes Concordat of Worms with Henry V.*
1100–40	Building of the great Cluniac churches (pointed vaults).
1120–70	Building of the great Cistercian churches (pointed windows from *c.* 1130).
1122–52	Conrad duke of Zähringen (Rector of Burgundy for a time).
1125–38	Under Emperor Lothar II Burg'ns still rebellious.

Hohenstaufen Emperors, Kings of Burgundy (1138–1254)

1147	*Second Crusade*
1152–86	Berthold IV Duke of Zähringen (Rector of Burgundy for a time).
c. 1160	Chanson de geste 'Gerard de Roussillon' (in a Burg'n dialect?)
1164–92	Hugh III Duke of Burgundy. Apparently the Duchy's first homage to a king of France.
1166	County of Forez becomes part of France.
c. 1170	Valdensian heresy starts (at Lyons).
1178	Frederick I (Barbarossa) crowned King of Burgundy at Arles.
1182–92	Englishman John White Hands Archbishop of Lyons.
1186	Duke Hugh III seeks Frederick's help against Philip Augustus of France but latter defeats him.
1189	Third Crusade.
1193	Emperor Henry VI (1190–7) assigns crown of Burgundy to Richard Lionheart.
1204	*Fourth Crusade. Western crusaders set up Latin Empire at Byzantium.*

Fall of Hohenstaufen; Rise of France, Provence and Savoy

1212–50	Frederick II Emperor and king. Conflict with Papacy comes to climax. Decline of imperial control in Burgundy.
1213, 1214	*France's victories at Muret (south) and Bouvines (north) symbolic of her rising power.*
1215	Innocent III proscribes Albigensian heretics. The crusade against them introduces French power into southern Gaul.
1215	*Magna Carta in England.*
c. 1220	Notre Dame de Dijon (Burgundian Gothic).
1244	*Jerusalem lost by Christians, never to be recovered.*
1246	Charles of Anjou Count of Provence.
1257–72	Richard of Cornwall (Henry III's brother) widely recognized as king.
1261	*Westerners lose Byzantium again to Greeks.*
1263	Savoy increasingly powerful from accession of Count Peter (lived from 1246 in London at Palace of Savoy).
1271–1312	French advances in southern Gaul.
1281–2	Charles of Anjou (and Provence) close to restoring separate Kingdom of Burgundy; Duke of Burgundy and English allied against French and Charles.
1281 onwards	Rebuilding of Dijon cathedral in Burgundian Gothic.
c. 1300	Saint-Thibault-en-Auxois built in French Gothic. 'Beatrice of Ornaciu' written in Burgundian.

Decline of France, Rise of Duchy of Burgundy

1309, 1337	Further opportunities for Angevins to gain crown of Arles.
1315 onwards	French generally in retreat in Burgundy and elsewhere.
1343	But they gain Dauphiné.
1346	*French military disaster at Crécy.*
1351, 1353	Strengthening of Swiss Confederacy through adherence of Zürich and Bern respectively.
1364–1404	Philip the Bold founds great Valois dynasty of Duchy.
1365	Emperor Charles IV crowned at Arles.
1384	Philip the Bold and wife Margaret inherit Flanders, Artois, Nevers, etc.
1386	Hapsburgs crushed by Swiss at Sempach.
1415	*French army destroyed at Agincourt.*

1415, 1416	Emperor Sigismund makes royal progresses through his Kingdom of Arles.
1416	Count Amadeus VIII made Duke of Savoy.
1420–35	Duchy of Burgundy, now separate from France, grows steadily in power.
1428	Philip the Good gains Holland, Zealand, Hainault.
1429	*Relief of Orléans by St Joan.*
1435	Congress of Arras. Philip ascendant.
1435–77	Duchy of Burgundy leading power in Europe.

Recovery of France, Fall of Burgundy. Final centuries

1436	*French recover Paris.*
1443	Philip gains Luxemburg.
1453	*English lose Guyenne, retain only Calais and Channel Islands.*
1467	Charles the Bold accedes.
1473	Conference of Trier. Charles made King of Burgundy, abortively. Daughter Mary's marriage to Maximilian Hapsburg arranged.
1475	English invade France. Treaty of Picquigny. Charles occupies Lorraine.
1476	Swiss defeat Charles at Grandson and Morat.
1477	Charles slain at Nancy. Mary marries Maximilian.
1477–93	France secures Duchy of Burgundy, Hapsburgs the rest of Charles's empire.
1526	Charles V briefly recovers Duchy.
1536–57	French masters of Savoy until Emmanuel Philibert defeats them at St Quentin.
1580–1610	Charles Emmanuel of Savoy aspires to crown of Burgundy. Occupies Aix-en-Provence etc. 1590–1.
1602	Charles Emmanuel fails to take Geneva. Duchy of Burgundy finally annexed to France.
1678	County of Burgundy ceded by Hapsburgs to France.
1713	Savoy becomes a kingdom (as 'Sardinia').
1860	Savoy annexed to France.

Rulers of Burgundy

The First Kingdom

Nibelungs

Gebicca	?late 4th C.	Gundobad	474
Gunther	by 413	(Godegisel,	
		king at Geneva	474–500)
Gundioc	437	Sigismund	516
Chilperic I	c. 470	Gundomar	523–34

Merovings

Clotar I	534–61	Clotar II	613–29
(also Francia	558–61)	(also Francia	613–23)
Guntram	561–92	Dagobert	629–39
Childebert II	593–95	(also Francia)	
Theodoric II	595–613	Merovingian kings'	
		control slight	639–751

Carolings

Also Francia:

		Burgundy, 'Lotharingia',	
		Italy only:	
Pepin	751	Lothar I	843–55
Carloman	768	Burgundy, 'Lotharingia':	
Charlemagne	771	Lothar II	855–69
Louis the Pious	814	Also Francia:	
Lothar I	840–55	Charles the Bald	869–77

The Second Kingdom

Lower Burgundy			
(Provence): Boso	879–87	Louis the Blind	887–928

Rudolfians

Upper Burgundy:		Reunited Burgundy:	
Rudolf I	888	Rudolf II	933
Rudolf II	912	Conrad the Peaceful	937
		Rudolf III	993–1032

Kings of the Second Kingdom who were mostly also kings of Germany and Italy:

(a) *Franconians*

Conrad II	1033	Henry V	1106
Henry III the Black	1037	Lothar II	1125
Henry IV	1056–1106		

(b) *Hohenstaufen*

Conrad III	1138	(Interregnum	1254–57)
Frederick I Barbarossa	1152	Richard of Cornwall	1257–72
Henry VI	1190	Alfonso of Castile	1257–72
Otto IV	1197		
Frederick II	1212		
Conrad IV	1250–54		

(c) *Later King-Emperors*

Rudolf I of Hapsburg	1274–91	Charles IV (of Luxemburg)	1346
Adolf of Nassau	1292	Wenceslas (of Luxemburg)	1378
Albert I of Hapsburg	1298	Rupert (of Palatinate)	1400
Henry VII (of Luxemburg)	1308–13	Sigismund (of Hungary)	1410–37
Louis IV (of Bavaria)	1314–47		

(d) *Hapsburgs*
(Kingdom of Burgundy or
  Arles increasingly
  shadowy)

Albert V	1438–9	Theoretically speaking	
Frederick III	1440	the last King of	
Maximilian I	1493	Burgundy was:	
Charles V	1519–56	Francis II	1792–1806

Dukes of Burgundy

Richard the Justiciar	880	Hugh III	1162
Raoul	921	Odo III	1192
Hugh the Black	936	Hugh IV	1218
Gilbert	952	Robert II	1272
Otto	956	Hugh V	1306
Henry the Great	965	Odo IV	1315
Otto William	1002–15	Philip of Rouvre	1349–61
Henry	1015	Philip the Bold	1364
Robert I	1032	John the Fearless	1404
Hugh I	1074	Philip the Good	1419
Odo I	1093	Charles the Bold	1467
Hugh II	1102	Maximilian of Hapsburg	1477–1519
Odo II	1143		

Savoy

Counts

Humbert I (White Hands)	c. 1000	Amadeus IV	1233–1253
(gains Bugey 1003, Val		Boniface	1258
d'Aosta 1025,		Peter II (the 'little	
Maurienne 1043)		Charlemagne')	1263
Amadeus I	c. 1048	Philip I	1268
Odo	c. 1057	Amadeus V	1285
(gains lands in Italy)		Edward	1323
Peter I		Aimon	1329
(shares with Odo)	d. 1078	Amadeus VI (the Green	
Amadeus II	1078	Count)	1343
Humbert II	1080	Amadeus VII (the Red	
	d. 1103	Count)	1383
Amadeus III	c. 1103	Amadeus VIII	1391
Humbert III (the Saint)	1149	(became Duke of Savoy	
Thomas I	1189	1416, Pope Felix V	
		1439–49, d. 1451)	

Dukes

Amadeus VIII, Duke	1416–34	Louis	1434

Amadeus IX	1465	Charles III	1504
Philibert I	1472	Emmanuel Philibert	1553
Charles I	1482	Charles Emmanuel I	1580
Charles II	1490	Victor Amadeus I	1630
Philip	1496	Francis-Hyacinth	1637
Philibert II	1497	Charles-Emmanuel II	1638
		Victor-Amadeus II	1675

Kings
Victor-Amadeus II becomes

King of Sicily	1713	and then on to:	
of Sardinia	1718	Charles Felix, last of	
		old House of Savoy	d. 1831
Charles Emmanuel III	1730–73	Victor Emmanuel II,	
		King of Italy	1861–78
		Victor Emmanuel III	1900–46
		Humbert (Umberto) II	1946
		(Republic declared 1946)	

Kings of the Franks to 814

(Often more than one king at a time. These are selected)

Merovech	?	Childebert I	511
Childeric I	*c.* 463	Clotar	511
Clovis	481	(sole king	558–61)
		Caribert	561

Kings of the West Franks
(sometimes of all Franks)

Chilperic I	567	Chilperic II	715
Clotar II	584	Theodoric IV	721–37
(sole king	613–28)	Childeric III	743–51
Dagobert I	628	(Charles Martel, Mayor	
(sole king	632–39)	of the Palace	737–41)
Clovis II	639	Pepin (Mayor 741–51)	751
Clotar III	657	Carloman	768–71
Theodoric III	670	Charlemagne	768
(sole king	679–90)	(Emperor 800–14)	
Clovis III	690		
Childebert III	694		
Dagobert III	711		

Kings of the Franks 814–936

Louis the Pious	814–40 (Emperor 814)	Louis II the Stammerer, West Franks	877–79
Lothar I	840–55 (Emp. 840, Middle Kingdom 843)	Charles the Fat, East Franks	876–87 (Emp. 881)
		Louis III, West Franks	879–82
		Carloman, West Franks	879–84
		Arnulf, East Franks	887–99 (Emp. 896)
Louis the German, East Franks	840–76	Charles the Simple, West Franks	898–922
Charles the Bald, West Franks	843–77 (Emp. 875)	Louis the Child, East Franks	899–911
Louis II, East Franks	855–75	Conrad I, East Franks	911–18
Lothar II, Middle Kingdom	855–69	Henry I the Fowler, East Franks	918–36
Charles, Provence	855–63		

Kings of the West Franks (France) from 898

Charles the Simple	898	Philip III	1270
Robert	922	Philip IV	1285
Raoul	923	Louis X	1314
Louis the Exile	936	Philip V	1316
Lothar	954	Charles IV	1322
Louis V	986	Philip VI (Valois)	1328
Hugh Capet	987	John II	1350
Robert	996	Charles V	1364
Henry I	1031	Charles VI	1380
Philip I	1060	Charles VII	1422
Louis VI	1108	Louis XI	1461
Louis VII	1137	Charles VIII	1493
Philip II (Augustus)	1180	Louis XII	1498
Louis VIII	1223	Francis I	1515–47
Louis IX (Saint)	1226		

Kings of the East Franks (Germany) from 936, Emperors from 962

Saxons		*Franconians*	
Otto I King 946, Emp.	962	Conrad II	1024–37
Otto II	973	(For his successors see	
Otto III	983	under Kings of Burgundy)	
Henry II the Saint	1002		

Abbots of Cluny

Berno	910	Odilo	994
Odo	927	Hugh	1048–1109
Aimar	948	Peter the Venerable	1122–55
Majolus	954		

Genealogical Tables

A   From Charlemagne to Frederick Barbarossa.
B   The Capetians (in Paris and Dijon), Castile and Portugal.
C   The Hohenstaufen (and some connections).
D   Provence 1112–1481.
E   The House of Savoy *c.* 1000–1630.
F   The Duchy of Burgundy 1102–1556.

The tables are extremely selective. They aim to identify personalities who figure in the story (and occasionally to illustrate claims to thrones).

The tables overlap to some extent and some links between them are shown, e.g. B indicates that he or she appears also in Table B.

Dates are mostly avoided so as not to overload the tables, but also because many appear in Appendix VII.

Numbers 1 2 3 indicate the order of birth; (2) indicates a second marriage; a wavy line indicates an illegitimate child; and a vertical dotted line more than one generation.

There are some obvious abbreviations, e.g. K France for King of France, D for Duke of, C Count, B Bishop, A'b Archbishop; d. for daughter (of), s. son.

Table A – From Charlemagne to Frederick Barbarossa

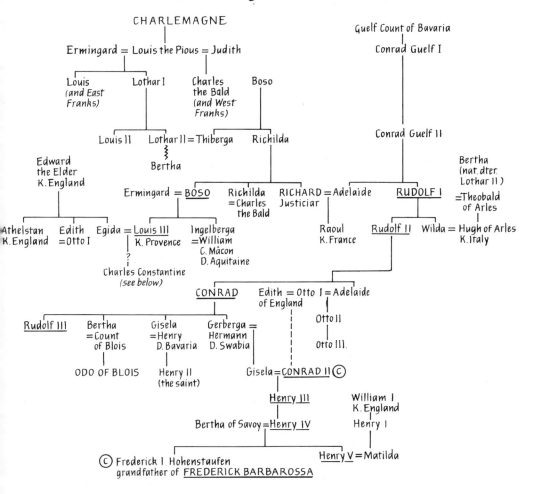

This table, in which Kings of Burgundy are underlined, covers c.800–c.1100. It shows the relationship of *Boso, Richard* and *Rudolf*, lords of the three Burgundies late in 9 cent., and the claims to Burgundy of *Odo* of Blois, and the Emperors *Henry II* (the Saint) and *Conrad II* in the 11th cent.

A matter of no significance in our story but of interest to readers impressed by the interrelationships of these ancient dynasties: on p. 64 I have followed sources which deny any sons to Egida of England and *Louis III* (the Blind), King of Provence (887–928) and briefly King of Burgundy and Emperor; other sources say that Hugh of Arles ousted their son *Charles Constantine* and demoted him to Count of Vienne, which title passed to his sons (i) Poltou, whose daughter Etiennette married William II, Count of Burgundy (Table C), and (ii) Amadeus, father of Humbert White Hands (Tables D and E).

Henry II counts as the last of the Ottonian emperors. His father Henry of Bavaria was Otto I's nephew.

See pp. 278–9 for many rulers appearing above.

Ⓒ denotes that he appears in Table C.

Table B – The Capetians, Castile and Portugal

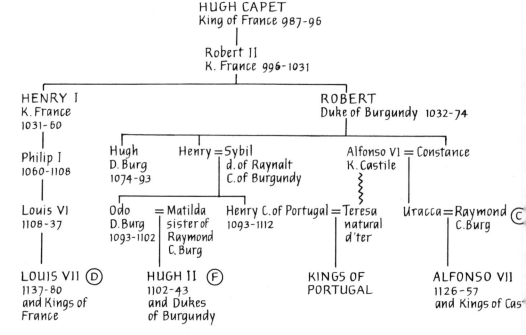

This shows the links between France and Burgundy (Capetian kings and Capetian dukes both died out in 14 cent.); between the Duchy and County of Burgundy (through Count Raynalt's daughter Sybil and granddaughter Matilda); between the Duchy and Castile (Constance marrying Alfonso VI); between the County and Castile (Raynalt's grandson marrying Alfonso's daughter); and above all between the Duchy and Portugal. In 1093 Constance called for her nephew Henry's aid in Castile; as reward he was married to her stepdaughter Teresa and made Count of Portugal. The Burgundian line were Kings of Portugal till 16 c.

Royal and near-royal families were interrelated in those days at least as closely as in modern times. A typical link between this tree and the tree in Table A: Raymond Count of Burgundy and his sister Matilda (ancestors respectively of the Kings of Castile and the Dukes of Burgundy) were the great-grandchildren of Charles Constantine shown in Table A. They were also the great-grandchildren of Otto William in Table C; and, via Charles Constantine, cousins of the House of Savoy (Tables D and E).

© denotes See Table C.

Table C – The Hohenstaufen (and some Connections)

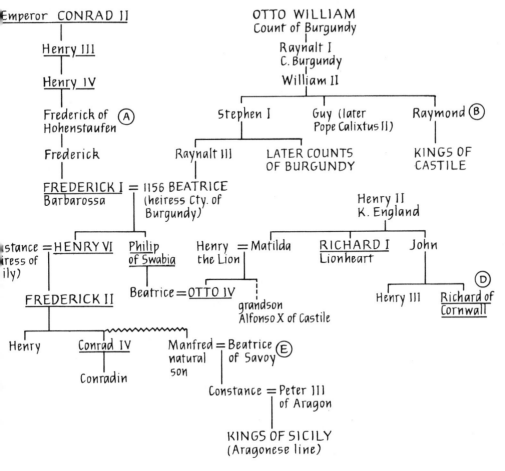

In Emperor Henry VI, who assigned the Kingdom of Burgundy to Richard Lionheart, ran the blood of Otto William, Count of Burgundy, as well as of the Franconian emperors. See Table A for the latter.

Kings of Burgundy are underlined, including some claimants not widely accepted, eg the English Richards and Philip of Swabia.

For the Angevins, rulers of Provence, claimants to Burgundy, but also rivals in Sicily and south Italy of the Hohenstaufen and Aragonese, see Table D.

Ⓐ denotes See Table A,   Ⓑ Table B etc.

Table D – Provence 1112–1481

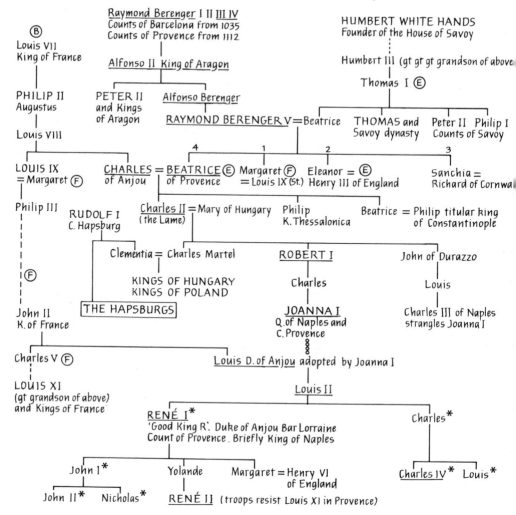

Counts of Provence (or claimants) dying 1471-81, leaving field to Louis XI of France

See the notes on p. 280.
Counts of Provence are underlined.
Ⓒ denotes See Table C.

Table E – The House of Savoy *c.*1000–1630

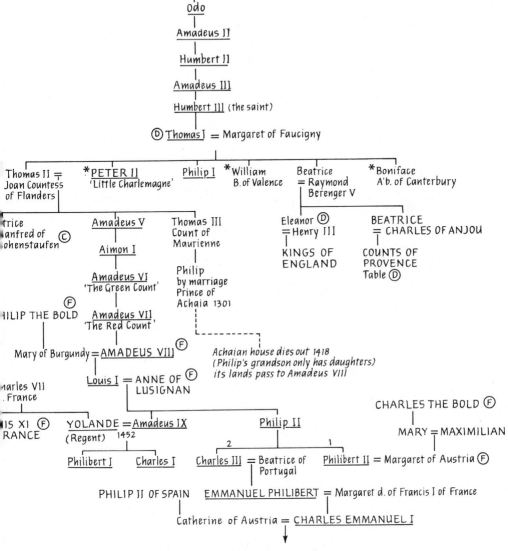

See the notes on p. 280.
Counts and (from 1416) dukes of Savoy are underlined. Several are omitted.
The uncles whom Eleanor of Provence brought to England are asterisked.
Ⓒ denotes See Table C.

Table F – The Duchy of Burgundy 1102–1556

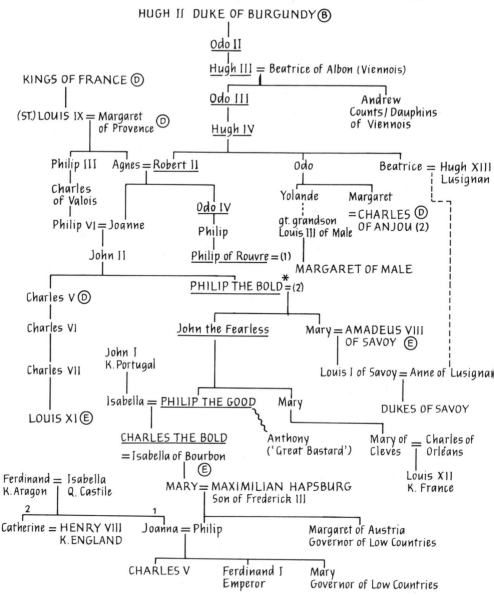

See the notes on p. 280.

Dukes of Burgundy are underlined. Some are omitted.

* Philip of Rouvre's marriage to Margaret had been settled when he succumbed to the plague (1361), and the Capetian line died out. Philip the Good married her nearly eight years later and they started the Valois dynasty.

Ⓓ denotes See Table D.

Index

Abbreviations: B. or Burg. Burgundy; B'n. Burgundian; F. France, French; F.P. Franco-Provençal; S. Savoy; *Ill'n*, see illustration; n footnote; etc.

Aeneas Piccolomini. *See* Pius II.
Aetius, imperial governor of the Gauls 38, 261
Agaune, S. Maurice d', abbey 41
Agincourt 161, 173
Agricultural revolution 11th cent. 74
Albigensians 92–3
Alexander the Great 28
Allemannia 45
Allemannic language(s). *See* Schwyzerdütsch.
Allemannic region of Burgundy: settlement by Allemans and Burgundians 42, Charles Martel and 58, in Rudolf's kingdom 62, not in Burgundian Romanesque area 84, area of Schwyzerdütsch 120, 142 *Map 13*, of Swiss Confederation and early Hapsburgs 144, Charles the Bold invades it 178f, survives as bulk of Switzerland 201, still distinct 203
Allemans: settle Switzerland 42, expel Burgundians 42n *Map 6*, as a cause of Burgundy's failure 229
Alpert (chronicler) 106
Alsace 29, 174, 178, 222
Amadeus VIII, Duke of Savoy, Pope Felix V 153, 154–7, 264 *Ill'n. Map 21*
Angevins 128f, 205. *See also* Charles of Anjou, Charles II, Joanna, René, Robert.
Anselm of Aosta, saint 91
Anthony of Coma and Vienne, saint 51
Anzy-le-Duc 81, 247, *Ill'n.*
Aosta (Val d') 19, 49, 104, 120, 208–11
Aquitaine 42, 45, 110, 113–4, 131
Arch chancellor of Burgundy 21, 107, 147
Architecture, Burgundian: characteristics 21, 84–5, 87, 202–3, 247, 249–50, area 21, 84, 215, 252 *Map 12*, church-building in Dark Ages 51–2, comparison with French 79–80, 87–9, part of 'First Romanesque' 80, role in evolving Gothic 80, 86, 99, Cluny III 80–3 *Ill'ns*, Burgundy's smaller churches 21, 84, Cistercians' 85f, its vast spread 85, 99, Burgundian influence in Italy, Germany, Iberia, France 85–7, 249–50, B'n. Gothic 87, 250–2, succumbs to French

influence 88, 251, influence in Normandy and England 89, 251
Architecture, English 80, 89–90, 249, 251
Architecture, French 79–80n, 86–9, 247–51
Architecture (generally) 247–50; rebuilding of churches around 1000 (Glaber) 74, 'First Romanesque' 80, transition from Romanesque to Gothic 86, 248, distinguishing styles 87, 248–50
Arelate (Arelatum): Kingdom of Burgundy comes to be called 51, 103n, 104, 113, frontiers 104, 147, 191–3. *See* Arles, Kingdom of, *and Maps 11, 17*
Arians, Burgundians as 38, 50
Arles 51–2, 54, 74 *Ill'n.*; coronations at 21, 108, 109, 147
Arles, Kingdom of: 104–48, 191–7; frontiers 104; 'permanence' 148; as Lower Burgundy, as distinct from Kingdom of Vienne, Transjuran B. or Upper B. 113n. *See also* Arelate, Provence, and Burgundy *notably references from 128 onwards*
Armagnacs 161
Arras, Congress of 161
Arthur of Britain 36, 38–9n
Athanagild, father of Brunhild 47
Augustine, saint, (of Canterbury) 36, 49
Austrasia 42, 45, 47, 120n
Austria. *See* Hapsburgs, Charles V, Frederick III etc.
Autun 51, 55: cathedral 81, 87 *Ill'ns.*
Auxerre 21, 43 *Ill'n.*
Avignon 19, 23, 74, 134, 138 *Ill'n.*
Avitus, Archbishop of Vienne 46

Basin, Saône-Rhône 23, 45, 216, 230, 234 *Map 2*
Basin, Thomas, on Charles the Bold 182
Basle 68, 104
Baux family 108, 115, 129, 131, 138
Bavaria 23n
Beatrice of Burgundy 110
Beatrice of Provence 128f

Beaujolais 19

Belfort 43, 174

Belgium 185, 187, 214: offered as 'Kingdom of Burgundy' 21, as successor state of B. 23, 201, 222, *see also* Netherlands

Bells, placing of, 21

Bern 144, 178f

Bernard, saint 78, 91, 234: culmination of Church's influence in Burgundy 75, influence on B.'s art 78, 87, 98

Besançon 21

Bibracte 19

Bishops, 'disappearance' in 8th cent. 54, 262

Bohemia 23, 148

Bornholm (Burgundarholm) 36

Boso, founder of Second Kingdom 62f *Map 10*

Bourg-en-Bresse 204–5

Bourguignon (dialects) 94, 120, 142, 184, 206, 242

Brabant 28

Bresse 110, 151, 154, 193

Britain 36, 38n. *See also* England

Brou, church of 204, 235 *Ill'ns.*

Brunhild (Brunehaut), Queen 47f, 52, 236–7; inspiration of the legend 47, importance 49, Burgundy's decline after death 53

Bugey 151, 154, 193

Burgundian, the language. *See* Franco-Provençal

Burgundian (region of) Burgundy 42, 43n, *120*, 231. *See also* Homeland.

Burgundian "national" consciousness 106–7, *140*, *145*, 153–4, 183, 218

Burgundian point of view, view of history 24, 232, 253

Burgundians: settle Homeland 21, 38–9, 42, 261, early B'ns. 'most Romanised of "barbarians"' 36, their migrations 36f, 260–1, their kingdom of Worms 38 *Map 5*, under Roman influence 38 *Map 5*, destroyed by Huns 38, their 'First Kingdom' 39f *Maps 7, 11*, their numbers 42, their culture in 'Dark Ages' 45, 50–5, 262, laws 45, in Spain and Portugal 77, characteristic realism and moderation 78, 235, resistance to invaders 41, 106–7, 183–4. *See also* 266–7

Burgundy: as wine country 19, 23, 74, 201, 235 *Ill'n.*, extent 19f, 29, 42–3, 62–4, 103–6, 120–4, 147, 161, 177, 215, 218 *Maps 4, 5, 7, 10, 11, 16, 17, 22*, 'milk' of B. 21, 184, B. as chimera 21, a kingdom in Charlemagne's empire 23, 103, an original kingdom of Europe, a long-lasting kingdom 23, 104, 231, disappearance of the kingdom 23, 201, 233, leaving few remnants

23–4, 201–2, comparison with England 23, 36, 49, no comprehensive history of 24, 231, 253–4, its case gone by default 24, 231–2, B. as might-have-been 24, 213–26, 231, its power under Valois dukes 27, 161–2, the Kingdom restored for Charles the Bold 29, 170f;

The Kingdom created by the Nibelungs 38, the First Kingdom 39–56 *Map 7*, taken over by the Merovings 41, settlement by Franks and Allemans as well as Burgundians results in emergence of four different regions 43, B.'s 'national' church 46, B. as a sub-Roman kingdom 50, survival of civilisation in 50f, 262, relatively slow decline 54, part of Mediterranean world in Dark Ages 55, Moors' invasion 57, Charles Martel administers B. in its four regions 58, distinctiveness from France 58, 66, 66n, 80, 97, 145, Vikings' attacks 61f, partial restoration of Kingdom by Boso 62;

The Second Kingdom 62–148 *Map 11*, Rudolf I's kingdom 62 *Map 10*, reunited with Boso's 64, emergence of Duchy of B. 66, the Kingdom certainly, the Duchy possibly, included in the Middle Kingdom created by the Partition of Verdun 66n, Magyars' attack 64, expulsion of Moors 67, decline and fall of Rudolfian kingdom 68;

B. sees flowering of culture c.1000 onwards 73f, monastic orders 76f, village churches 84, few philosophers 91, heresies 92f, B. a 'permanent feature' in Middle Ages 103–4, its administration as one of the Empire's kingdoms 106–7, offered to Richard Lionheart 112f *Map 15*, prospects c.1200 119, 124, the four regions of B. recapitulated 120–3, B. likely to break into those four regions 124–5 *Maps 16, 17;*

Charles of Anjou and the Angevin attempts to restore the Kingdom (now generally known as the Arelate) 128–39 *Map 18*, the four regions follow different destinies 142f, Savoy a continuation of Kingdom of B. 153, Duchess Yolande and Charles the Bold's designs on the Kingdom 158;

B. as 'new monarchy' 160, its strength in 15th cent. 161f *Map 22*, consolidation by Charles the Bold 162, 172, court and culture in 15th cent. 164, Kingdom reconstituted for Charles 171, abortively 172, B. given federal institutions 172, war with France 173–7, extent of Charles's control over B.'s four

regions 177–8, war with Swiss 179–81, B.'s
alliance with England 181–2, proposal to
restore Kingdom end 16th cent. 183, the Low
Countries as 'Burgundy' 184–5, 218f, B. a
'better bet' than Austria 187, Charles
Emmanuel's attempts 191–7 *Map 23*;
B.'s end and remnants 201–3, notably Savoy
203–5, and Alpine patois 208–12, B. as
'Middle Kingdom' 201, *217–21*, 221–4,
reasons for B.'s failure 181–2, *229–31*, place
in history 233–5.
See also County and Duchy of Burgundy,
Allemannic region, Frankish region,
Homeland, Provence, Savoy, Charles the
Bold, Charles of Anjou, Charles Emmanuel,
Phoenix, *etc.*
Architecture, importance of B.'s, 81, 85, 88–9,
98–9, 247–52; *see also* Architecture.
'Burgundy proper': and 'Abbé Chaume 43, 215,
recapitulation 123, as possible survivor 215–7;
Compared (or contrasted) with England 23, 36,
49, 69–70, 73, 112, 162 *Map 2*, France 58, 66,
88, 226, Germany 215, 226, Ireland 227–8,
Italy 215, 226, Scotland 228;
Contribution to European civilisation 76f, 79f,
98–9, 146, 233–4;
Extent at different periods 19f, 29, 42–3, 62–4,
103–6, 120–4, 147, 161, 177, 215, 218 *see also*
Frontiers *and Maps 7, 11, 16, 22*;
Failure, reasons for 181–2, *229–31*;
First Kingdom of, the 39–56 *Map 7*: created 39,
taken over by Merovingian Franks 41, why
kept intact by them 42f, its four regions 43,
civilisation of 45, 50f;
Frontiers relatively stable 64, 103f, 124, 147; *see
also* Frontiers *and Maps 11, 14*;
Golden age of 73f, *98–9*, 233–4;
'Greater Burgundy': successor to six Roman
provinces 42, becoming the First and later the
Second Kingdom (*which see*) *Map 11*,
recapitulation 123, Charles the Bold and
177–8, Charles Emmanuel and 193;
Hub of Europe, at 73, 233 *Map 14;*
'Lesser Burgundy' (the Inner Kingdom): and
Godegisel 42, restored by Rudolf I 62,
increasingly distinct from 'Greater Burgundy'
123, as it coalesces in the form of Savoy 142,
146–7, 149f; *see also* Homeland, Savoy;
Links with England or Britain 38n, 49, 64, 78,
89–90, 109f, 152, 169, 173f, 181, 197
Lower Burgundy; *see* Provence, Boso;
Middle Kingdom, as (part of) 29, 66n, 146,
217–21, 221–2;
'Might-have-been', as 24, 181, 213–26, *esp. 215,*
218;
Second Kingdom of, the 62–148, *Map 11*:
founded by Boso 62 and Rudolfs 64, decline
68, under Franconian emperors 69f, 103f,
Hohenstaufen emperors 108f, several
contenders 116f, Hapsburgs 124, 142, 144,
Charles IV 147–8; *see also* Arelate;
'Separate and intact' 45, 55, 62, *103*, 116, 126;
Significance of 98–9, 124, 233–5;
Transjuran Burg. 62; *see also* Rudolf I,
Homeland.

Capetians 64, 68, 125, 145, 188
Carolings, Carolingian empire 55, 58–9, 103, 123,
Map 9
Carthusian order 78, 90
Catalonia: architecture 80
Cathars 92–3
Cattle, the Burgundians' 21, 43
Census of 1863 208, 240
Chalon 47
Chaluz 114
Chambéry 191, 225
Champenois 96–7, 206
Chancellor of Burgundy 107
Chapaize 80, 247, *Ill'n.*
Charlemagne 59, 103, 109, 188: empire of C. as
heartland of western Europe 21, compared with
original EEC 23, *Map 3*
Charles II of Anjou (Charles I) 54, 128f, 142, 205,
224, *Ill'n. Map 18*: marries Beatrice of Provence
129, King of Sicily 130, designs on Kingdom of
Burgundy 130f, Sicilian Vespers 134–5, *Ill'n.*
character 135–6
Charles II of Anjou (the Lame) 131–4, 135, 138
Charles of Provence (Caroling) 59
Charles IV, Emperor 115, 147–8
Charles V, Emperor 165, 183–4, 189
Charles VI of France 147–8
Charles VII of France 148
Charles VIII of France 188
Charles III of Savoy 189
Charles the Bald (Carolingian emperor) 59f *Map 9*
Charles the Bold (the Rash), Duke of Burgundy: at
conference of Trier 1473 27–31, 170–2, *Map 4*,
power of his state 27–8, 161–2, invested as
Duke of Guelders 28, Kingdom of Burgundy
reconstituted for him 29, 170, report of his
coronation 31.
Accession 161, controls Lorraine 162, court and

Charles the Bald – *cont.*
culture 164f, contrast with father 168, character
as probably read by Frederick III 171, betrayed
by F. 172, organises his empire 172 *Map 22*, war
on France with Edward IV 174f and its failure
176–7, speech in Nancy 177, war on Swiss 179,
death 181, reasons for failure 181–2, final
comment 182, *Ill'ns.*

Charles the Fat 62

Charles Emmanuel I of Savoy 106, 116, 190–7,
205, 224: first attempt on Kingdom 191, second
193, defeat 195–6, *Ill'ns. Map 23*

Charles Martel 57–8: C.M.'s division of Burgundy
58

Charles Martel of Naples-Provence-Hungary 131,
135

Charlieu 83, *Ill'n.*

Charter of the Burgundians 145

Chartres 87, 89

Chaume, abbé Maurice, 43, 140, 253–4

Chilperic, father of Clotilda 39

Chilperic, King of Neustria 46–7

Church, the Burgundian: as national unifier 46,
importance in Dark Ages 51, 53–4, gaps in
bishops 54, 262, driving force 10th cent.
onwards 76–7, and heresies 91–4, 234,
ecclesiastical provinces 84, 103–4, 261, *Map 12.*
See also Architecture, Cistercians, Cluny.

Churches (particular): 80f. *See also under town
names and Appendix III.*

Cistercians: order founded 78, contrast with Cluny
78, links with England 78–9, 89–90, spread
early (half-) Gothic 78, 85, develop and spread
technology 79, 99, C.'ns and English wool
industry 79, architecture 80, 85, examples 85,
89, 249 *Ill'ns.*, C'n. half-Gothic in England 89,
Ill'n. reforming influence 91, contribution to
European civilisation 98–9, 234. *See also* Saint
Bernard.

Cîteaux 78, 80

Cities: decay in Dark Ages 51, 54

Clairvaux 80

Clementia Hapsburg 131

Clotar I, son of Clovis 46

Clotar II 55

Clotilda, saint 39–41

Clovis 39–41

Cluny, Order of: founded 75, part in European
renaissance 76–8, crusades in Spain and
Portugal 77–8, idealism tempered by moderation
78, spreads Romanesque 78, 80, its arts and
architecture 79, Cluny II 80, 85, 98, 247, Cluny

III 80–1, 85–6, 98, 248 *Ill'ns.*, sculpture 81–2
Ill'ns., painting 82 *Ill'n.*, influence in France 86,
England 89 *Ill'n.*, reforming influence 91,
contribution to European civilisation 98–9, 234,
Cluniac churches 249 *Ill'ns.*

Commynes, Philip de, 167, 176, 182

Conrad of Burgundy (the Peaceful) 66–8: victory
over Magyars and Saracens 67

Conrad II, Emperor 69, 103, 107

Conrad IV (Hohenstaufen) 116, 129

Conradin Hohenstaufen 130, 134–5

Constance, Council of, 21, 104

Constantinople 28, 109, 164

Coronations: Frederick I 21, 108, Charles IV 147

County of Burgundy (Franche Comté) *passim*:
Burgundians settle Sequania 38, south part in
Homeland 43, Otto William count 68,
architecture 79f, 84 (*apply largely to C. of B.*),
south speaks Franco-Provençal 120, north
speaks Franc-Comtois 120, united with Duchy
of Burg. 146, absorbed by France 183–4, 228,
today 202n, part of Burgundy proper 215

County as unit of administration 42

Crécy 139, 145, 147, 173

Crown of Burgundy 21, 69, 69n, 108–9, 114, 147

Crusades 67, 77, 92, 109–10, 114

Dagobert 53

Dark Ages 'not so dark' 36, 50–1, 54–5, 262–3

Dauphin (of Viennois) 138: viceroy of Arelate 104,
148

Dauphiné (or County of Viennois) 23, 29, 38, 106,
191: becomes French 139, 148

Dialects 120, 142, 184, 205–12, 213–4, 239–46:
suppression in France 206f, 212. *See*
Bourguignon, Franco-Provençal, Provençal,
Schwyzerdütsch *etc. and Maps 13, 24*

Dijon 23, 43, 68, 68n, 165f, 173, 183–4:
Notre Dame 87n *Ill'n.*

Dodo, Burgundy as, 23

Dominican order 93

Duchy of Burgundy: beginnings with Richard the
Justiciar 62–6, separation from Kingdom 66,
Capetian dynasty established 68, 77n, monastic
orders and the arts 77–89, D. speaks
Bourguignon and Bas-Bourguignon 120, first
regular homage to France 145, but Duchy
continues to defy Paris 145, Capetians die out
and Philip the Bold establishes Valois dynasty
145–6, inheritance of Low Countries prepares
ground for Dukes' 'Middle Kingdom' 146;
Peace and prosperity in 15th cent. 160–1,

relatively compact state 162, good prospects 162, under Charles the Bold 162, 169f, court and culture 164–8, taken over by France 183–4, briefly restored to Hapsburgs 183, last separatist 'fling' 184, prospects late 15th cent. compared with Austria's 186–7, the Dukes diverted from their natural destiny 215f, reasons for failure 229f.
See also Burgundy (*particularly when the Kingdom and Duchy shared history and culture*), Frankish region of Burg., Bourguignon, Charles the Bold, Mary of Burgundy.
Durham 80–1

Early English architecture 89 *Ill'n.*
Ebroin 55–6
Edward I of England 132, 144
Edward IV of England 169, 173
Egida, English princess 64
Eleanor of Aquitaine 113
Eleanor, wife of Henry III of England 128–30, 132
Electors of Holy Roman Empire 107, 147
Emmanuel-Philibert, Duke of Savoy 189–91 *Ill'n.*
England: comparison with Burgundy 23, 36, 49, 69–70, 73, 112n, links with Burg. 37n, 38, 49, 64, 78–9, 89–90, 128, 144, 161, 188, conversion by Augustine and Felix 49, architecture 89–90 *Ill'ns.*, Eng. archbishops in Burg. 90, Richard Lionheart 'King of Burg.' 112f, Eng. involved in alliance against Charles of Anjou 132, as 'new monarchy' 160, alliance formed with Burg. 169, 174f, Edward IV bought off 176, importance of English alliance to Burg. 181–2, as buttress of the Middle Kingdom 219. *See also* Savoy and *names of Kings.*
Ermingard 62
"Escalade" 194–6 *Ill'ns.*
Estavayer 178–9 *Ill'n.*
Eugene of Savoy, Prince 188
European Economic Community 23n

Federates, Burgundians as Roman, 37n
Felix, saint 49
'First Romanesque' architecture 80 *Ill'ns.*
Flanders. *See* Belgium, Netherlands, Painting.
Forez 19, 104, 120, 203
Franc-comtois. See Bourguignon, County of Burgundy.
France *passim*: as kingdom in Charlemagne's empire 23, extent in earlier times 24, 54n, 66, author's links with 24, 232, Charles the Bold's lands in 29, Clovis's kingdom 39, Merovingian

Francia 42f, distinct from Burgundy 55, 58, 66, 79, 88, Burg.'s achievements naturally credited to 79, 88, literature 96, 98, acquires allegiance of Forez 104, help to Charles of Anjou 131, Hundred Years' War 138, wins Dauphiné 139, and Provence 139, defied by Duchy of Burg. 145, temporarily gains Savoy 158, F. as new monarchy 160, expulsion of English from F. 160, Edward IV bought off 176, F. absorbs Duchy of Burg. 183–4, and County 184, and Savoy 198, suppression of regional languages/dialects 206–8, 'F. twenty nations' 208, expansion under Louis XIV 219–21, and Napoleon 222, F.'s absorption of Burg. 229, *Map 26. See also* Francia, Franks, French, Merovings, Carolings, Capetians, Valois *and names of kings.*
Francia: divided by Merovings 42, 44–5, extent 54n, 66, attacked by Vikings 59, 61. *Now see* France.
Francien (early form of French language) 24, 58, 96, 206. *See also* Langue d'Oil.
Francis I of France 183, 206
Franciscan order 93
Franconian emperors 69, 73, 103, 124
Franco-Provençal (language): extent in modern times/today 19, 208–12, 240–1, develops in the Burgundians' Homeland 43n, F.P. and 'French' distinguished c.8th cent. 58, every-day use 94, literature 96, area 120, not spoken by German kings or French dukes 140, spoken by counts of Savoy 154, F.P. as one of Europe's languages 206, three million speakers late 19th, early 20th cent. 209, resurgence in NW Italy 209–11, situation recently and today 211–2, 240–1, history, characteristics, etc 241–5, *Maps 13, 16, 20, 24, 25, Ill'n.*
Frankish region of Burgundy 42–3, 43n, 58, 64, 120, 142, 177, 202: settlement by Franks and Burgundians 42, becomes Duchy of Burg. 62–3, speaks Bourguignon 94, 120, 142. *See* Duchy of Burgundy.
Franks: in NE Gaul 39, masters Pyrenees-Weser 42, settle NW Burgundy 42, practice Roman liturgy, Salic Law 46n, accept that Burg. is a separate kingdom 55, their devastation of Burg. 58. *Now see* France, French.
French *passim*: claim to natural frontiers (Rhine, Alps, Pyrenees) 24, 221, 229, view of history 24, 231, 253, leadership in architecture 86, 234, 'invention' of Gothic 86, 'le style français' 88, architectural triumphs 89, F. power in south Gaul after Albigensians crushed (Muret) 92,

French *passim. – cont.*
215, F. language in Middle Ages 94, literature
96–8, F. expelled from Sicily 135. *See also*
France.
Frederick I (Barbarossa), Emperor 21, 108–9
Frederick II, Emperor 128f
Frederick III, Emperor 27–9, 106, 164, 170f, 186,
230: as astologer 171, 186
Friars 93
Friesland 29, 177
Frontiers of Burgundy 29, *42–3*, 45–7, 51, 62–6,
104–6, 124, 161, 177; of France 54n, 66n, 86n,
110, 112

Gallican liturgy 46n
Gambetta, Lex. *See* Lex.
Gaul, Burgundy as 66n, 107, 263
Geneva, Lake Geneva (lac Léman) 19, 151–2, 177,
193 *Ill'n.*: as center of Homeland 21, first capital
of First Kingdom 39, early churches 51–2, 52n
Ill'n., rebuffs Dukes of Savoy 156, 158, allies
with Swiss Confederation 158, 'immediacy' from
the Emperor 193, 226n, attacked by Charles
Emmanuel 194–6
Gerard of Roussillon 59–61; *chanson de geste* 59, 96,
233
Germany: as kingdom of Charlemagne's empire
23, ditto Holy Roman Empire 103, 106,
Burgundy compared with 106, 215, 226.
Gerson 104
Gilbert (Gislebertus) 81, 235 *Ill'n.*
Girard, Girart. *See* Gerard.
Glaber, Rudolf 67, 74, 140: description of church-
building 74
Godegisel 39, 42, 62, 123: his 'inner kingdom' of
Burgundy 42, 62
Godomar 41
Golden age of Burgundy 73f, *98–9*, 233–4
Golden Bull 107, 147
Goldsmith's art 52 *Ill'n.*
Golden Fleece, Order of 164f
Gothic 86f, 248f: Burgundian G. 87f, 250; area 252
Goths 21, 35–6, 42, 45, 55
'Grand Dukes of the West' 164f
Grandson 179, 231 *Ill'ns.*
Gregoire, Abbé 208
Gregory the great, Pope 49
Grenoble 21, 108
Guelders, Charles the Bold invested with 28
Gundioc 38, 42
Gundobad 39–40, 42, 123: law giver 39, 45
Gunther (Gunnar, Gunthiar) 35–6, 38, 236f

Guntram 46, 49

'Half-Gothic', Burgundian 78, *85–7*, 89, 249 *Ill'ns.*
Hapsburgs: emergence 124, 144–5, 213, 221, 226;
Frederick III 170f, Maximilian 183, Charles V
regains Duchy of Burgundy 183, H. gain most of
Charles the Bold's empire 185, marry to world
power 186, 'worse bet' than Burg. 187
Henry III, Emperor, 103
Henry VI, Emperor, 103, 109–115, 119, 263
Henry IV of France 184, 193, 196
Henry VI of England 29n
Heresy(sies) 91–4, 234
Héricourt 174, 178
History, waywardness of 24, 213–4: Burgundy a
'better bet' than Austria 187, frontiers of Europe
not preordained 15, 213–4
Hohenstaufen emperors 21, 106–16, 128. *See also*
Frederick I, Henry VI, Frederick II, Conrad IV.
Holland 29, 219. *See also* Netherlands
Holy Roman Empire 28, 103, 106. *See also*
Hohenstaufen, Hapsburgs, Frederick III
Homeland, the Burgundians' *38–9*, 62: settled 21,
38–9, Geneva center of 21, extent defined 42–3,
about equals Wales 43, B'ns.' Romance language
develops in 43, H. redefined 120, ruled by
House of Savoy 142. *See also* Burgundy proper,
Burgundy (Lesser), Savoy.
Honoratus, saint, 51
Howden (Hoveden) 109, 113
Hugh, Count of Arles 64
Hugh of Cluny, saint, 75–6, 80, 83
Hub of Europe, Burgundy as 73, 233
Humbert I White Hands of Savoy 149
Humbert III of Savoy 149–50
Humbert II of Viennois (Dauphiné) 138, 147
Huns 21, 35–6, 38
Hussites 94

Iceland 21
India and Suez analogy 106
Inner Kingdom of Burgundy (or of Godegisel). *See*
Burgundy, "Lesser Burg.", Homeland, Savoy.
Innocent III, Pope 93
Italy 49, 54–5, 64, 67–8, 85, 96, 149, 160, 165,
191, 198, 203, 205, 221, 223, 233–4: as kingdom
in Charlemagne's empire 11, as successor-state
of Burg. 24, 201, subject to Franks 45, kingdom
in Holy Roman Empire 103, 106–7, Charles of
Anjou and 130f, compared with Burg. 106, 215,
226. *See also* Lure of, Savoy, Piedmont, Franco-
Provençal.

Joan, saint 39, 161
Joanna of Naples and Provence 139, 147
John of England 110, 114, 149
John the Fearless 146n, 161, 182
John II of France 145–6, 228
John II of Portugal 160
John XXIII, Pope 21, 104
Jordanes 38
Jura 19, 23
Justin II, Byzantine emperor 49

Lance of St. Maurice. *Ill'n. See* Regalia
Language: as map-maker, state-maker 213–4, 227,
    as hallmark of a nation 97
Langue d'Oc 97–8, 142, 205, 214, 245. *See also*
    Provençal
Langue d'Oil 94, 142, 205, 214, 245. *See also*
    Francien, Bourguignon, Champenois, Picard
Law(s), Gundobad's, 39, 45, Gambetta 45, early
    ecclesiastical 46
Lear, King 21, 184
Léger, saint 55, 260
Lex Gambetta 45, 202
Literature, medieval Burgundian 96–7, 233:
    comparison with others 96, 98; lit. in 15th cent.
    Duchy 167–8
Lombards 49
Lorraine 162, 173–6, 178, 222. *See also* Nancy,
    Lotharingia.
Lost kingdom, lost country, Burgundy as 231;
    other lost kingdoms 126
Lothar II (Meroving). *See* Clotar II.
Lothar I (Caroling) 59, 66n, 188, *Map 9*
Lothar II (Caroling) 59
Lotharingia 29, 66n, 120n, 177, 188. *See also*
    Middle Kingdom *and Maps 4, 9, 22*
Louis of Provence 64
Louis IX of France, saint, 128–31
Louis X of France 145
Louis XI of France 29, 139, 160, *174–8*, 182
Louis XIII of France 184
Louis XIV of France 165, 184 *Map 26*
Low Countries. *See* Netherlands
Lower Burgundy. *See* Provence, Kingdom of
    Arles.
Lure of Italy (Burgundy's involvement with) 64,
    68–9, 197–8, 225, 230; Angevins' involvement
    130–9, 230
Luxemburg 147, 175, 201, 222, 225
Lyons, Lyonnais 23, 39, 43, 45n, 46, 52, 74, 104,
    106, 108, 120, 128, 193; churches 88
    Poor of Lyons. *See* Valdensians.

Magyars 64–7, 73
Majolus, Abbot of Cluny 67, 77, 80, 98
Manfred Hohenstaufen 116, 129–30, 134, 136
Manteyer: and Burgundy's four regions 43n
Map of Europe, language and 24, 213–4
Margaret of Male 146
Margaret, wife of Louis IX 128f
Marseilles 54, 74
Martin IV, Pope 131, 137
Mary, Duchess of Burgundy 28–9, 174: betrothed
    to Maximilian 28, 170, foreseen as heiress to
    Kingdom of B. 29, marries Maximilian 183
Maurice, saint, 41, 69n, 152–3, 156
Maurienne. *See* Savoy
Maximilian, Emperor, 27–8, 172, 183
Mercia 57, 126
Merovings, Merovingian empire 41, *42f*, 46f, 50,
    52f, 103 *Map 8*
Middle Kingdom (media Francia) 59: still awaiting
    its creator 29, briefly created by Partition of
    Verdun 59, 66n, Valois dukes' lands the basis for
    a M.K. 146, France's long struggle to wrest the
    M.K. from Germany 188, Valois dukes create a
    M.K. 217–21, Charles the Bold's M.K. (177,
    182), 217–24, end of M.K. 1945 223–4
Monasticism, Burgundian. *See* Carthusian order,
    Cistercians, Cluny. Beginnings of 51
Montagne, La (high ground north of Burgundy)
    43, 61
Moors 57–8, 67, 123. *See also* Saracens.
Morat 179–80 *Ill'n.*
Muret, battle of (92), 215, *Map 15*
Music in 15th cent. Duchy 166–7

Nancy (162) 172, 175, 177–9, 180–1, 218
Naples (or Sicily), Kingdom of, 109, 130f, 135,
    138–9, 143, 174. *See also* Charles of Anjou,
    Charles II, René, Robert.
Napoleon 188, 198, 222, *Map 26*
Nation States 24, 221. *See also* New Monarchies.
National consciousness in Burgundy, resistance to
    foreigners 53, 68, 106–7, 140, 145, 183
Nationalism 140–2, 230
Navarre 23
Netherlands 21, 146, 183f: as successor-state of
    Burgundy 23, 201, 222
Neustria 42, 45, 47, 120n
New Monarchy(-ies) (153), 159–60
Nibelungenlied 21, 36n, 38, 236
Nibelungs 36, 38, 45, 123: extent of their kingdom
    39
Nicetius, Archbishop of Lyons 46

Nicholas III, Pope 130–1
Normans 73, 124
"Northern Burgundy". *See* Netherlands

Occitan. *See* Provençal
Odo of Blois 69
Offa, King of Mercia 57
Options, Burgundy's, at its mid-point 119
Orange 51, 108, 115, 185. *See also* Baux.
Otto I 67, 103
Otto of Freising 107
Otto William 68–9
Ottonian emperors 67f

Painting, in medieval Burgundy 83 *Ill'n.*, in
  14–15th cent. Duchy 166
Paray-le-Monial 81, 85, 251 *Ill'n.*
Paris 47, 66n, 103
Payerne 247
Peter II of Savoy 151f *Ill'ns.*
Philip II of Spain 193
Philip II of France (Augustus) 110–4, 263 *Map 15*
Philip III of France 128, 131
Philip VI of France 139
Philip of Rouvre(s) 145
Philip the Bold 145–6, 161–2
Philip the Good 161, 164f, *168–9*, 181–2 *Ill'n.*
Philosophers, medieval Burgundian: few 91
Phoenix analogy *126–7*: attempts to raise ph. 23,
  70, 119, 124, 129f, 168, 170f, 193f, fall of 68f,
  'reduced to ashes' 70, Austria as Burgundian ph.
  186, Savoy ditto 204–5
Picard, Picardy 80, 86, 88, 96–7, 206
Piedmont 104, 154, 158, 190, 195, 198: first links
  with Savoy 149, 153, reunited with S. under
  Amadeus VIII 154. *See also* Savoy.
Pirenne 54, 262–3
Pius II, Pope 27–8, 156
Place-names, evidence of 43, 261–2
Pliny, earliest mention of Burgundians 119, 260
Poland, Burgundians in 36, 45, 260
Poor of Lyons. *See* Valdensians.
Portugal, Burgundians in 77; as new monarchy
  160f
Priscus, Archbishop of Lyons 46
Probus, Emperor 37n
Proudhon 208
Provençal 58, 94f, 120, 142, 242. *See also* Langue
  d'Oc.
Provence *passim*: 43, 54, 58–9, 64, 98, 113, 177:
  'promised' to Charles the Bold 29, 178, 178n, in
  First Kingdom but has few Burgundians 42, long

retains identity 43, in Dark Ages 45, 54–5, Boso
  king of 62, expulsion of Moors 67, 77, revival 73,
  architecture 79f (*apply largely to P.*), heresies in
  91f, literature 96f, language 120, Charles of
  Anjou and Beatrice 129–34, its prosperity
  129–30, Queen Joanna and 139, France gains
  139, 178n, survival of Provençal 142, the
  Angevins and Italy 143, Charles Emmanuel
  occupies 191–2, today 202
Prussia 23n

Raymond Berenger V 128–9
Recapitulation *119–25*
Regalia of Burgundy 41, *69n*, 153 *Ill'n.*; *also* 171
Regions of Burgundy, the four (language-based)
  42–3, 43n, *120–3*, 142, 202: Charles Martel and
  58, Charles the Bold and 177–8, survival today
  202. *See also* Allemannic, Frankish, Homeland,
  Provence.
Renaissance of 11th and 12th cents. 73–5, 233
René of Anjou, 'King of Naples', Count of
  Provence ('Good King René) 29n, 134n, 139:
  his 'promise' to Charles the Bold 29, 178n
René II, Duke of Lorraine 162, 174, 178n, 180
Reuss, river 39, 104, 124, 203
Rhône Basin. *See* Basin, Saône-Rhône.
Richard the Justiciar, "first Duke of Burgundy" 62,
  66
Richard I of England (Lionheart) 109f, 263: King-
  designate of Burgundy 112–5 *Map 15*
Richard of Cornwall, King of the Romans 116,
  128–9, 152
Ricimer 39
Riothamus 'king of the Britons' 38n
Robert of Naples 138–9, 143
Robert II, Duke of Burgundy 145, 169
Romainmotier 80, 247
Roman liturgy 46n
Romanesque, Burgundian 78f, 247: its area 84,
  252 *Map 12*
Rudolf I (Hapsburg), Emperor, 130, 144
Rudolf Guelf (Rudolf I of Burgundy) 62–4, 124
  Map 10
Rudolf II of Burgundy 64, 103
Rudolf III of Burgundy 68–9
Rudolfians: accession 62, decline 68f, 128, patrons
  of the Church 74–5

Sagas 21, 236
Saint Denis 86, 249–50
Saint Martin des Champs, Paris 249–50
Sanchia, Queen of the Romans 128–9

Saône Basin. *See* Basin, Saône-Rhône

Sapaudia 38. *See also* Savoy.

Saracens 57–8, 67, 73, 92

Sardinia, Kingdom of, 23, 197–8, 203, 205, 212, 221

Savaric, Bishop of Bath 110f, 263

Savoy *passim*: language of 19, Kingdom of Sardinia 23, territories in Italy awarded to Charles the Bold 29, Burgundians settle S. (Sapaudia) 38, in Rudolfian kingdom 62, counts aim at crown of Burgundy 124–5, S. and Charles of Anjou 132, 137, Charles IV recognises effective independence 148;

Early story 149f, Peter II builds Savoy palace in London 152, his conquests 152, S.'s constant frontiers 153, consolidation 154, becomes duchy 157, Duke Amadeus VIII viceroy of Burg. 157, Holy Shroud 157n, 190n, decline 158, recovery under Emmanuel Philibert 189–90, Charles Emmanuel 190f, becomes kingdom 197, chooses union with France 198, as remnant of Burg. 203, 205, modern autonomy movement 225. *See also* Sardinia, Amadeus VIII, Yolande.

S. as the political form of the Burgundians' Homeland 142, 157, 203, 225, as a 'mini-Burgundy', the Inner Kindom of B. 146, 153, as a durable (the most durable) form of B. 146, 205, 225, as the continuation of the Kingdom of B. 153, 205, 225, as the B'n. phoenix 205, as a B'n. 'might-have-been' 224–5. *See also* Homeland.

S.'s correlation with the B'ns.' language 120, 142, 146, 154 *Map 20*

Compared with Scotland 154

Contacts with England 93, 151–2, 188, 197

Links with Italy 149, 154, 191, 196, 197–8. *See also* Piedmont.

Saxony 23n

Schools in Merovingian Burgundy 52–3

Schwyzerdütsch 142, 242

Scotland, Savoy compared with, 154; Burgundy ditto 228

Sculpture, in medieval Burgundy 81 *Ill'ns.*, Burgundian influence in France 87, sc. in 14–15th cent. Duchy 165–6 *Ill'ns.*

Selective nature, lack of balance, of the book 24, 106n

Sens-en-Bourgogne 47, 140

Sequania 38. *See also* County of Burgundy.

Settlements, Burgundians' 38–9, 42, *43*, 120

Sicily (or Two Sicilies or Naples) 23, 109, 130f;

Sicilian Vespers 134–5 *Ill'n. See also* Naples, Charles of Anjou.

Sidonius Apollinaris 38n, 45, 50

Siegfried 47, 236–7

Sigebert, King of Austrasia 47, 236

Sigismund, King of Burgundy 41, 42, 51

Sigismund, Emperor, 104, 148, 157

Spain 47, 54, 57, 85, 98; Burgundians in, 77, 85; as new monarchy 160

Speyer 80, 110, 113

'States make nations' 24, 214

Stephen Harding of Cîteaux 78

Strasbourg oath 96

Successor-states, Burgundy's 23–4, 201, 222

Suez and India analogy 106

Suger, Abbot 86–7, 248–9

Suisse Romande (western Switzerland) 43, 120, 201

Susa 49, 104, 120 (201)

Swiss: included in Charles the Bold's kingdom 29–31, their rise 144–5, defeat Hapsburgs 144–5, alarmed by Charles the Bold's designs 178, defeat him 179–80

Switzerland: as part of Burgundy 21, as successor state of Burg. 23, 201, 222, largely in First Kingdom 38f, in Rudolfian kingdom 62, beginnings of the Confederation 144, an aberration of history? 213. *See also* Suisse Romande, Schwyzerdütsch.

Tapestry, Burgundy's 166 *Ill'n.*

Tarascon 134–5, *Ill'n.*

Thought, medieval 91

Toulouse, County of 92–3, 112

Tournus (64) 269, *Ill'n.*

Toynbee, Arnold: and likely rulers of Burgundy 216, and Middle Kingdom 223–4

Transjuran Burgundy, Kingdom of, 62. *See also* Burgundy, Inner Kingdom.

Trier, Archbishop of, 21, 107, Conference of, 27f, 170–2

Tristan legend 61, 233

Troubadours 92, 96–7

Troyes-en-Bourgogne 47, 140, 202

Turin 191, 193, 196, 198, 211, 225. *See also* Piedmont

Turks 164

Uchizy 80

Universities in Burgundy 91

Val d'Aosta. *See* Aosta.

Valdez, Valdensians 92–4, 234: V'ns.' influence in Bohemia 93, survival in Italy 93, Milton's tribute to 93, 197, literature 96.
Valence, Valentinois 74, 108, 154
Valois dukes of Burgundy 146, 217f. *See also* Charles the Bold, John the Fearless, Philip the Bold, Philip the Good.
Valois kings of France 138, 145, 188
Verdun, Partition of 29, 59, 60n, 66n. *See also* Middle Kingdom.
Vexin 110
Vézelay 61, 81, 249 *Ill'ns.*
Vicars, Imperial, 107, 112, 116, 124, 148, 157
Viceroyalty of Roman provinces 42–3, 261
Viceroys of Burgundy. *See* Vicars, Imperial.
Vienna 164
Vienne 39, 49, 59, 74, 107–9, 132, 138, *Ill'n*; Kingdom of, 113, 115. *See also* Arelate.

Viennois, Count(s) of. *See* Dauphin. County of, *see* Dauphiné.
Vikings 59f, 73
Vinegrowing, recovery of, 10th cent. onwards 74
Voga 19
Volsungasaga 38, 47, 236–7
Vosges 19, 23

Wagner (and '*The Ring*') 38, 47, 236
Western civilisation, threat to, around 900 64
William the Silent 185
Wipon, chaplain to Conrad II 107
Worms, Burgundian Kingdom of 38 *Map 5*; agreement of (1193) 112
Württemburg 23n, 37

Yolande of Savoy, Duchess 157, 174

Zähringen (dynasty) 152–3

South-eastern France and its neighbors

Miles
0

AUBE
Sens
Troyes
Bars/Seine
Chaumont
Tonnerre
Châtillon
HAUTE
MARNE
Langres
Luxeuil
VOSGES
Épinal
HAUT
RHIN
GERMAN
Basle
Zü
Auxerre
YONNE
Vézelay
MORVAN
La Charité
NIÈVRE
Nevers
Saulieu
CÔTE D'OR
Dijon
HAUTE
SAÔNE
Belfort
Aar
Solothurn
Reuss
Luzern
Besançon
DOUBS
Bern
Beaune
Dole
Doubs
Pontarlier
Sarine
Fribourg
SWITZERLAND
Autun
Chalon
SAÔNE ET
LOIRE
JURA
Lons
VAUD
Lausanne
Rhône
Brig
Moulins
ALLIER
Allier
Vichy
Cluny
CHAROLLAIS
Mâcon
BEAUJOLAIS
Roanne
RHÔNE
BRESSE
Bourg
AIN
DOMBES
St Claude
Ain
VALROMEY
Geneva
Chillon
Sion
St Maurice
CHABLAIS
FAUCIGNY
VALAIS
Martigny
Stresa
PUY DE
DÔME
LOIRE
Feurs
FOREZ
St Étienne
Lyons
Rhône
Vienne
Albon
ISÈRE
BUGEY
GENEVOIS
HAUTE-SAVOIE
Annecy
Hautecombe
Chambéry
TAREN-
TAISE
Aime
Moutiers
SAVOIE
MAURIENNE
Aosta
Dora Baltea
Ivrea
Nova
HAUTE LOIRE
Le Puy
Valence
Isère
Grenoble
Vizille
La Mure
Briançon
Dora Riparia
Susa
Turin
ITAL
PIEDMONT
LOZÈRE
ARDÈCHE
Rhône
Drôme
Die
DRÔME
HAUTES-ALPES
Embrun
Cuneo
Aygues
BASSES
ALPES
Orange
VAUCLUSE
Avignon
Arles
Durance
PROVENCE
BOUCHES DU RHÔNE
VAR
Marseilles
ALPES
MARITIMES
Nice
San Remo
Cannes
Lérins

South-eastern regions
of modern France

Medieval
Burgundy

Bourgogne
Franche-
Comté
Rhône-
Loire
Rhône-
Alpes
Provence-
Côte d'Azur